Signifying Nothing

Signifying Nothing

Truth's True Contents in Shakespeare's Text

Malcolm Evans

The University of Georgia Press

Athens

Published in the United States of America in 1986
by the University of Georgia Press
Athens, Georgia 30602

© 1986 Malcolm Evans

First published in England in 1986 by Harvester Press

Printed in Great Britain

LC 85-28945
ISBN 0-8203-0837-4

For Gareth
in memory of Robert Evans

Cryf oedd calon hèn y glas glogwyni,
Cryfach oedd ei ebill ef a'i ddur,
Chwyddodd gyfoeth gŵr yr aur a'r faenol
O'i enillion prin a'i fynych gur.

Contents

Acknowledgments

I would like to acknowledge here the assistance and support of Maurice and May Evans, and the contribution of the following friends and colleagues, who have helped in various ways and at different stages in the preparation of this book: John Bartholomew, Homi Bhabha, Tish Blackstone, John Burnes, Bill Corporandy, Howard Davies, Arnold Evans, Lucy Gent, Dave Goldwater, Ken Guy, Terence Hawkes, Trevor Hemmings, David Jarrett, Peter Middleton, Toril Moi, Sean O'Hagan, Colin Parfitt, Christine Richards, Angie Salfield, Matthew Sweeney, John Thieme and Don Van Vliet. My particular thanks go to Catherine Belsey, Daniel Baron-Cohen, John Drakakis and Colin MacCabe for arranging seminars held in April and May 1983 on earlier versions of some of this work, and to their colleagues at U.C. Cardiff, Oxford English Ltd, the University of Stirling and the University of Strathclyde, respectively, for many helpful comments and criticisms. Opal Cerdan collaborated on the final version of the last section in Chapter 6, 'Goodnight Ladies/If I Were a Woman'.

The sections dealing with Edward Harrison's journal and papers could not have been written without the co-operation of Michael Dangerfield or the tenacity of Marc Ratner, my exchange partner from California State University, Hayward, whose second year at the Polytechnic of North London made it possible for me to retrace Harrison's route around British Honduras (now Belize) in the summer of 1980. I would also like to thank the present owner of the manuscripts, Kenneth R. Harrison, for joining me on the latter part of the journey, for his constant help and encouragement throughout this project and for his permission to quote from the journal. In connection with this part of the research I am indebted to the following for their interest and hospitality: Kathy Harrison in Port Dinorwic, Bernard and Wendel LeMott in Cayo and Belize City, Esther Ann Thomas in Tulum, Ahsid Joseph in Dangriga and Harry Min at Placencia.

Finally, my thanks go to my publishers, and my editor Sue Roe, who have shown great patience in waiting for me to produce this book, and to the staff of the British Library, the Statsbiblioteket, Århus, and the library of the Polytechnic of North London, particularly Christine Fuller and Susan Gardiner.

Earlier versions of some of the material in Chapters 2 and 5 appear in *Shakespeare Quarterly* 26 (1975) and *Glyph* 9 (1986). This material is used here by permission of the editors. The lines quoted in the dedication are from 'Cerdd yr Hen Chwarelwr' by W. J. Gruffydd.

Department of Language and Literature
Polytechnic of North London
January 1985

1
Introduction

I do not approve of anything that tampers with natural ignorance. Ignorance is like a delicate exotic fruit; touch it and the bloom is gone. The whole theory of modern education is radically unsound. Fortunately in England, at any rate, education produces no effect whatsoever. If it did, it would prove a serious danger to the upper classes, and probably lead to acts of violence in Grosvenor Square. What is your income?

(Lady Bracknell in *The Importance of Being Earnest*)

Proverbs for Paranoids . . .
If they can get you asking the wrong questions, they don't have to worry about the answers.

(Thomas Pynchon, *Gravity's Rainbow*)

The Myriad Problems of Life and Eternity

Half way through her 1982 Christmas broadcast to the people of Great Britain and the Commonwealth, Queen Elizabeth II turned from an expression of support for the Conservative government's South Atlantic war earlier in the year to more traditional, less controversial matters. "No man is an island entire of itself", she reminded her subjects in the immortal words of John Donne, "every man is a piece of the continent, a part of the main". And how true this message remained, especially on Christmas Day, for the great family of races and nations gathered for the duration of the tape to share a moment of reflective festivity with its sovereign. During the reign of Elizabeth I, the critic who later commented that the line about the island and the main went some way towards backing Argentina's territorial claim on the Falklands/Malvinas would probably have ended up in the Tower, and quite rightly.[1] Drawing attention on such ceremonial occasions to the *embarras de richesses* in poetic language is as unseemly as pointing out that the monarch is wearing no clothes. If encouraged, this kind of thing would spread from the indiscretions of the literary text to those of humbler discourses. While showing viewers around the new home on the eve of the royal wedding in 1981, a television commentator remarked: "Here's a billiard-room where Prince Charles can entertain his friends while Lady Diana's beavering away in the kitchen".[2] Without due respect for the intentions of the speaker and proper standards of interpretation, the routine sexism in this unctuous evocation of domestic life would collapse into a Joycean intertext of cheap romantic fiction and hardcore pornography, the rhetoric of estate agents and the language of conservationism. Much virtue in "beaver".[3]

An attentive Elizabethan school-child, trained in elementary rhetoric, would have recognized in the queen's "island" and the BBC commentator's "beaver" instances of *aporia* or "the Doubt-full" (Puttenham, 1589, p. 189), the unfortunate lapse that spoils the 'finish' of an utterance, disclosing the processes of production and manipulation behind what seems to be a plain statement of perfectly natural truths and sentiments—in this case those constituted in a peculiarly parochial discourse on the

3

royal family, which affirms at once the virtues of bourgeois domesticity and a decayed imperial power's continuing delusions of centrality. In contrast the modern viewer or listener, whose formal induction into the arts of language would be centred on literature, might still be thinking about the quotation from Donne and, depending on whether her or his education was 'basic' or 'advanced', experiencing the 'taste', 'refinement' and 'sensibility' connoted by the literary as either the exclusion proper to a humble subject or a sharing of cultural landmarks based on some knowledge of Donne, his work and his period. Across these divisions of response there remains the common unity of a national language and culture. If we are English then this tradition is, supposedly, ours however little we know of it. The eternal grandeur of great literature may still be ministered to us, directly in the form of appropriate quotations and indirectly in the language of those who have absorbed its spirit and can therefore speak with a greater cultivation and authority. If we are foreigners who speak English, this literature, by virtue of its 'humanity' and universality, is ours by proxy and its citation reaffirms our special relationship with a culture which, unlike others less fortunate than itself, has a history and tradition stretching back through many centuries, during which great men have given elegant and forceful utterance to basic truths about human nature that we can still recognize today. This second category would, of course, give special priority to products of British colonial or post-colonial education systems and, pre-eminently, to citizens of the United States where—to cite some modern instances germane to the present study—Shakespeare has been represented as "a constant companion of American development" (Dunn, 1968, p. 3) whose contribution to the enrichment of American speech was almost as great as that of the Bible (Westfall, 1939, p. 1), and whose birthplace is an essential landmark on the itinerary of tourists in pursuit of their English historical and cultural roots (Marder, 1964, p. 233). From this latter vantage point, with its own more recent assumption of an imperial centrality, the insular British discourse on the Anglo-centric universe remains, nevertheless, a source of surprise and amusement.

"While literary critics have been cultivating sensibility in a minority", claims Terry Eagleton, "large segments of the media have been busy trying to devastate it in the majority". (Eagleton, 1983, pp. 215–16) In Britain this devastation is nowhere clearer than in the long-running soap opera concerning the royal family, which, because it is 'above politics', is an inexhaustible source of conservative representations that are not answerable to the media's notorious doctrine of 'balance'. And if academic English has been remiss in not turning sooner to these discourses, which pose the greatest contemporary threat to a broad critical awareness, it has also been unbalanced in its teaching of literature—the cultivation of 'sensibility' being itself a rather one-sided activity.

Ideologically, the 'effect' of literature, as Pierre Macherey and Etienne Balibar argue, is not just in "the domain of 'feeling', 'taste', 'judgment', and hence of aesthetic and literary ideas; it sets up a process itself: the rituals of literary consumption and 'cultural' practice" (1978, p. 12). This second domain, many of the main features of which become apparent when the queen quotes Donne, is given no formal recognition in most Anglo-American criticism, although critical discourses are themselves inscribed in its rituals and practices. Because these considerations determine perceptions not only of the 'aesthetic' and 'literary' but of the text itself as an object of study, they cannot be filed away in a separate drawer marked "Sociology of Literature" and conveniently forgotten. The production of 'literature', or rather the process of dignifying a loose assembly of texts and discourses with that name, is itself subject to ideological and sociological analysis. The fact that everyone knows what literature is does not change the fact that literature, in concrete terms, is nothing in particular. Donne's "no man is an island" comes not from a poem, play or novel but from one of a series of 'meditations', and if Donne's meditations are literature for some reason, those of Karl Marx or Abiezer Coppe, to pick two random examples, are not. Nor are all fictional or poetic works deemed to be literature—no one in their right mind would publicly affirm the eternal verities of the human condition or even the solidarity of the British Commonwealth with reference to the immortal words of Barbara Cartland, William MacGonagle or Desmond Bagley. 'Literature', then, is the product of a value-judgment, already a normative exercise in refinement and taste before it begins to nurture or question the refinement and taste of the reader, and this category, with its obvious potential for incorporation in other discourses, is continually reproduced and revitalized in the rituals and practices of education.

In 1921 a British government report praised Shakespeare Day, an annual commemoration held in elementary schools, as a great bond between English-speaking children in the United Kingdom, the empire and the United States of America. The same document noted with satisfaction that this day of celebration had also been recognized in the schools of France (Newbolt, 1921, p. 319). As Shakespeare is the national monument whose legs must clearly bestride the aesthetic and the ideological, and because his special day was a key ritual in the construction of English Literature as a compulsory subject in schools, this is as good a place to start as any.

The observance of Shakespeare Day followed a pattern derived from religious worship. The official tercentenary programme, addressed to "Children Brave and True of the Great Mother-Tongue" who will be "Lords of an Empire as wide as Shakespeare's Soul", suggested the following schedule: "I. Reading (from *Ecclesiasticus* XLIV); II. Singing of a Shakespeare Song; III. Discourse on Shakespeare; IV. Another Shakespeare Song; V. Scenes and Passages from Shakespeare; VI. Another Shakespeare Song; VII. 'God Save the King'." (Gollancz, 1916, p. 6) Most of the passages recommended for reading display Shakespeare's "boundless love of country", which, as the programme explains in notes to be incorporated into the "Discourse on Shakespeare", is "no mere poetic fervour" but "solidly based upon his belief that English ideals make for righteousness, for freedom, for the recognition of human rights and liberties". His example shows all English boys and girls "how it behoves us as patriots to strive to play our part in war and peace, and how best to maintain our faith in the ultimate triumph of a noble humanity". This appeal goes beyond divisions of education and privilege as Shakespeare's genius was essentially democratic, happily destined "to teach all classes of his countrymen—lords, gallants, scholars, and unlettered groundlings". Although his compatriots are especially blessed, "his sovereignty has become well-nigh universal—England's

most cherished possession, shared and adored by all the world".
And this genius which crosses national and cultural boundaries
is also immortal, Shakespeare's being "the power to please and
enrapture, and to instil into men's hearts his manifold observations on the myriad problems of life and eternity" (Gollancz,
1916), pp. 10–12, 21).

Among the members of the Newbolt Committee, which
praised Shakespeare Day in its report to the British Board of
Education, were Caroline Spurgeon and John Dover Wilson,
whose criticism still features as recommended reading on
Shakespeare courses, and many of the assumptions central to
this particular production of 'Shakespeare' remain, for the most
part, unchallenged: Shakespeare's "exalted genius", the universality and immortality of his appeal, the power of his work to
'humanize', its concern with fundamental, unchanging problems of human life, and an aesthetic capacity to please and even
'enrapture'. The programme's concern with patriotism,
national unity and what it calls "English ideals" is specifically
associated with its date of publication, in the second year of the
Great War, but these preoccupations, as we shall see, also
characterize other texts written in less immediately threatening
circumstances but equally concerned with a cult of Shakespeare
as national hero and, built around this, an English Literature
which can be at once a great source of unity and pride and a
subject suitable for study in schools and universities. So
sentiments expressed in this call to patriotism and national
unity are, historically, a major factor in establishing the present
status of English Literature in the curriculum, and the process
of indoctrination so obvious, in retrospect, in Shakespeare Day
has not altogether disappeared.

This propagandist image of England and its national poet
was, we should recall, dispensed to children obliged by law to
be present in school, and not old enough to have read much
Shakespeare or to have formed their own opinions about him.
For the majority, who would leave school after a 'basic'
education and in whose lives 'high culture' would subsequently
play only an indirect part, it would constitute the educational
establishment's concept of 'the minimum everyone should
know about Shakespeare'. For the small minority who would
proceed to higher education and so to subtler, less aggressive

formulations of the dominant ideology, this would remain the formative matrix within and against which they would have to think. For all these children there would be no escape from the work of Shakespeare, presented here not as a set of historical documents in a language already to a marked extent 'foreign' but as an essential and supreme element of the "Great Mother-Tongue", which will condemn those who do not master it to a kind of exile within their own language. Whether they like it or not, they will all be Shakespeare's subjects, and a process of subjection illustrated here in very specific terms remains a part of schooling inseparable from ideologies of the 'purely' literary or aesthetic:

> *Formally* literature, as an ideological formation realised in the common language, is provided and destined for all and makes no distinctions between readers but for their own differing tastes and sensibilities, natural or acquired. But *concretely*, subjection means one thing for the educated dominant class: 'freedom' to think within ideology, a submission which is experienced and practised as if it were a mastery, another for those who belong to the exploited classes: manual workers or even skilled workers, employees, those who according to official statistics never 'read' or rarely. These find in reading nothing but the confirmation of their inferiority: subjection means domination and repression *by* the literary discourse *of* a discourse deemed 'inarticulate' and 'faulty' and inadequate for the expression of complex ideas and feelings.
>
> (Macherey and Balibar, 1978, p. 12)[4]

Imagined Corners

Signifying Nothing is a study of Shakespeare based on contemporary theories of the subject, the sign and ideology. As an introduction aimed primarily at students, it is necessarily indicative rather than exhaustive, addressing a wide range of issues in cultural studies, literary theory, theatre history and the history of Shakespeare teaching and criticism, while also offering detailed readings of *The Tempest* and *Love's Labour's Lost* (Chs. 3 and 4), *Macbeth* and *Hamlet* (Chs. 5 and 6), *As You Like It* (Ch. 6), *A Midsummer Night's Dream*, *King Lear*, *The Winter's*

Tale,[5] Peele's *The Old Wives' Tale* and Kyd's *The Spanish Tragedy* (Ch. 7). This study aims to introduce some measure of the self-reflection that characterizes its main object, the Shakespearean text, into a critical process previously inclined to minimize its own *productive* role, and to contribute to the development of a Shakespeare criticism that works knowingly on a text always already "occupied" or "incrusted" by other critical discourses,[6] which function within the institutions, rituals and material practices of ideology.

Such a project is hampered by the preponderance in Shakespeare studies of an idealist criticism which always purports to recover (at last) some hitherto inadequately revealed aspect of the text "as in itself it really is". This orthodoxy needs to be engaged on several fronts and it would take four or five carefully interrelated volumes to develop the case against it. These would include a history of the Bard as a cultural signifier, which might range from the refusal by the worthies of Stratford to permit performances of Shakespeare in the town in the early seventeenth century, through Garrick's bicentenary celebrations, the nineteenth century's construction of the national hero, to Shakespeare Day, the Newbolt Report, the interpretative and formalist academic criticism that reinforced the institutional monumentality of Shakespeare without ever having to stoop to vulgar bardolatry, and on to the moment when deconstruction stands poised, vibrantly suspending itself at the impossible threshold of a text with no outside. The models for such a book already exist in recent criticism—in the work of Chris Baldick (1983), for example, and in some of the contributions to *Re-reading English*.[7]

But this history would call for a companion-study of 'the words on the page'—a description of the semiotic processes that have accommodated at once the closures of each new interpretation or analysis of form, genre, and so on, and the inexhaustibility of the 'aesthetic' object which is mobilized by these discourses and which keeps them in circulation. Such a description would involve a deconstruction of the unified signs, subjects and texts delivered by more traditional Shakespeare criticism, a restoration to the plays of the 'play' denied them by the institutional process of translation into the literary 'work' in which the uniquely gifted author addresses the sensitive reader on the myriad problems of life and eternity. This Derridean or Lacanian version of Shakespeare calls in turn for another volume of the multiple critical commentary, one which, following Foucault (1970) and Elam (1984), begins to account *historically* for the text's particular preoccupation with—and manifestation of crisis in—representation and the signifier. And beyond this lies the task of relating Robert Weimann's work (1978) on the hybrid forms of Elizabethan drama, its divided acting space and contending theatrical modes to the larger divisions and discontinuities in representation, the subject and the sign.

Signifying Nothing is none of these books, but a sketch for all of them. A number of factors suggested the need for such a hazardous project. First, at the time when the book was being planned and drafted, literary theory had already been a major issue in British and American English departments for some years but appeared to be having very little impact on the teaching and criticism of Shakespeare.[8] Second, the more established forms of criticism were beginning to consolidate their position and to curb an embarrassing proliferation of interpretations promoted by the pressures of careerist academic publication, a corrective move particularly apparent in 'lets be sensible about this and agree on a middle way' criticism, the work of Levin (1979), Powell (1980) and Rabkin (1981) for example, which assumed a consensus on the unified subjects, signs, texts and 'culture' traditionally kept in place by the ideology of academic literary studies. The present work is written against that consensus, which has taken upon itself the task of pre-empting the challenge of contemporary literary theory before it has even reached Shakespeare in any concerted form. A number of recent studies have reaffirmed Shakespeare's 'meaning' and mimesis with a vengeance, along with the need for a 'flexible' and 'humane' response, in other words one that does not disclose its theoretical position. At the same time, a caricature of the "radical formalist" has been prepared for the expected enemy, who will close all windows and doors against the fresh air of 'real life' to indulge in a spiral of meta- and inter-textual navel-gazing.[9]

Because *Signifying Nothing* aims only to open the gate and to begin mapping a different terrain, it is marked by a degree of eclecticism. At certain points, Chapters 5 and 6 for example, a deconstruction which may tend towards formalism is turned against the metaphysical assumptions of traditional Shakespeare criticism. At other points certain tendencies within deconstruction itself are criticized from the perspective of more historical and political modes of reading that focus on questions of ideology rather than the strategies of metaphysics. In some ways each chapter is a critical experiment of a different sort. Time and space dictate an ending at some point, but if this project were to continue and to move towards homogenizing some of its own tensions and discontinuities, its theoretical model would be more centrally that of the political and ideological 'unconscious' outlined in Macherey (1978), Eagleton (1976), and Jameson (1981). In more concrete terms the 'single' mode of *Hamlet* and *Macbeth* (see Ch. 5) would be located more firmly in a historical account of Tudor absolutism and its apologists.[10] And the reading of "truth's true contents" in *As You Like It* (see Ch. 6) would be related to the social and economic history of the family, enclosures and engrossments, beginning with the work of Montrose (1981) and Skipp (1970). Chapter 9 would be on the English history plays, Chapter 10 about *Julius Caesar* and *Coriolanus*.

Another chapter, or another volume, would extend the account of Shakespeare as a signifier of 'culture', focused here on Shakespeare in England and specifically in the English and colonial education systems, to North America. I mention below in passing Shakespeare in Hollywood, the Exxon Shakespeare, the Gallup Cultural Olympics and Pepsi-Cola's appropriation of the rival claimant's issue, but I have had to omit a large amount of other material—on Shakespeare in performance and in American education, for example, on the polarization of opinion over his Englishness and 'universality' during the struggle for independence, on *Othello* and the fear of miscegenation, and on Shakespearean burlesque in blackface minstrelsy. The studies of Shakespeare in the United States are now outdated or too unsystematic but the present work, already stretched in too many directions, is not the place to put this right.[11] The decision to concentrate here on the institutions and rituals of a specific national culture represents a conscious avoidance of a specious mid-Atlantic 'universality' and invites fuller parallel studies of the American material. The sections on

theory, inevitably, draw much more extensively on American
and European sources and here I am able to take the exemplary
contributions of Lentricchia (1980) and Ryan (1983) as read,
and to focus on other issues—such as the Cambridge 'structuralist' controversy of 1980/81—which have not yet been given
this kind of critical attention.

I write at length about Shakespeare criticism in subsequent
chapters, and I will briefly note here only the major influences
on this study. I take my bearings primarily from the attempt at
a conjunction of contemporary theories of the subject, the sign
and ideology in Coward and Ellis's *Language and Materialism*
(1977), from the work of Catherine Belsey and Terry Eagleton,
and from the teaching and published criticism of Terence
Hawkes. I owe in each case a debt too deep for mere footnotes. [12]

I am also indebted to a number of studies of Shakespeare's
language and the problems of interpretation it poses, studies
which, without benefit of the horizons of contemporary critical
theory, remain open to polysemia and play in a text which
refuses to be finally contained by the unities of the dominant
critical tradition or by the view of literature expressed by M. H.
Abrams (quoting Wordsworth against Derrida and his followers) as "a man speaking to men". These studies include sections
of Empson (1953), Hulme (1962), Grivelet (1963), Danson
(1974) and Booth (1969 and 1977). Stephen Booth's attack on
a critical tradition which mistakenly assumes that "in *Hamlet*
we behold the frustrated and inarticulate Shakespeare furiously
wagging his tail in an effort to tell us something" (1969,
p. 138) is a particularly acute anticipation of some of the main
preoccupations of deconstruction. [13] A number of books produced in the 1960s and 1970s on Shakespearean
'metadrama'—including Righter (1962), Forker (1963), Calderwood (1971), Egan (1975) and Van Laan (1978)—also point
to areas of the text that are useful for a post-structuralist or
post-Althusserian criticism, however much either might dis-
agree with the notion of an authoritative 'meta' level of
discourse which exists within the plays and determines what or
how they signify. The present study has also drawn on several
accounts of popular festive and/or dramatic traditions, ranging
from Barber (1959) and Bakhtin (1968) to Bethell (1944),

Hawkes (1973), Hattaway (1982) and, pre-eminently, Weimann's *Shakespeare and the Popular Tradition in the Theater*.[14]

The most promising current line of inquiry for Shakespeare studies, evident in the work of Dollimore (1984), Stallybrass (1983) and Sinfield (1983), is a historically based analysis which takes recent theoretical developments in semiotics and deconstruction into account, but anyone concerned with Shakespeare in relation to contemporary critical theory must also be aware of the work of Lacan (1977b), Sibony (1977), Felperin (1977), McDonald (1978), Girard (1980), Dawson (1982) and Calderwood (1983). Keir Elam's *Shakespeare's Universe of Discourse* (1984) was published too late to be referred to in the chapters that follow but represents an important contribution to this area, albeit one that stops short of any consideration of the subject, ideology or the post-structuralist appraisal of the Saussurean sign and the implications of this critique for any contemporary semiotics or analysis of discourse.[15] With Dollimore and Sinfield (1985) and Drakakis (1985), which also appeared too late to be discussed in any detail here, the long overdue assault of contemporary critical theory on the basic assumptions of Shakespeare studies has begun in a conscious and concerted fashion. Dollimore and Sinfield's volume, which includes essays by Greenblatt and Tennenhouse, and cites work by Montrose, Orgel and Marotti, also enlists the New Historicism to a "cultural materialism" which implies an allied political and pedagogic critique.[16]

In the first three chapters of the present work I quote extensively from an unpublished diary kept by Edward Harrison between September 1929 and March 1933, a document now in the private collection of Mr K. R. Harrison of Port Dinorwic, Gwynedd, who is currently preparing selected entries for publication. Edward Harrison taught Shakespeare appreciation in Placencia, British Honduras, between 1929 and 1930, and his teaching notes suggest a point of embarkation very different from the one taken by orthodox academic criticism in the years immediately following the Newbolt Report. Harrison was born in Worcester in 1900, of an English father and Welsh mother, and spent the two years immediately prior to his departure for the Caribbean and Central America in and around Cambridge. The journal itself is a large format

(30.5 cm. by 32 cm.) petty-cash book, with hard boards and leather spine and corner pieces. Its pages—of which pp. 32 to 35 inclusive have been removed—are numbered from 1 to 100, with facing pages bearing identical numbers. Inside the back cover there is a circular stationer's label which reads "Tollit & Harvey Ltd, 40 Gresham St, E.C.".

Included with the journal are several letters from Harrison's friend at Cambridge, Michael Dangerfield, one of which— dated 18 March 1930—contains a number of cryptic references to the "experiment" and a quotation, attributed with page reference, from I. A. Richards's Practical Criticism, which was published in 1929. The critical judgments of unmarked texts that make up the body of this "natural history of human opinions and feelings" (p. 6) were produced, Richards informs us, by anonymous undergraduates in various subjects. There is at least an intriguing possibility[17] that Edward Harrison's only piece of published criticism, prior to the extracts from the journal now quoted below and the reading of *The Tempest* reconstructed from notes in Chapter 3, was the extract quoted in Dangerfield's letter—evidently an attempt to deal with what Richards called his piece of "field-work in comparative ideology" (p. 6) by throwing a spanner in the works. The passage in question is on the subject of Donne's Holy Sonnet VII, "At the round earths imagin'd corners, blow":

> After repeated readings, I can find no other reaction except disgust, perhaps because I am very tired as I write this. *The passage seems to be a rotten sonnet written in a very temperamental kind of iambic pentameter. Not even by cruel forcing and beating the table with my fingers can I find the customary five iambic feet to the verse*; the feet are frequently not iambic, and there are sometimes four, and even six accented syllables to the verse. In structure the passage sounds like the first labours of a school boy. Particularly displeasing are verses 5, 6, and 7. Yet the idea seems really worth while.
> (Richards, p. 48)

Notes

1. Julian Barnes, "A Surfeit of Hush and Plush", *Observer*, 2 January 1983, p. 48.

2. BBC 1 "Nationwide", 22 July 1981, showing viewers around the new home on the eve of the royal wedding.
3. On the semiotics of the beaver, *see* Vonnegut, 1974, pp. 30–1.
4. My italics.
5. All references, unless attributed to other editions, are to Hinman, 1968.
6. On the "occupied" text, *see* Bennett, 1979, p. 137; on the "incrusted" text, *see* Macherey, 1977, p. 4.
7. *See* Doyle 1982, in particular.
8. As a convenient barometer of this, "self-knowledge" would always heavily outscore "semiotics", conveniently placed nearby, in the subject index of the annual *Shakespeare Quarterly* bibliography, most articles on the latter topic being in Italian.
9. *See*, for example, Nuttall, 1983 and Rabkin, 1981, p. 1. While Elam, 1984, states quite clearly that "the 'self-activity of the word'" in Shakespeare's comedies "amounts not so much to the autonomy of verbal form as to the identity of that form with the dramatic concerns of the plays" (p. 2), one of the book's first reviewers ignored this disclaimer and leapt in with this predictable attack: "The 'universe of discourse' in drama is not autonomous, and it is disingenuous to act as if it were" (Brian Vickers, "The Wantonness of Language", *Times Literary Supplement*, 21 September 1984, p. 1045). In subsequent chapters of the present study the 'deconstructive' *platea* action is viewed always *in relation to* a qualified mimesis, and the disposition or modality of language regarded, in Kristeva's terms, as "heterogeneous to meaning" is always "in sight of it or in either a negative or surplus relationship to it" (Kristeva, 1980, p. 133).
10. Beginning with the account of the feudal "parcellisation of authority" and division of power in Anderson (1978, pp. 152–3, 193) and the placing of the absolutist state at the point of a break between feudalism and capitalism in Poulantzas (1975, pp. 155–67).
11. *See* Dunn, 1968 (first published in 1939); Westfall, 1939; Marder, 1964; Shattuck, 1976.
12. Belsey, 1981, suggested one of the epigraphs and the conclusion of Chapter 7 below, in addition to a number of other points more easily acknowledged in the course of the argument.
13. Booth, 1977, also supplies a wealth of material that would tend to support the account below, in Chapter 6, of the permutations of 'truth', 'true' and 'contents'. *See* pp. 201–2, 227, 233, 242, 327, 348, 374, 390, 403–4.
14. According to the criteria employed in Chapter 7, below, many of the critical works listed in this and the next paragraph also reaffirm some aspect of a more conservative version of Shakespeare—the phonocentrism of Hawkes, 1973, would be a case in point, as would Hattaway's

recuperation of a 'Brechtian' Shakespeare and Felperin's use of Russian formalism to advance an argument about the quality of Shakespeare's engagement with experience. Felperin uses formalism to argue a case ultimately not unlike the one Nuttall later develops by attacking formalism. My intention in these two paragraphs is simply to acknowledge borrowing, a degree of parallelism, and *bricolage*.

15. Elam attempts to combine semiotics with speech-act theory and other aspects of English linguistic philosophy (Searle and Austin) attacked in some of Derrida's most polemical work.

16. It is significant that this critique is pursued most vigorously in Part 2 of *Political Shakespeare*, which emerges from a British academic context. Some of the reservations expressed by Ryan (1983, p. 103) in relation to the institutional role of depoliticized North American deconstruction must also apply, provisionally at least, to the New Historicism.

17. Michael Dangerfield refuses to confirm or deny this.

2
Some Subtleties of the Isle

> You do yet taste
> Some subtleties o' th' Isle, that will not let you
> Beleeve things certaine.
>
> (*The Tempest*, Act 5, Scene 1)

> If the world had any ends, British Honduras would certainly be
> one of them.
>
> (Aldous Huxley, *Beyond the Mexique Bay*, 1934)

Edward Harrison's Journal

The first entry in Harrison's journal is dated 9 September 1929 and written at the settlement of Placencia in British Honduras, the outpost of the empire on the American mainland. It begins with notes on the colony, including some quotations from a popular travel-guide:

> 17 day sea-crossing. 5,700 miles from Liverpool to the capital, Belize. Jamaica 3 days away. New York 9. New Orleans 14. Green and gold islets and cays edge the coastline. Palms towering over a city of wooden houses, a few raised on piles against hurricane and flood. "The Indian inhabitants include persons of African descent coming from the West Indian islands; aboriginal Indian residents in the interior; and Caribs. Creole woodcutters are the most numerous." Negroes = 'Indians'! Back to Caliban. But Maya, blacks, mestizos all seem to enjoy each other's company. Even Prospero is not resented. Offering perhaps some bulwark against the territorial claims of Guatemala, always threatening on the Western frontier. Rugged Cockscomb Range rises to 3,700 feet in the South. To the North acres of Mangrove swamp dissected by slow, treacly rivers. Malaria. Finest known mahogany, rosewood for inlay, Santa Maria wood for masts and beams, cedar, balsa, chicle, coconuts, guava, bananas, copra, logwood, grapefruit, plantains. "The Colony is larger than Wales and slightly smaller than Palestine." 1638 first British inhabitants settle after shipwreck ("Yare! Yare! We split! Who now will work the peace of presence?") 1662 arrival of logwood cutters. 1774 failure of attempt to settle convicts. 1798 masters and slaves combine to repulse Spanish invasion. 1834 end of slavery. 1890 opening of ice factory. 1929 enter Harrison bearing culture for the natives. Weather hot. (Harrison, p. 1)[1]

Harrison goes on to describe a few days recently passed on Cay Ambergris, an island to the north, and an encounter on the way to Placencia with an American visitor obsessed with airships, who recounts in tedious detail the Orient flight of the *Graf Zeppelin* in March of that year and leaves a tattered article on the event torn from the *San Jose Mercury*. At one point the American hallucinates (at least as far as the sceptical Harrison is concerned) a United States Navy dirigible in cloud above the eastern horizon. This episode brings into sharp focus the epigraph, from *The Tempest*, for the entry as a whole: "You do yet taste some subtleties o' th' Isle, that will not let you Beleeve things certain".

The record is as much commonplace book as journal. Fragments from *The Tempest*, a particular preoccupation, jostle Harrison's own observations and his extracts from other reading. He has with him, in addition to the Shakespeare, three travel volumes that serve as his introduction to the Caribbean islands and the eastern seaboard of Central America—Dr Thomas Gann's *Maya Cities* (1927), *Roaming Through the West Indies* by Harry A. Franck (1920) and a new book on Haiti, W. B. Seabrook's *The Magic Island* (1929). There is also evidence, at this stage of his journey, of some reflection on three unpublished essays, primarily on Marx, sent by his friend and contemporary at Cambridge, Michael Dangerfield, and still retained with the manuscript. The assignment that takes Edward Harrison to Placencia, a month of teaching English at the local school, keeps Shakespeare very much to the foreground. A hired purveyor of culture, he aims to repay his debt by "arming Caliban, 300 years later, against Prospero" (p. 8). Everything he writes is, unconsciously, an elaborate circumstantial reading of *The Tempest*, or rather Harrison's immersion in the play feeds back into his observations and reading on the way to Placencia. In this the journal inadvertently and obliquely reproduces the assumptions of an emerging critical position left far behind in Cambridge. With the young F. R. Leavis in the third and final year of his probationary faculty lectureship, Harrison's *Tempest* becomes a splendid *reductio ad absurdum*, or strong misreading *avant la lettre*, of the Leavisite moral fervour and indignation, unique imaginative response of the individual to the work of art, and inextricable relationship between 'literature' and 'concrete experience'. The road to Placencia could equally have led, in a year to two, to a *Scrutiny* meeting where Edward Harrison, corrected of reductive Marxist leanings, might have forgotten his reservations about academic English in "the creative interplay of real judgements—genuine personal judgements, that is, of engaged minds fully alive in the present" (Leavis, 1963, p. 5). Having missed the boat, or prematurely caught another, at the dawn of the movement that was to claim for his discipline the guardianship of English culture as a whole, Harrison finds himself despairing of institutional literary criticsm. He ironically sums up the whole business in two lurid quotations from Seabrook's exotic guide to Haiti: "'Blood-maddened, sex-maddened, god-maddened, they danced their dark saturnalia'" and "'If you will ride with me to-morrow night, yes, I will show you dead men working in the canefields; close even to the cities there are sometimes *zombies*'" (Harrison, p. 9; Seabrook, 1929, pp. 48, 95).[2] Harrison's *Tempest* is to be quite simply a political weapon. His other text, for no immediately apparent reason, is *Love's Labour's Lost*.

The entry for 9 September ends with some impressions of Placencia—in prose then in verse. The next entry (for 11 September) is another poem, this time in narrative form, celebrating the national day of British Honduras, which falls on 10 September and commemorates the victory at St George's Cay in 1798 of the 'Baymen', white log-cutters and their slaves, over an armada under the command of the Spanish admiral Arturo O'Neill. A laconic footnote adds that writing became impossible on National Day and that the first entry, which runs to some 5,000 words, was relieved by the better part of a bottle of cane rum. This may explain, in retrospect, the movement from a hesitant noting of the words of others, through Harrison's fragmented speculations, into the embrace of a stilted Caribbean muse. In later entries writing itself becomes increasingly the central problem. Towards the end of his stay in Placencia, Harrison notes that the record obscures and impinges on the experience: "At best the immediacy can only be *found* elsewhere. Congealed and washed up in other writing" (p. 19). Caught between the island and the page, his faculties "scarce think their eyes do offices of truth, their words are natural—we split, we split, we split" (p. 20).[3] Later still a complete original sentence seems beyond him. In places the record consists only of scraps of dream or poetry, ideas for ideas, lines of thought suddenly diverted to take in unacknowledged words spoken in the background or glimpsed through the corner of the eye in open books or newspapers. On 24 December 1929 Harrison comments on the despondency that descends when he writes, or which provokes him to pick up a pen in the first place. Because of this, and for other reasons, "the written character may have nothing to do with the person who writes" (p. 28). To say he is beside himself by this point is only to recognize where Harrison has been all along, "doubly alien to the role of Crusoe/Prospero and in the very act of writing" (p. 3).

9 September 1929

> Big sea on night journey down. Grow fins. Get back in the water again. But beware the marauder. These days, when they will not give a doit to relieve a lame beggar, they will lay out ten to see a dead Indian. And the one who exercises his virtue and humanity is the most lethal. He feeds on the fall of the other. He will carry this island home in his pocket, and give it his son for an apple. And sowing the kernels of it in the sea, bring forth more islands.   (Harrrison, p. 1)[4]

So begins the opening sequence, dealing with Cay Ambergris, which runs Shakespeare and Dr Thomas Gann's *Maya Cities* together. The island is named, writes Gann, after an immense and valuable lump of ambergris once washed up here. Inhabitants of the cays and coast still live off the providence of tide and storm, particularly on the jettisoned cargo of vessels running contraband from Colombia to the United States. "Cheerly, cheerly, my hearts . . . Play the men" (Harrison, p. 1).[5] Ambergris, Harrison notes, is a waxy intestinal emission of the whale, and a source of perfume: "An ounce of civet, goot apothecary, to sweeten my imagination . . . the base effluent of cat . . . travellers must be content" (p. 1).[6] The use of quotation, which is always approximate, returns to Gann: " 'The interior is a desert of mangrove swamp, scrubby bush and sour grass savannah, interspersed with waterways and small lagoons' " (p. 1; Gann, 1927, p. 95). The interjection comes again from *The Tempest*—"the ground indeed is tawny", "perfumed by a fen", "as if it had lungs and rotten ones" (Harrison p. 1)[7]—and leads into an encounter from earlier in the journey of the archaeologist Gann, during a night on "a weird islet" off the coast of the Yucatan peninsula:

"I reached behind my pillow for the electric torch and, pulling up the mosquito-curtain, turned the light on to the floor of the tent, where a truly disgusting sight met my eyes. The whole floor was literally covered with enormous, greyish green crabs, so crowded together that there was not standing room for all of them, and they were crawling over one another's backs, their great claws producing a faint clicking noise and their loathsome bodies exhaling their disgusting earthy odour. They had probably been attracted by the remains of a tin of lunch tongue left on the floor of the tent, and, having devoured it, were seeking anything else edible. Fortunately they were unable to get on top of the cot, being baffled in the attempt first by the thin steel legs which supported it and by the fact that the mosquito-net was tucked under the camp mattress. I slew a dozen or so of them, but these crabs showed no inclination to retire, but rather a determination to stop and devour the corpses of their friends and relatives. I could not reach my boots, and had no intention of stepping down in my bare feet among the seething mass of filthy crabs to get at them, but, sitting on the low cot, I managed to do tremendous execution with my long machete amongst the disgusting cannibals, until, slowly and reluctantly, the survivors at last retired."

(Harrison, pp. 1–2; Gann, pp. 46–7)[8]

In photographs Gann is a gaunt, quixotic figure, towering by at least a head above the Maya Indians who greet him. Harrison interpolates Ariel's song as performed by Amado, a faithful mestizo companion always referred to as "Muddy" by Gann: "Full fadom five thy father lies. Those are the pearls that were his eyes. Doth suffer a sea-change into something rich and strange. Bones of coral. Choral. Shells and crabs" (Harrison, p. 2). This initiates a characteristic spell of distraction marked by a series of anagrams of 'ambergris' and a return to Thomas Gann's idyl of the cays, offered without comment. Now, on a smaller, uninhabited island near Cay Ambergris:

"The shore, which is hardly ever visited, is a receptacle of the flotsam and jetsam of thousands of miles of ocean. The most varied collection of objects has drifted ashore here. A great mast, five feet in circumference, mute witness of a tragedy somewhere in the Caribbean, and a good ship gone to the bottom; several small casks, two wicker-covered galephones, a new gasolene drum, two lifebuoys, a number of mahogany

logs—probably broken adrift from rafts of the wood being
towed down from the interior—curious brass-tipped standards
of unknown use, and innumerable smaller objects."

(Harrison, p. 2; Gann, p. 98)

There is much more from Gann's *Maya Cities*, again taken
without comment but for odd scribbled remarks, perhaps from
later, alongside the copperplate of the original entry made,
Harrison tells us, in the light of a hurricane lamp on a pine
table itself more than likely a survivor of some wreck. This
section ends with a transcript of a whole paragraph, virtually
unaltered. Here, back on the mainland, Gann describes a beach
terraced by the tide:

> "On this virgin page of sand the tracks of everything that had
> passed across it were as clearly marked as upon new fallen snow.
> Everywhere were visible tracks of wading birds, from the great
> crane, known to Creoles as 'full-pot', for obvious reasons, to the
> tiny sandpipers, found in great flocks all along this coast. Here
> a small tiger-cat had strolled down from the upper terrace to
> take a closer view of the sea, but evidently finding nothing to
> interest it, had returned on its own tracks; farther on was
> plainly written on the sand the account of a battle between half
> a dozen john crows, or black vultures, over the extremely rotten
> carcase of a stranded rock-fish, fragments of the bones, head,
> and skin of which were still left to identify it. The tracks which
> intrigued and puzzled me most, however, were found in great
> abundance crossing each other and running in every conceivable
> direction. One of these consisted of a wide, shallow, concave
> trench, such as a medium-sized snake leaves, upon each side of
> which were lines of oblong indentations, placed very close
> together. The whole track was about four inches in breadth.
> The second of these tracks consisted of a double row of parallel
> indentations, much smaller than those of the first. The size of
> these indentations, and the space between them, varied very
> much in these second trails, showing that they had been made
> by individuals of the same species, but of different sizes. Both
> tracks ran in all directions, and ended sometimes in the seaweed
> by the water's edge, sometimes in the scrub covering the upper
> terrace."   (Harrison p. 4; Gann, pp. 101–2)

Harrison's estrangement, the shock of arrival and loss of
familiar cultural landmarks, leads him to prop up a shaken

identity not only on the stability and concreteness of other writings but, within these, on reassuring lists of palpable marks and objects. Like medieval blazons, his quotations act as metonymic rivets to pin down an observable reality. The same need is apparent when he turns to the conversation and article on the *Graf Zeppelin*, where the detailed itinerary of the Orient flight becomes a key item. On a wet March morning the giant airship is unmoored from its base at Friedrichshafen. It flies south to hover above the French fleet anchored off Toulon, then on the Cannes, Nice, Monte Carlo and to Rome, where the ship circles and the captain, Hugo Eckener, sends a telegram of greeting to Mussolini. Dinner, served over the Straits of Messina, gives Harrison the security of a list within a list, as the invited gathering of dignitaries and politicians sit down to "turtle soup; ham and asparagus; roast beef with vegetables; salad; Roquefort cheese; and German nut cake" (p. 5). The passengers wake and view Crete from the promenade deck windows, proceed to breakfast—with another itemized menu—and on to the library or the asbestos-lined smoking room, lodged between vast flexible bags of explosive hydrogen. By late afternoon, the journal reports, they are over Palestine, "the drumming of the engine so soft that the clamour of children and dogs is distinct in the villages below" (p. 5). The farthest outward point of the journey is Egypt, where the British colonial authorities refuse entry into their airspace—"the outrage of outmaged Prospero" (p. 5)—and the zeppelin turns, three miles off the coast, to head back for the Alps and home.[9]

Lists and schedules secure a new centre on the margins of Harrison's past conception of the world and reinvent a Europe now pushed to the periphery. But the poetic landscape crossed by the shadow of the airship can no longer be safely domesticated by metonymy. It is already the space of transformations, a marginal other-world of romance. As the account of the Orient flight proceeds, it passes from the metonymic solace of lists to a metaphorical exploration of limits. In moonlight the *Graf Zeppelin* hovers over the Dead Sea, reducing height until cliffs and mountains tower all around. As it hangs only a few hundred feet above the opaque surface of the sunken lake, the airship is in fact a thousand feet *below* sea level. Looking down from the promenade deck at this impossible point, Edward

Harrison imagines himself returning from Placencia to Friedrichshafen. A day out, above dense cloud, pitching in a
south-easterly gale, the airship reduces speed, and lookouts in
the control cabin watch for a glimpse of the Atlantic. After five
hours, a gap at last appears in the cloud directly beneath,
"spiralling down through floating scraps of mist to a tortured
vortex" (p. 6). Then the rocky coast of Newfoundland slowly
crosses from behind as the ship, which has made no headway
east against the storm, drifts backwards still burning fuel.
Again, projecting a polar flight for two years later in 1931,
Harrison, on 9 September 1929, looks down on vast icefields
cut by blue channels and across, through mirages produced by
the mingling of warm and cold air masses, "to the place where
Placencia, Cay Ambergris and then Cambridge slip slowly by
to the south" (p. 7).

Robinsonade

> Whatever their charge of fantasy, islands, for the English, are
> only copies or shadows of one original. That other Eden. That
> little world. That precious stone set in a silver sea. That earth.
> That realm. That bull. Other islands are still places where they
> kill and die for nothing. Calculate profit and loss. Serve the
> yellow slave who blesses the accursed, makes the hoar leprosy
> adored, places thieves, and gives them title, knee and appro-
> bation, with senators on the bench. Makes foul fair, wrong
> right, base noble, old young, coward valiant.
>
> (Harrison, p. 7)[10]

Caught between the pull of conflicting centres and peripheries,
Harrison's writing stays fixed for a time in paradox and the
identity of opposites, accepting its own vertigo and drift. In
terms of Sebastian and Antonio's words, quoted earlier without
acknowledgment, he appropriates and then disseminates Placencia in his own idiosyncratic meanings:

> *Seb.*   I thinke hee will carry this Island home in his pocket, and
>   give it his sonne for an Apple.
> *Ant.*   And sowing the kernels of it in the Sea, bring forth more
>   islands.
>
> (*The Tempest*, II. i. 762–4)

At the end of the zeppelin interlude, order is restored not in the solid untrammelled 'self' of a Crusoe or Prospero, but through the clarification of a system of political purposes. The apple, in the other dimension of Shakespeare's text, is plucked to mark the loss of political innocence. These words are, after all, an ironic prologue to the naive Golden Age that Gonzalo will aim to instate on the island. The son's legacy, and his sowing of seeds, are no longer an anarchic semiotic scattering but the construction of an all too pressing reality—that of colonial and imperialist expansionism.

There are still moments of distraction. At one point the journal breaks off to describe a misanthrope at the nearby, predominantly Carib, town of Dangriga who has trained huge, deadly wasps to protect his house against intruders. But the focus is now on the work in prospect. Harrison notes Marx's warnings against the dreams of island-dwellers, of would-be Crusoes, expressed in eighteenth-century ideas of an irreducible individualism given by nature. The host of 'Robinsonades' that follow Defoe fantasize original, unique, independent men who, from this beginning, can freely enter the relations of reciprocal connection figured in Rousseau's *contrat social*. Harrison writes:

> More than anything I must beware my *self*. No trite and painful Augustinian self-awareness, but to know that self produced in relations of domination, empire. Produced. Not participating in. Not in flight from. Here, even more than in the gospels, the first shall be last. The seeming *a priori* is in fact the secondary, epiphenomenal. Immerse everything in the relations. Book, teacher, taught, the Bard himself all in a network. Each terminal experiencing and, through automatism, ignoring historical relations that make object, subject, commodity what they are. These relations are forever at work in each. What are these pieces washed up by the various tides but *this*?
>
> (pp. 7–8)[11]

In rough notes he sketches an outline for his project at the school in Placencia. *The Tempest* and *Robinson Crusoe* are to be read "from the island" as island myths of European colonialism. A cryptic comment on 'negation' in Marx and Hegel breaks down into a chorus of nonsense phrases from *The Tempest* and other plays: "Cock a diddle dow, diddle dow, diddle dow, sessa, double double" (p. 8). This gives way to a rough agenda for *The Tempest*:

> Hegel on master-slave explains Caliban. Miranda no better off. Everyone is subjected to P. The conjuror in the twilight. Here he darns a huge hole in the fabric. Behind him the sound of tearing. Miranda is trained to be at last as foolish as Gonzalo. Brave new world to the old man's debacle. Combines indulgent mother and unknowing, defenceless infant. Here on the island itself (in the still vexed Bermoothes) it's a different play. How otherwise? At the heart of Empire there is a stillness, totally enclosed. It imagines an eternal truth. Blind. Culpably so. They say is Prospero perfect from the start or only at the end? Cracking whips and constriction of the middle passage. They make their wantonness their ignorance.   (p. 8)[12]

In an afterthought, Harrison wonders at the difficulties of talking about this in school with adolescent natives:

> More than Shakespeare they need ammunition. But Stephano, or Trinculo, calls his bottle his book. I'll sink it more deeply than doth plummet sound, arming Caliban, three hundred years later, against Prospero. I come not to praise . . . but to bury . . . *Love's Labour's Lost* will do it by babble babble babble and pointlessness. Wee Willy Winkie. How follows that? Fit in his place and time. Only Caliban speaks as eloquently as even Thomas Gann.   (p. 8)[13]

The American Standard in Sanitation

An oblique line abruptly divides the page here. This is, of course, not finished criticism in any sense, nor intended to be read. There is nothing to suggest that Edward Harrison, in his final draft, could not have abided by the conventions of the current critical discourses and expunged the awkward first impressions, primary motivations and personal ideological commitments as adroitly as a Bradley or a Dover Wilson.[14] As the entry proceeds, however, it offers something related and more coherent in a synopsis, with some comment and extensive quotation, of Harry A. Franck's *Roaming Through the West Indies* (1920).

This journey begins in the southern United States in 1919 where the traveller comments on a primitive order of segregation and lynch-law with all the liberal indignation of a northerner. But as the journey proceeds it becomes increasingly a foil to Harrison's own. At Key West, Florida, Franck is disturbed by the cigar workers' own Spanish-language newspapers, which proclaim new victories for the international proletariat. In Cuba, Puerto Rico and Santo Domingo such aberrations associated with the "Latin temperament" accumulate and begin to undermine him. Everywhere there is gambling, instability and an unproductive noise of humanity. Transport and amenities are inadequate and unreliable. Ticket sellers for the national lottery attempt to overcharge him. Franck praises the seizing of Santo Domingo in 1916 by the United States Marines and their continuing presence. A history of repeated revolts and growing debt calls for an injection of order. The foreign invaders are, in his terms, "security forces" and the guerrillas "outlaws"—" 'You are under arrest', said the colonel, dryly. 'Caramba!' cried the outlaw, while a detachment of marines disarmed his seventy followers" (Harrison, p. 9; Franck, p. 237).

Edward Harrison's notes taken from Franck's book record that United States forces have occupied Puerto Rico since 1898, Haiti since 1915 and Nicaragua, off and on, since 1912. Harrison adds his own comment, that "those who will not choose the American version of freedom and democracy must have freedom and democracy thrust upon them". From his island he sees all around:

> the Great Wall of America which protects the homeland. Built of the cheapest raw materials: rotten fruit and corpses. Beyond it, the Atlantic and the Panama Canal, which serve it in the office of a moat defensive to a house. Against infection, the hand of war and the envy of less happier lands. Against the threat of invasion from the inhabitants of the Azores or Ascension Island. From its own comic-opera tyrants on the southern continent. (p. 9)[15]

In contrast to a massive systematic oppression imposed by the fruit and mineral companies, assisted when necessary by United States military forces, Harry A. Franck's attitudes strike Harri-

son as almost genial. He cites examples of Franck's qualified
approval of a rich historical and architectural heritage and his
remarks on a modern literary tradition. In Cuba, writes Franck:

> "three or four residents of the island are producing occasional
> volumes of the usual Spanish-American type of novel, over-
> florid in description, heavy with details, and intimate beyond
> the point of decency according to our standards, yet with a
> nicety of style seldom attained by our own present-day novelists
> and now and then catching a true reflection of a tropical
> landscape or a native idiosyncracy."
>
> (Harrison, p. 9; Franck, p. 237)

But in the predominantly negro islands, which lack even this
saving grace of 'culture', Franck becomes increasingly debili-
tated. Casual obscenities greet him everywhere. No one works
or seems to him to want to work. He is troubled by the heat,
the flies and the white women who, virtually without exception, "'grow scrawny, nervous and weak-eyed, their pasty
complexions sprayed with freckles under their veils'" (Harrison, p. 10; Franck, p. 368). Next to a series of quotations
which chart the decline of this refined sensibility in contact
with what it calls the "'lowest species of the human family'",
Harrison scribbles "the horror! the horror!"

Against the historical backdrop of the world's first black
republic, established with the successful slave revolt of 1804,
and his own colourful variations on the standard themes of
voodoo and bloodshed, Franck presents Haiti as a typical
instance of a broader malaise: "'Abuse of authority is a fixed
fault in the Haitian character, as with most negroes'". The
American occupation of the country is "'ample proof of the
advantage of having the negro ruled over by the whites, even
though that rule be faulty, instead of letting him run wild'"
(Harrison, p. 11; Franck, pp. 128–9, 161). In Puerto Rico the
whites themselves have been contaminated by hookworm, a
condition which serves Franck as a metaphor for what he
regards as a generally corrupting presence: "'The disease was
brought by African slaves—along with most of the troubles of
the West Indies'" (Harrison, p. 11; Franck, 1920, p. 297).
Having maintained a decorous silence for some time, Harrison
now bursts in with a chorus from *The Tempest* and Conrad:

These whelps, hag-born, not honoured with human shape!
Slave! Devil! If thy nature will receive no print of goodness, thy
back shall receive stripes. You taught me your language, and
all it profits me is to curse. Exterminate the brutes.

(p. 11)[16]

Harrison wonders who but the United States could be the
creator of such a protagonist:

Dickens, Conrad, Dostoyevsky? No. There is a common
ancestor. It is you that have chalked forth the way that brought
us here. Prospero. Ariel buys the whiteface pills. Caliban
invests in a gun. What ho! Slave! For this, be sure, tonight thou
shalt have cramps. Side-stitches shall pen thy breath up. Thou
poisonous slave, got by the devil himself. (p. 12)[17]

The selection of items from Franck's *Roaming Through the West
Indies*—much more extensive than quoted here—seems init-
ially to make up another of Harrison's lists, another intinerary,
and to show signs of an increasing fatigue. Everything so far has
been written at one sitting, on the night of 9 September 1929.
But the pattern in the quotations is unmistakable, with its
return to an assumed 'cultivation' shared by Franck and his
reader and its insistent presentation of historical relations of
oppression and economic exploitation in terms of unchanging
essences of nationality or race. In some ways Franck is unique, a
comic grotesque, another character in Harrison's narrative who
peeps out through the jalousies of expensive hotels, or ventures
into the streets and market-places to encounter the populace in
the spirit of Thomas Gann's night meeting with land-crabs.
But what troubles Harrison most, along with Franck's complacent assumption of his own liberalism, is that there is
nothing unusual in his basic attitude, one shared by the
zeppelin-lover encountered on the journey from Cay Ambergris
and implicit in the North American commercial, political and
military presence in the region.

Edward Harrison left Europe at a time when fascism was
already established in Italy, and National Socialism was emerging as a political force in Germany. Lloyd George's promise in
1918 of a land fit for heroes to live in had led to no substantial
changes in the English class sytem. In 1924 Fleet Street's

anti-Soviet propaganda based on the forged 'Zinoviev letter', supposedly from the head of the Third International, inciting British workers to open revolt, helped bring down the first Labour government. Military forces intervened in the General Strike of 1926, while the police and right-wing press formed a united front against the working-class movement. In April 1930 Harrison records news from England of two and a half million unemployed and a year later of the means test which keeps social security payments to a minimum (pp. 53, 94). Washed up on his island, conditioned by a literary education to expect sea-changes and cleansed perceptions, he sees more of the same:

> The New World is the Old World. Structures of oppression masked and misrepresented. 'What do you expect?' asks Miranda. 'It's only human nature after all.' Here the blacks there the reds. Cock a diddle dow. History to be read? Or suffered? Or made?   (p. 12)

The concluding words of his modern Prospero, Harry A. Franck, offer a glimpse of the future of these structures, in Europe in the late 1930s and early 1940s and three decades later in South-East Asia. At one point Harrison cites Franck citing a symptomatic mis-spelling in a journal kept by George Washington while in Barbados during the winter of 1751/52. Franck mentions the phrase in question, "the fields of *cain*", for no other reason than to show that even the father of American democracy cannot be perfect. Harrison notes that "the obvious implications for the brotherhood of man are missed" (p. 10). In his last extract from *Roaming Through the West Indies*, the closing sentences of the book, the intimations of genocide which may appear in retrospect are clearly as unintentional as they are in the words of George Washington. Franck, referring to the recent purchase from Denmark of the United States Virgin Islands, meditates on the future of what Harrison, elsewhere, calls "the American ramparts" (p. 33), "the pineapple fringe" (p. 78) and "the great wall of bananas" (p. 42):

> "That there would be certain advantages to the United States in acquiring possession of, or political control over, all the islands on our southeastern seaboard goes without saying . . . But there

is little doubt that they are outweighed by the disadvantages, at least all those of a material nature. Sentimentally it would be pleasant to see our flag flying over all the Caribbean . . . But with the Virgin Islands as an example, we would be paying dearly long after we had parted with an acceptable price which would bring the European West Indies under our flag. Merely to raise them to the American standard in sanitation would be a colossal task, to say nothing of adding materially to our already troublesome 'colour question'. As some joker has put it, 'We could well afford to buy all the West Indies on the basis of the price paid to Denmark, *if the sellers would agree to remove all the population*; any other arrangement would probably prove a poor bargain."   (Harrison, p. 13; Franck, pp. 485–6)[18]

Horizons

When Edward Harrison, towards the end of the first entry in his journal, describes himself as "Sitting on a bank, mourning again the king my Father's wrack" (p. 14), it is difficult to know whether he is misquoting *The Tempest*, first performed in 1611, or Eliot's *The Waste Land* published, complete with footnotes in 1922. But since 1929 was also the year of I. A. Richards's *Practical Criticism*, this distinction should be unimportant. After Richards the reader could be expected to respond to form and significance in the text without regard to where and how he or she was situated, when it was written, or who wrote it—Shakespeare, Eliot or, for that matter, Harrison. *Practical Criticism* bequeathed to the academic study of English one of its most abiding rituals in which the student, temporarily purged of affiliations of class, race and sex, confronts a passage shorn of author, date and other contextual markers in a historical void. A successful outcome to this *pas de deux* will disclose the student's refined sensibility and enhanced critical awareness, but the very fact that the activity involved is 'practical' removes from this 'refinement' any embarrassing connotations of aristocratic taste. The 'practical critic' is a gritty, blue-collar type of operator, one who has renounced the salon of *belles lettres* for the workshop where hands may be dirtied and texts thoroughly overhauled.

By its very practicality, this mode of criticism sets itself apart from theory, valuing the humane, flexible, imaginative response. But its own underlying assumptions, including its construction of the relationship between theory and practice, constitute an undisclosed theory, based on an amalgamation of empiricist and idealist positions which its practice covertly reproduces under the guise of a liberal privileging of the unique communion of individual reader and text. Its idealism permeates the basic 'tools of the trade', the linguistic and generic 'forms' given by tradition and suspended outside their changing institutional bases and historical uses. These norms are seen to precede the text and to shape its author's purposes, transcending its material contingencies just as art, in its absolute idealist sense, transcends ideology. This discourse's empiricism belongs to a philosophy which, particularly in the English tradition, is part of received wisdom and 'common sense'. This philosophy, in its vulgar forms, washes its hands of philosophy itself. But empiricism is at root metaphysical, involving an initial act of faith in a theory which amounts, in its own way, to a theology. Its first principle, the absolute priority in all knowledge of what can be verified by the senses, is itself an idealism, unverifiable by the sense.[19] The theory of no theory is founded on a hidden contradiction as acute as the one through which Tertullian and Sir Thomas Browne, for example, willingly and openly embraced Christian dogma: "certum est quia impossibile est".

Pierre Macherey has described the text as never being simply itself but always irrevocably marked and transformed by "everything which has been written about it, everything which has been collected on it, become attached to it—like shells on a rock by the seashore forming a whole incrustation" (Macherey, 1977, p. 4). All commentary is a *production*, which is then assimilated to the text as part of its material history. While Harrison, in Placencia in 1929, worked towards these perceptions of reader and text as processes produced in specific historical relations of production, in Cambridge Richards was launching the flagship course of modern English Literature—a course which erases these determinants of the text by purporting to restore it in its pristine empirical presence, and postulates the ideal reader as a unique floating sensibility, a Crusoe of the spirit. Whereas the former position is preoccupied with history, the latter banishes it. While Harrison begins with a declared political position, the 'flexible' response required by practical criticism rules that any unpurged residue of the reader's place in a specific social or ideological formation is likely to yield a subjective or reductive analysis. But the concealed theoretical agenda of practical criticism is itself profoundly political. Idealism assumes unchanging essences, while the contradictory mediations of empiricism construct an unmediated 'reality' directly available to the senses. Together they propose a world given and readable rather than constructed and therefore available to be rewritten. They transform historical practices dependent on specific relations of production into a conservative vision of the apparently universal and perfectly natural.

Edward Harrison's journal is not accessible to practical criticism. Crossed by and caught up in a network of other texts, the entry for 9 September 1929 is largely only the unconscious processes of more finished productions—the readings of *The Tempest* and *Love's Labour's Lost*—devised like their originals for oral performance, the originals at the Globe Theatre and Blackfriars and the readings in the classroom at Placencia. Harrison has said nothing of Shakespeare's intentions in *The Tempest* or of his attitude to Sylvester Jourdain's *Discovery of the Barmudas* (1610) and other sixteenth- and early seventeenth-century texts on colonization. But in establishing and very tentatively theorizing a position "on the island" set against the "eternal truth" imagined at the "blind heart of Empire", he suggests that no retrieval of these intentions or decoding of their historical determinants could be altogether innocent or disinterested. From this point on, his own intentions become more difficult to retrieve. It is late at night and the weather, as Harrison has said, is very hot. It was no less so in London, which was experiencing an Indian summer. *The Times* for Monday 9 September records a temperature of 88 °F on the previous day. The most important news is that Flying Officer Waghorn beat off the Italian challenge and flew his seaplane to victory in the Schneider Trophy race. The *Manchester Guardian*'s editorial recommends that diplomatic relations with Moscow be resumed as all Soviet attempts at subversion have patently failed to achieve their objectives.[20] The main items of interest during the previous week appeared in sections devoted

to "Imperial and Foreign News". The third in a series of bombs
had exploded in the Reichstag and communists were being
blamed. There were riots in Palestine. Arab sources alleged
Jewish atrocities against Palestinian women .and children,
while Egypt requested that the British government revoke the
Balfour Declaration.[21] The British response to these events,
delivered by the prime minister in a speech to the League of
Nations, reaffirmed the law of Prospero and the magisterial
stillness of self-evident imperial values. Deploring an "outburst
of criminality and murder" to which "no civilized nation could
ever yield", Ramsey Macdonald pronounced:

> There is no racial conflict in what happened in Palestine the
> other day. It is not a conflict between Arab and Jew. It is an
> uprising of lawlessness and disorder, whatever its motive may
> be, and so far as we are concerned we do not care what their race
> and what their religion and what their culture may be[22]

On his island, Harrison finally subsides into verse. There is
little in the remainder of this entry, or in the one for 11 September, to amplify either his specific readings of Shakespeare or his
view of the conditions that determine any such reading or teaching. In later, more eccentric entries, Prospero becomes Matthew
Arnold, seen not as the nineteenth century's apostle of culture but
in his professional capacity as an inspector of schools who supported the suppression of the Welsh language among school-
children (p. 71).[23] Caliban, concomitantly, is not only the
Indian and the negro Harrison takes him for elsewhere but the
pupil left at the end of the day wearing the board marked 'Welsh
Not', who would be flogged for speaking the language (pp. 39,
71). This seems to be connected in his mind with a mythic Welsh
presence in the Americas based on absorption rather than
conquest—at other points he deals with Madog, Prince of
Gwynedd, who supposedly reached the New World three
hundred years before Columbus, and with reports of the discovery of Welsh-speaking tribes deep in the Amazon jungle
(pp. 53, 57). Mercifully none of this appears in his teaching notes
for Placencia, but an element of nostalgia does emerge at the end
of the first entry. Here the last two lines of an *englyn*, "Y Gorwel",
mark the meeting point of an oblique gaze to the north-east from
Placencia and west from the coast of Pembrokeshire:

> Hen linell bell nad yw'n bod,
> Hen derfyn nad yw'n darfod.

These words describe the horizon as "That distant non-existent line /Infinity of limits".[24]

Notes

1. The source of the quotations and much of the information is Hunter, 1926, pp. 185–192. See also *The Tempest*, I. i. 8–42.
2. In all cases of direct quotation by Harrison I cite the journal page reference first, followed by the source.
3. *The Tempest*, I. i. 73 and V. i. 2125.
4. *The Tempest*, II. i. 762–764 and II. ii. 1070–1.
5. *The Tempest*, I. i. 11–18.
6. *King Lear*, IV. v. 2571–2; *As You Like It*, II. iv. 800 and III. ii. 1265.
7. *The Tempest*, II. i. 721–9.
8. Gann, 1927, pp. 46–7. There are some minor omissions in Harrison's transcript.
9. The details of this and other flights described in Harrison's journal are confirmed in Eckener, 1958, pp. 49, 60, 128.
10. *Richard II*, II. i. 681–91; *Timon of Athens*, 1630–40. Michael Dangerfield, in one of the essays still retained with the manuscript, quotes the citation of the second passage in Chapter 3 of *Capital*.
11. Harrison's comments on the 'Robinsonades' follow closely those in Dangerfield's essay. Cf. Marx, 1973, p. 83; Marx, 1976–81, I, 169f.; and Engels, 1947, pp. 191–200.
12. *The Tempest*, I. ii. 348; *Hamlet*, 1. 1801–2.
13. *The Tempest*, II. ii. 1174; *Love's Labour's Lost*, I. 106.
14. For an illuminating account of some historical and ideological determinants in Dover Wilson's criticism, *see* Hawkes, 1983.
15. *Richard II*, II. i. 689–90.
16. *The Tempest*, I. ii. 410–11 and 492–504.
17. *The Tempest*, I. ii. 457–64, 493, and V. i. 2184–5.
18. My italics.
19. *See* Norman, 1976, p. 12.
20. *The Times*, 9 September 1929, pp. 12, 13; The *Manchester Guardian*, 9 September 1929, p. 8.
21. The *Manchester Guardian*, 3 September 1929, p. 6; 4 September, p. 8.
22. *The Times*, 4 September 1929, p. 11.
23. For confirmation of this point, *see* Arnold, 1962, III, 296–7; and Rowse, 1976, pp. 86–7.

24. My translation. I have been unable to find a source for these lines. The authenticity of the Harrison journal is in considerable doubt. I would ascribe to it here no more authority or truth than if it were, in fact, only a work of literary fiction.

3

The Converse of Breath

All writing is pigshit.

(Antonin Artaud)

The use-value of things is realised without exchange, by means of a direct relation between things and men, whereas their value is realised only in exchange, only in a social process. Surely, in this connexion, every one will recall the excellent Dogberry's instruction to neighbour Seacoal: 'To be a well-favoured man is the gift of fortune, but to read and write comes by nature.'

(Marx, *Capital*, Ch. 1)

The Triumph of Speech

Paid to bring Matthew Arnold's religion of culture to the natives of British Honduras, Edward Harrison, *Complete Shakespeare* in hand, promises to drown his book and do as little damage as possible (Harrison, p. 8). Historically his dilemma is particularly complex. His arrival with a book is a return to the earliest scene of colonization, where literacy was a key factor in distinguishing Europeans from their subjects in the New World. Caliban regards Prospero's books with awe, "for without them/Hee's but a Sot, as I am." (*The Tempest*, III.ii. 1446–7) The return of *The Tempest* to Placencia is, in this sense, a redoubling of its action, the 'magic' of the book now that of a cultural commodity, its mythicized use-value based on the power to bestow a guaranteed personal 'refinement' and its exchange-value inscribed in the 'centrality' and 'universality' of European concepts of cultivation. But the reference to 'drowning' the book comes from the play itself (V.i. 2007) and points to a more critical dimension in the text that puts it at odds with its later uses in the ideological work of a colonial education system. If Prospero's books mark his power over Caliban, they have also been his downfall in Milan. When his library becomes "Dukedom large enough" (I.ii. 209), the dukedom itself passes to Antonio. Prospero, "rapt in secret studies", becomes a stranger to his "state" (171), which signifies not only Milan but his own condition. Study here is an escape, a form of intoxication—Stephano's bottle is his "Booke" (II.ii. 1174)—and the library is a place set aside from active social duty. *The Tempest*, performed less than 150 years after the introduction of the first printing presses into England and at a time when the majority of English men and women remained illiterate,[1] echoes some strong reservations, common in the sixteenth and early seventeenth centuries, about the cultural impact of books and reading. Its reproduction of specific elements in a contemporary debate on speech and writing may, in a later institutional context which takes literacy and the values of a literary culture for granted, allow the text—a printed version of an *oral* performance—to be turned against itself. Harrison's 'book', if read historically, could be drowned in the reading.

Caxton promoted the printing press in England by praising

writing—a secure 'memory' for cultural and religious truths—
at the expense of speech, seen as intrinsically "perisshing, vayne
and forgeteful" (Caxton, 1928, p. 51). This distinction was
common in the Renaissance humanist account of the 'Dark
Ages' before the rediscovery of classical learning as a period of
'unlettered' ignorance and barbarism,[2] based on assumptions
that imply an even sharper denigration of the wholly illiterate
societies of the New World. The Protestant recovery of the
'true faith' was also represented in these terms, with Scripture
the sole authority against the 'unwritten verities' of apostolic
tradition on which the Roman Catholic Church based such
doctrines and practices as papal supremacy, the ceremony of the
Mass, purgatory, pardons and clerical celibacy.[3] John Foxe, in
the mid sixteenth century compared printing and the dissemination of Bibles to the Gift of Tongues, and insisted that the
papacy, in order to survive, must now root out all literacy and
learning and "excommunicate God himselfe" (Foxe and
Haddon, 1581, *Fol.*481r.). Seventy years later the puritan Dr
John Bastwick, eventually mutilated and given a life sentence
for his attacks on the popish complexion of the state Church
under Archbishop Laud, proclaimed from the pillory against
the censorship which had extended even to Foxe's great *Book of
Martyrs*: "Were the press open to us, we would scatter
[Antichrist's] kingdom" (Hill, 1980, p. 83).

The reverse formulation of this relationship between the
spoken and written word presents writing and print as the
source of pedantry, legalism and misunderstanding, and speech
as a means of living, flexible communication directed to the
specific needs and capacities of the hearer. "It more avayleth a
student to discourse one hour with his like," says Anniball in
Guazzo's *Civic Conversation* (translated into English in 1581)
"than to study a whole day by himselfe in his studie", repeating
a common contrast between the efficacy of words "lively
pronounced" and the sterility of language "set downe to be
reade in dead letters" (Guazzo, 1925, I, 43, 126).[4] This
contrast took on a particular urgency in Roman Catholic
polemic which, from the earliest attacks on such dissident
groups as the Waldensians and the Lollards to the later, more
general resistance to vernacular Bibles and the Protestant
'priesthood of all believers', warned against the fatal conse-

quences of the letter.[5] An element of this remains in the doctrinal compromises of the Church of England in the early seventeenth century. John Donne, for example, could still claim that the eye was "the devil's doore" and the ear "the Holy Ghost's first doore", so those wishing to obey the biblical injunction "Search the scriptures" should do so not by reading but by seeking knowledge from a priest (Donne, 1952, p. 278).

If the *locus classicus* for secular arguments about the inherent inferiority of writing was Plato's *Phaedrus*, the biblical authority for such a belief was St Paul's "The letter killeth but the spirit giveth life", (2 Corinthians 3:6) in which the *pneuma* or *spiritus* (literally 'breath') denotes an essential *presence* more immediate in the "natural breath" of speech (*The Tempest*, V.i.2125) than in the obstructive materiality of the written.[6] When Dogberry claims that "to write, and reade, comes by Nature", (*Much Ado About Nothing*, III.1355) a misunderstanding of the cultural character of language in general is pointed by the doubly 'unnatural' mediations of writing. According to this construction of the duality, the 'breath' of speech connotes the primary and the living while the 'letter' suggests the merely supplementary, death, distance, inflexibility. Set against a narrative on the destructive consequences of immersion in books, the 'education' of Miranda places in the foreground a dialectic which attends specifically to her involvement and needs—"Do'st thou attend me?" (I.ii.173), "I pray thee marke me" (186), "Do'st thou heare?" (203) and, finally, "Heare cease more questions/Thou art inclinde to sleepe; 'tis a good dulnesse,/And give it way" (395–8). "Your tale, Sir", says Miranda, "would *cure deafnesse*" (202). While Faustus offers to burn his books too late, Prospero willingly drowns his. At the end of *The Tempest* his dukedom will be Milan not his library, the pattern of the good governor his nurturing of Miranda.

The book is an unequivocal sign of Prospero's power over Caliban, but its drowning is a prerequisite of the "brave new world" to be instated at Milan. The dissymmetry between these two versions of the common speech-writing opposition is produced in *The Tempest* from a range of ideological materials centred on the gesture of defining each term in its essential character and in relation to the other. In one sense, writing is dead and speech living; in another, writing lives on while speech perishes at its moment of utterance. There is, of course, no end to this movement, and the figure becomes a battleground in which polarities may be reversed within a single text, depending on the position to be defended or the case to be argued. The breaking of the clerical monopoly of literacy and the expansion of secular education in the sixteenth century followed a broadly humanist programme based on the notion of an authoritative wisdom enshrined in the best of classical writings, a bastion against the 'barbarism' of illiteracy, but the fundamentally rhetorical orientation of educational curricula emphasized speech as the main instrument of society and rhetoric as an essentially oral, social practice, distinct from writing and justified in the last analysis only by *actio*, the efficacy of the performance or delivery. "Arte without utterance can do nothing", wrote Thomas Wilson on this subject in 1560, but "utterance without arte can doe right much" (Wilson, 1909, p. 218).[7] In Reformation sources the combinations are still more complex and potentially contradictory. Protestant polemic, for example, upheld the Scriptures against 'unwritten verities' but maintained equally, following the example of Christ who "himself wrote nothing, but only spoke",[8] that the gospel was an *oral* ministry. This emphasis on preaching, sustained by the essential priority of speech, made the pulpit in England from the Reformation through to the Restoration a key platform for the theological debate which was the main site of ideological struggle, and also for directly political propaganda. The 'letter' went through other transformations in this continuing conflict. Valued by Protestants as the bearer of the literal sense of the Bible, still recoverable in spite of being treated as a 'nose of wax' to be moulded at will by the allegories and *multiplex intelligensia* of Catholic exegetes, it was also despised as the idol of a Judaic legalism, regarded as being still manifest in the Roman Catholic Church's insistence that justification should not be by grace alone but also by merit before the law.[9]

In general terms and in the context of larger historical processes, the attacks on writing, and specifically print, defended a traditional feudal and Catholic order against the progressive religious and economic forces of the time. The first signs of secular literacy appeared among the merchant classes of the Italian city states in the twelfth century, and its expansion in England in the sixteenth century owed much to an educational revolution which brought about an unprecedented social mobility in providing a bureaucracy for the Protestant nation state consolidated under the Tudors.[10] Throughout northern Europe the expansion of literacy and the printing industry may, broadly, be associated with the rise of capitalism, Protestantism and individualism and the challenge to the feudal mode of production and the authority of the Church.

But the intricacies and contradictions of the various debates on speech and writing show the relative autonomy of ideology from the deeper economic and political changes which were to eventually lead to widespread literacy and the culture of the book. The speech-writing opposition offered no formal or metaphysical certainty but could be used in many different ways, even undoing itself in the metaphorical distinction between 'letter' and 'spirit' as a hermeneutic construct which applied equally to speech and writing, indicating the presence in both of a material order of words or signifiers and the 'ideas' or 'intentions' of the signified, and ensuring that if writing is always a shadow of speech, speech is no less marked by the materiality of writing. There are also obvious ironies in the fact that the classical and biblical sources cited in claims for the superiority of speech had survived in manuscript to add authority to works attacking letters in print.

Finally the Protestant justification of vernacular Bibles on the grounds that the Holy Spirit, the *speaking* Word of God, would descend to illuminate the understanding of the diligent reader—or, in Calvinist theology, the Elect—was transformed at its outer limit into the doctrine of the 'Free Spirit', in which the inner voice replaced Scripture as the sole authority, and all forms of external constraint— textual, legal, moral or institutional— became the oppressive structures of the 'letter'. With this promise of the universality of the Spirit goes the assurance of God's mercy which, in the antinomian tradition of Joachim of Fiore, the Brethren of the Free Spirit and Thomas Müntzer's Anabaptists, will make sin meaningless and herald a universal perfection.[11] The flowering of this doctrine in the most radical aspirations and practices of the English Revolution brought proclamations of the equality of all men and women—harlots, cutpurses, bishops and lords—and an end to all title-deeds and legal protection of private property, to all "Gospell ordinances" and "stinking family duties". [12] Less than thirty-five years after Shakespeare's death, the Ranters struggled for a final overturning of the 'letter' in all its manifestations, preaching a social gospel of "perfect freedom, and pure Libertinisme", in the name of God-in-man (Coppe, 1649, I, p. 1). At this point, beyond what was, in terms of the traditional disputes on religious authority, the triumph of writing over speech, a political programme emerges which parallels other visions of a world *before* writing. In Gonzalo's Golden-Age utopia too, which recalls the more positive, idealist sixteenth-century appraisals of the communities of the New World, "Letters should not be knowne" (*The Tempest*, II.i.827). [13]

However equivocal the relationship between the power of Prospero's book and the call for it to be drowned, speech triumphs at the end of *The Tempest*. The balance comes down on the side of 'breath' when Prospero invites the response of the audience, underlining an immediate reciprocation and community attributed to the oral performance:

> But release me from my bands
> With the help of your good handes:
> Gentle *breathe* of yours, my Sailes
> Must fill, or else my project failes
> Which was to please:
>   (*Epilogue*, 2330–4)

Here the theatrical context is all-important. There is no evidence to suggest that Shakespeare prepared any of his plays for publication or wished to see them in print. [14] There were, indeed, sound financial reasons why a major shareholder in an acting company who prepared scripts for performance in repertory, with the option of reviving successful plays time after time, should keep them out of the hands of the printers. [15] If printed attacks on reading tended to undermine their own case, an affirmation of the immediate 'breath' of speech in the Jacobean theatre was a different matter.

In *The Tempest*, however, this affirmation is itself suspended, wrapped in layers of acknowledged mediation, and in its way as distant and compromised as the ideal community envisaged by

Gonzalo. Earlier in the play, at the end of another performance, Prospero has already brought the audience into the action, comparing the world to a stage and drawing attention to the Globe Theatre itself:

> And like the baseless fabricke of this vision
> The Clowd-capt Towres, the gorgeous Pallaces,
> The solemne Temples, the great Globe it selfe,
> Yea, all which it inherit, shall dissolve,
> And like this insubstantiall Pageant faded
> Leave not a racke behinde: we are such stuffe
> As dreames are made on; and our little life
> Is rounded with a sleepe:
>
> (IV. i. 1822–9)

The island, the second world of romance, is identified with the theatre and both stand in the same relation to the world as dream to waking experience. But this distinction too fades and is transformed as the world itself becomes as insubstantial as the pageant or the dream.

As the text redoubles its dreaming, opposites become identical and its signs, produced from the raw materials of history and ideology, are "rounded with a sleepe" which covers the traces of their origins and claims for them an autonomy that spreads from the immediate 'breath' of the theatre to colonize the larger 'pageant' of the world. This apparent autonomy is, however, an effect not of the spontaneous generation of signs but of their over-determination, and their historical determinants speak through the dream as an ideological and political 'unconscious' which works not only in the manifest content of the text but also in its strategic repressions. [16] When Trinculo, for example, suggests that Caliban could be displayed in England for profit—"when they will not give a doit to relieve a lame Begger, they will lay out ten to see a dead *Indian*" (II. ii. 1070–2)—the sleep that purports to seal off the play's *metaphysical* discourse of 'nature' and 'art', the 'base' and the 'noble', and its legitimation of political and familial authority *per se* is momentarily broken by an incursion of the historical processes and more visibly ideological discourses in which such concepts were sustained. These would include the Tudor Poor Law, the enclosures of common land and engrossment of estates, six-

teenth-century inflation, the role in this, and in the primary
accumulation of capital, of the influx of gold from the New
World, and the ideological mirror of the Americas which could
reflect contradictory images—of the civilization of the European face and also of its barbarism. The Tupi interviewed by
Montaigne in France in 1562 observed that:

> there were men amongst us full gorged with all sortes of
> commodities, and others which hunger-starved, and bare with
> need and povertie, begged at their gates: and found it strange,
> these moyties so needy could endure such an injustice, and that
> they tooke not the others by the throte, or set fire on their
> houses.   (Montaigne, 1892, I, p. 231)[17]

As much as by what it 'says', the text is shaped by what it
endeavours to keep silent, which speaks anyway in the tracks of
the sign that betray its home in ideology even as it appears,
nominally transmuted, in the "baseless fabricke" of art. What
holds true for its relationship to ideology in general also applies
to *The Tempest*'s re-presentation of its own specific mode of
production in the theatre. Here the conjunction of mimesis and
acknowledged illusion, humanist learning and popular, oral
traditions of miming and performance, the written script and
the voices and movements of the actors, reappears as the
immediate converse of stage and audience in the "naturall
breath" of speech, which bears nevertheless the imprint of the
dream and traces of the various sixteenth-century and early-
seventeenth-century transformations of the speech-writing
opposition. Those silenced in *The Tempest* surface elsewhere—
letter and spirit or merit and grace in *The Merchant of Venice* and
Measure for Measure, the immortality bestowed by writing in the
Sonnets, the escape from conversation and experience into
literary stereotypes in the Comedies generally, and the conflict
between the "breath of Kings" and the "Inky blottes and rotten
Parchment bonds" of delegated authority in *Richard II*. In spite
of the self-contained egalitarianism of *The Tempest*'s version of
itself as a theatrical transaction, fitting in its way to the theatre,
which Alfred Harbage described as a "democratic institution in
an intensely undemocratic age" (1941, p. 11), the text can
never free itself from the historical processes inscribed in these
images specific to its mode of production and in the ideological

materials it reworks. Nor can its reproduction in later institutional forms of reading and performance be an innocent decoding of an essential signified, recoverable in its pristine presence and capable of being separated from, and thrown into relief by, a detachable historical 'background'.

Our own points of reference and practices of reading are located, as Robert Weimann points out, in "the same historical process that is both reflected in and accelerated by Shakespeare's contribution" (Weimann, 1978, p. xiv). If one vector in *The Tempest*'s ideological 'unconscious' moves from the 'letter' and 'spirit' of medieval exegesis towards a later recovery of Shakespeare's 'intentions' or 'essential meanings' from the canonical text under the auspices of Arnold's religion of culture, institutionalised in academic English Literature, another incorporates the vision of a world in which "Letters should not be knowne" and points from Müntzer's attempt to re-establish a primitive Christian communism to a utopian overturning of the 'letter' proposed by the more radical movements of the English Revolution. The 'letter' in this sense implies not only "Gospell ordinances" rejected by the Ranters but also the Norman legislation written so that "the poor miserable people might be gulled and cheated, undone and destroyed" and attacked, in the name of a more fundamental, natural and unwritten law, primarily by the Diggers and Levellers whose activities were foreshadowed in rebellions in Northamptonshire and Shakespeare's native county, Warwickshire, as early as 1607.[18] Projected forward from a utopian to a more 'scientific' socialism,[19] this second historical vector crosses Edward Harrison's journal, at odds with his institutional location in the first as professional expounder of the most sacred texts of the English culture, and proposes not only other ways of reading the Shakespearean text but also of reading the ways in which it is (and has been) read.

Here the text itself is inseparable from its ideological materials, manifest and suppressed, or from its continuing historical incrustation, reproduced as a cultural commodity and valorized within the fluid idealist category of 'literature' which, as far as twentieth-century constructions of the seventeenth century are concerned, can incorporate productions as diverse as Shakespeare's, the speculations of Sir Thomas Browne, Bacon's

Essays, and the sermons of Donne and Lancelot Andrewes, but not the work of John Bastwick, Gerrard Winstanley, Abiezer Coppe or the authors of *An Agreement of the People*. The division between this perspective and that which purports to recover the 'spirit' from the 'letter' of Shakespeare within the "pure intellectual sphere" of Arnold's critical inquiry[20] is accentuated in the colonial context, particularly in relation to *The Tempest*. For Edward Harrison's purposes the contradiction between the triumph of speech in the play, however problematic, and its appropriation to the needs of a liberal literary education will serve as a beginning. The book to be opened in the classroom at Placencia is a fundamental transformation of the Jacobean performance, '*The Tempest*' being not so much a label for a solid, unchanging document as a play on words no longer identical, if it ever was, with itself. What Harrison does not say about the "babble, babble, babble" of his other text, *Love's Labour's Lost*, is that this in its way is an even more powerful weapon for 'barbarism' against the culture that brandishes the literary masterpiece.

Bookmen and Barbarism

In the 1598 Quarto, the earliest extant text of *Love's Labour's Lost*, the closing line is set without speech-heading in a type conspicuously larger than that used for the rest of the play: "THE WORDS OF MERCURY ARE HARSH AFTER THE SONGS OF APOLLO". The striking presentation gives the initial impression that this is an extrinsic comment rather than an integral part of the action. Most modern editors have favoured the revised Folio ending of 1623, which gives these words to the 'Braggart', Armado, and adds an appropriate exit line:

> *Brag.* The Words of Mercurie
> Are harsh after the songs of Apollo:
> You that way; we this way.
> (IVb 2896–9)[21]

The two most influential modern editions, however, have followed the original ending. The *New Shakespeare* editors do so, arguing that the Quarto compositor would hardly have taken out a fresh case of type unless prompted to do so by a strong directive in the copy (Quiller-Couch and Wilson, 1923, p. 185). In the Arden edition Richard David follows suit, suggesting that the Folio revision could have been the work of someone else connected with Shakespeare's company, perhaps a stage-manager or prompter (David 1951; p. xix). The precise significance of "the words of Mercury" and "the songs of Apollo" has never been established. E. K. Chambers would have nothing to do with the line, claiming that Mercury is not at all relevant to what precedes (Chambers, 1930, I, p. 338). Other commentators, preferring the Folio version, have treated the line as a functional device for bringing the play to an abrupt halt after the songs of Spring and Winter, which could only be marred by a return to the prose of the orator Mercury.[22] But its climactic position, Delphic ambiguity and portentous tone—all emphasized in the Quarto by typographical presentation—suggest something more interesting and central than this, and this promise is fulfilled through the association of Mercury and Apollo with writing and speech.

Love's Labour's Lost opens with Ferdinand, the King of Navarre, and two of his friends intent on withdrawing from society into a separate world of silence, seclusion and book-learning. Their attempt to conquer the senses and resist all worldly desires is more than a scholarly asceticism. The purpose of the project is to transcend time, mortality and the "present breath" of life—to live for ever:

> Let *Fame*, that all hunt after in their lives,
> Live register'd upon our brazen Tombes,
> And then grace us in the disgrace of death:
> When spight of cormorant devouring Time,
> Th' endevour of this present breath may buy:
> That honour which shall bate his sythes keen
>   edge,
> And make us heyres of all eternitie
> Therefore, brave Conquerours, for so you are,
> That warre against your owne affections,
> And the huge Armie of the worlds desires.
> Our late edict shall strongly stand in force,

> Navar shall be the wonder of the world.
> Our Court shall be a little Achademe,
> Still and contemplative in living Art.
>   (I, 5–18)

Through the dream of immortality as the end of great learning, Renaissance humanism added another dimension to the medieval ideal of the contemplative life, increasing the attractions of scholarly retreat. The Academy founded at Florence in the mid fifteenth century on the model of Plato's and placed by Cosimo de' Medici under the guidance of Marsilio Ficino created a vogue for similar institutions, which spread throughout Italy in the late fifteenth century and France in the sixteenth century.[23] Ferdinand's concept of learning as a struggle against the senses to achieve knowledge normally beyond their scope is firmly in the tradition of Ficino's Neoplatonism, in which the body must be purged of its carnal grossness before the original lustre of the soul is restored to the point where "its natural light shines out, and it searches out the order of natural things" (Ficino, 1944, p. 159). This knowledge is only possible after the battle against the "affections" and "the huge Armie of the worlds desires" has been won. To this end, Ferdinand's edict stipulates that "no woman shall come within a mile of my Court" (I.129)

On entering the Academe, Ferdinand and his courtiers leave a world governed by time, the senses and mortality for a new world of personal immortality achieved through fame and a knowledge which, being beyond the scope of the senses, is itself held to be imperishable. This new world is specifically that of books. The end of study is to discover "things hid & bard . . . from common sense" (I.61), but what study in fact amounts to, as Berowne complains, is "painefully to poare upon a Booke" (79). This remark develops into a prolonged attack on book-learning which maintains that both the fame sought by Ferdinand and knowledge seemingly beyond the senses are effects of an illusory immortality bestowed on language by writing.

Berowne's attack begins with the claim that those who read books "to seeke the light of truth" will find that "truth the while/Doth falsely blinde the eye-sight of his looke" (80–1). This repeats a complaint against reading made by Montaigne[24]and in Nashe's *Summer's Last Will and Testament*, which warns against schoolmasters who, by enforcing study, "will infect you, marre you, bleare your eyes" (Nashe,. 1904–10, III, p. 279). Berowne's comment recalls again the Neoplatonic 'inner light' which shines out to illuminate things concealed from the senses, now beguiled and atrophied by another light, the uninterrupted beam of writing which, inviting no response, brings only passivity, acquiescence and darkness:

> Light, seeking light, doth light of light
>   beguile:
> So, ere you finde where light in darkenesse lies,
> Your light growes darke by losing of your eyes.
>   (82–4)

All that then remains for those who, like Ferdinand, Dumaine and Longaville, would study hard and long is to uncritically accept the ideas of others, fixed in the form of the written word: "Small have continuall plodders ever wonne,/Save base authorite from others' Bookes" (90–1). This 'base authoritie' is a mere appearance of knowledge, equivalent to the "semblance of wisdom" which Socrates, in the *Phaedrus*, claims is the only fruit of studying the "external marks" of writing (Plato, 1952, p. 157). Here the Neoplatonic project of the Academe turns against itself. The aim of the war against the senses is to free the soul, previously "plunged into the abyss of the body as though into the river of forgetfulness, oblivious at the moment of itself" (Ficino, 1944, p. 159). But to embrace writing is to accept another form of materiality, another oblivion:

> If men learn this, it will implant forgetfulness in their souls; they will cease to exercise memory because they rely on that which is written, calling things to remembrance no longer from within themselves, but by means of external marks.
>   (Plato, 1952, p. 157)

Socrates, quoting the Egyptian king Theuth, goes on to say that writing will create a breed of ignorant pedants who, priding themselves in their wisdom, will be a burden to their contemporaries. Montaigne compares such wisdom to counterfeit coins or, in an image echoed in *Love's Labour's Lost*, (IVb.

2240–1) undigested seeds in bird-droppings (Montaigne, 1892, I, 137–38). Written words remain secondary, external to the learner. For Berowne, those who learn from books achieve no more genuine knowledge than the "earthly Godfathers of heavens lights" who "walke and wot not what they are" (I. 93–6).

Here the presence of Mercury, as patron of solitary learning, begins to assert itself. Berowne alludes to the early astronomers, such figures as Thales, Anaxagoras, Pythagoras and Prometheus who were types of this kind of study,[25] which is represented in the tirade against books as a pursuit of useless knowledge. Humanist texts depict Prometheus not as the fire-stealing rebel of Shelley and Nietzsche but as the model of the pious philosopher, champion of learning against the ignorance of the illiterate. To this end, emphasis is placed on the later stages of the myth when Prometheus, for his crime against the gods, is chained to the highest peak in the Caucusus, where, through solitary ratiocination, he discovers the motion of the planets. In popular sources, however, the *topos* of the *sapiens Prometheus* is inverted to present the vain and arrogant astrologer, proof of the pointlessness of study. In *Summer's Last Will and Testament* Prometheus appears, with Thales and Pythagoras, as a member of the "company of ragged knaves" who "told fortunes, juggled, nicknam'd all the starres,/And were of idiots term'd Philosophers" (Nashe, III,p. 274). When Berowne ridicules the "earthly Godfathers of heavens lights" the play echoes this tradition, also manifest in some Renaissance emblems, of debunking the ideal *sapiens*, and *Love's Labour's Lost* follows the emblem-books in associating Prometheus with the Icarus motif (I.i.89–90) to exemplify the false pride which accompanies deficient practical wisdom and self awareness.[26] In pursuing the ideal of the *sapiens*, Ferdinand and his friends come under the tutelage of Mercury who, in the legend, bound Prometheus to his task, assuming the role of patron of learning. When Berowne later leads his fellows from books to the "true *Promethean* fire" (IVa. 1654) which springs from women's eyes, the text underlines this connection, doubly present from the outset in Mercury's association with Prometheus and in his traditional function as inventor of letters.[27]

Berowne's attack on reading concludes with a couplet which questions again the value of the timeless world of books and of the fame his friends hope to achieve through study: "Too much to know is to know nought but fame:/And every Godfather can give a name (I.i.97–8). Readers may appear to learn a great deal, but this, echoing again the words of the *Phaedrus*, is only of superficial value. The pun on "fame" incorporates the sense implied by the allegorical figure who appears in Chaucer, Hawes, *The Mirror for Magistrates*, in the induction to *2 Henry IV* as Rumour "painted full of tongues", and in the "Lady Fame" mentioned in *Much Ado About Nothing* (II. 618–19).[28]

It is in this sense, of 'report' or 'rumour', that the 'fame' of the "bookmen" reaches the Princess of France and her companions.[29] The play on "fame" further undermines the heroic quest of the Academe. Knowledge found in books may seem useful but writing, which 'blinds', leaves the reader capable only of accepting the 'authority' of others. It imparts, for all its apparent permanence and substance, knowledge as insubstantial as that of rumour, the least reliable agency of the world of speech. Those who achieve fame through learning become the authorities for other readers, who derive a knowledge which is only 'fame' in its second sense and thereby acquire the glory that will blind those who enter this debilitating spiral at its next turn. Books and the pursuit of fame are, in this construction, a death in life rather than a means of transcending this "present breath" and living for ever. Although Berowne retracts this condemnation—"I have for barbarisme spoke more,/Than for that Angell knowledge" (I. 121–2)—its point is reinforced in a burlesque action. Holofernes and Nathaniel are grotesque caricatures of learning whose desire to be "singled from the barbarous" (IVb. 1815) recapitulates both the withdrawal into academic seclusion and the inner struggle against the "huge armie of the worlds desires". The pretensions of learning are heavily underlined when Nathaniel defines the literate elite, which excludes the 'barbarous' and 'unlettered' constable, Dull, in terms which parody the Eucharist:

> Hee hath not fed of the dainties that are
> Bred in a booke.
> He hath not eate paper, as it were:
> He hath not drunke inke.
> His intellect is not replenished.
>
> (IVa, 1175–8)

When the curate relegates Dull to the status of an animal, then that of a vegetable, the monopolistic claims of the literati on the distinctively human are explicit. At stake within the text's conflicting accounts of reading is the definition of man, and the 'natural' is constituted on both sides of the debate as that from which writing escapes or recedes. Before the oath is finally sealed, Berowne offers a parting shot for 'nature' and 'barbarism' against books. As the attack on study reaches its climax, Ferdinand and Dumaine object to its contradictory coherence and sophistication—language marked by books and learning is being turned against learning and books. In reply, Berowne abandons 'reason' in an apparent *non sequitur*: "The Spring is near when greene geese are a breeding" (I. 103–4). Here the language of rational argument suddenly assumes a density and play that break through the limit of denotation. Dumaine asks how this "follows" and protests that it is "In reason *nothing*" (105, 107). But the ambiguity is right for the moment, like the spring and the green goose "Fit in his place and time" (106), and if it is "nothing" in reason it is "Something then in rime" (108). In the spring and the goose, which connote youth, sexuality and renewal, the fertility repressed by the "barren tasks" of study returns from inside the productive play of language. Moth's enigmatic poem revealing the changes that occur behind a woman's painted face is "a dangerous *rime* . . . against the *reason* of white and redde" (I. 411–12). In the same way, Berowne's "rime" acts out the transformations that belie the transcendent ideality of Neoplatonic forms, the universality of metaphysical "reason" and the solidity of words in books and names on "brazen Tombes". Being "nothing" it seems to share a common lack of substance with that "present breath" of life doomed to end in the "disgrace of death", but reason and writing provide only an illusory transcendence. Death cannot be defeated and sexual passion will not be contained by force—"for every man with his affects is borne,/Not by might mast'red, but by special grace" (I, 162–3). This is the moment when Apollo, god of rhyme, the seasons and speech, begins to take issue with Mercury.

Penned Speech and Decorum

While one term in the conflict established during this opening sequence of *Love's Labour's Lost* is clearly writing, the other at first appears to be 'nature' or 'barbarism'. But as the play proceeds, speech becomes increasingly the main antagonist of letters, and just as Mercury emblematically links the concepts grouped around the written word, so Apollo serves a similar function for the spoken. In Renaissance iconography Apollo presides not only over the Muses but also the Hours, who regulate day and night and the cycle of the seasons,[30] two functions that coalesce in Berowne's "rime" as it passes from spring and the green goose to a celebration of "each thing that in season growes" (I. 116). Apollo also serves as patron of speech and protector of the vocal chords, the anatomical equivalent of his lyre,[31] and the spoken word, with the other features that promote the cause of the "affections", is barred from the Academe. By edict any man "seene to talke with a woman within the tearme of three years" will suffer public shame", (128–9), while any woman approaching within a mile of the court will lose her tongue (122). When the women of France make their entrance they observe that it is a "silent Court" (II. 515) and, speech being "conceit's expositor" (564) or, in the terms of a Renaissance commonplace, that which "most shewes a man",[32] assume that this must be an "unpeopled house" (582). Language, as Ben Jonson recorded in another commonplace, is "the instrument of society"[33] and this, made specific to speech, is the force of the Princess's later summary of everything that has taken place in the park at Navarre as "the converse of breath" (IVb. 2693). The implications of Berowne's attack on books are developed in the more positive associations of speech and conversation that recur in relation to the women. Even when speaking in jest they observe a reciprocal pattern which stands in contrast to the blinding beam of writing described by Berowne. After one such exchange the Princess congratulates Katherine and Rosaline with an image from tennis: "Well bandied both, a set of Wit well play'd" (IVb. 1916–17).

"In talke", says Annibal in *The Civile Conversation*, "the speaker and the hearer ought to agree to take turnes, as it were, like as they doe at tennis" (Guazzo, 1925, I, p. 151). From this principle of reciprocal exchange Guazzo elaborates a whole art and ethic of conversation in society, always set against the sterility of words "set downe to be reade in dead letters". In this process the speaker is at once *revealed* and *shaped* in a network that constitutes the proper relations of language. The basic ground-rules are also formalized in *The Courtier* and in other courtesy books. In Della Casa's *Galateo* for example, translated into English in 1576, the vice of disrupting an acceptable pattern of speaking and listening is discussed alongside other such objectionable habits as exposing the genitals in public, insisting that a companion sniff a foul-smelling object found at the side of the road, or blowing your nose and then opening the handkerchief "to glare uppon thy snot, as if yu hadst pearles and Rubies fallen from thy braynes". These latter practices are objectionable because "that which offendeth the senses, may also offend the mind", but breaches of a conversational code offend the mind directly.[34]

The main classical source for this formal conversational ethic was *De Officiis*, a standard Elizabethan grammar-school text, in which Cicero maintains that speech is "the most comprehensive bond that unites together men to men and all to all" (Cicero, I, p. 51) and that, "as in other things, so in general conversation", the speaker "should think it not unfair for each to have his turn" (I, p. 134).[35] At the centre of this process is the model of the Socratic dialectic (I, p. 134) and the principle of *decorum*, explained as a special adaptation of the term employed in literary theory, which implies both an appreciation of what is fitting and an ability to make this appreciation apparent in appropriate behaviour.[36] *Decorum* in conversation means avoiding all the indiscretions attributed by Socrates in the *Phaedrus* to writing, which does not know how to match its discourse to the needs of a particular hearer, is never fully present and is always unable to explain or justify itself (275D-E). According to this version of the relationship between spoken and written words, the standard Renaissance definition of literary *decorum* as "none other than what is fitting to places, times, and persons" (Cinthio, 1968, p. 56) is, paradoxically, precisely what writing cannot achieve. As a social principle *decorum* is much more than a nicety or a matter of form: "Such is its essential nature, that it is inseparable from moral goodness; for what is proper is morally right, and what is morally right is proper" (Cicero, I, p. 94).[37]

What the courtesy books have to say about *decorum*, translated as 'decencie' or 'seemlyeness' by Puttenham in *The Arte of English Poesie* (1589), offers useful historical evidence about behaviour, and particularly the regulation of the bodily functions—information which illustrates an increasing concern in the late sixteenth century with the demarcation of private spheres exclusive to the individual and the family.[38] But as far as conversation itself is concerned, concrete instances of contemporary practice—of privilege and priority between generations, classes and the sexes for example—tend to be overshadowed by the ideal order of *decorum* and reciprocation derived from Cicero and Isocrates, and validated by an origin myth of civil society in which the linguistic skills of the first orators are instrumental in calling men and women together from their scattered dwellings in caves, woods and on mountains.[39]

This emphasis on language as a founding contract and a free exchange informs Jonson's view of speech as "the instrument of society" and the women's images of verbal tennis and a "converse of breath" in *Love's Labour's Lost*. This is the order violated by the elites who have gorged themselves on paper and ink. It remains in place as a norm by which to judge the apparent conversion of Ferdinand and his courtiers from learning and solitude to love and renewed conversation—a transformation wholly compromised in the language of the play by an underlying persistence of the letter and its associated values. When Berowne supplies the intellectual justification for breaking the oath, his friends accept what he has acknowledged all along, that "Learning is but an adjunct to our selfe,/And where we are, our Learning likewise is" (IVa. 1664-45). But what seems to be a movement from the world of Mercury to that of Apollo conceals a more fundamental continuity. One academe, one text, one connotation of Prometheus has simply been exchanged for another. Women's eyes are now "the Ground, the Bookes, the Achadems,/From whence doth spring the true *Promethean* fire" (1652–4) and Berowne's sophistry, which rationalizes the breaking of an oath, is only an elaboration of Dumaine's continuing contempt for the "breath" which signi-

fies both speech and mortality: "Vowes are but breath, and
breath a vapour is "(1401). Like book-learning, this new-found
romantic idealism amounts to no more than a spurious means of
transcendence, a false promise of escape from the mortal into
the superhuman. In his catalogue of the lover's enhanced
powers, Berowne claims that his eyes "will gaze an eagle
blinde" (line 1684) reversing the earlier description of plodders
dazzled by the sun of written wisdom. The readers have become
writers and appropriately their wooing is now conducted in
letters, poems and the "pen'd speech" of rhetorical set-pieces
(IVb. 2039, 2334), not through the *decorum* of true conversation.

In the later stages of the play, writing invades the "converse
of breath" time and again, only to be rebuffed on each occasion.
Costard, confirming the Socratic dictum that the written word
does not know how to approach the right people and avoid the
wrong (*Phaedrus* 275E), delivers letters from Berowne and
Armado each to the wrong woman. Even when a message
reaches its right destination, writing is no adequate supplement to or substitute for speech, communicating nothing
but its own intrusive materiality:

> *Ros.* O he hath drawne my picture in his letter.
> *Qu.* Anything like?
> *Ros.* Much in the letters, nothing in the praise.
> *Qu.* Beauteous as Incke: a good conclusion.
> *Kat.* Faire as a text B in a Coppie booke.
>   (Vb. 1927 30)

The women confront rhetorical "penned speech", which aims
not to elicit a response but to captivate and enchant, with the
same measure of scepticism. Ferdinand and his friends, like
Moth in the prologue to their masque of the Muscovites, are
repeatedly "put out" by disruptive interventions that cut across
speeches memorized like an actor's part (IVb. 2442–61). Their
mode of approach is as oblivious as writing itself to the
personality of the receiver. Each courtier, concealed behind his
vizard and rhetorical smokescreen, presents his favour and
declares devotion to the wrong woman (IVb. 2052–82).

In the *Phaedrus* Socrates' condemnation of writing extends to
declamatory rhetoric, which brings the limitations of the

written word into the sphere of oral discourse. (277E) The men's "penned speech" in *Love's Labour's Lost* repeats this explicit connection while underlining the continuity between their two roles as students and as lovers. These associations are confirmed, and taken to an extreme of literal absurdity, in the language of the comic pedants. The latinate vocabulary and syntax of Holofernes, crammed with scraps of bookish erudition, matches his insistence, against such "rackers or ortagriphie" as Armado (IVa. 1759), that words should be spoken exactly as they are written, with an emphasis in 'ca*l*f', 'ha*l*f', 'de*b*t' and 'nei*gh*bour', for example, on the normally silent consonants.[40] But Armado himself speaks writing in another sense, his language being based on the precepts of textbook rhetoric read in a comically literal-minded way.[41] Infatuated with Jacquenetta, he also threatens to "turne Sonnet" and bids "Devise Wit, write Pen, for I am for whole volumes in folio" (I. 486–7). Caught between an abject devotion to the stereotyped goddess of a debased petrarchanism and the body of the "base wench" Jacquenetta, Armado's predicament parallels that of Berowne, who is tormented by the gulf between an ideal, literary Rosaline and the dark mortal who can threaten him with horns. If one is the conventional *donna sapienza* whose gaze replaces books as the source of knowledge and power, the other is "pitch and defiles" (IVa. 1337) or one of the "Light Wenches" who may "prove plagues to men forsworne" (III. 1136). When Armado, humiliated in front of Jacquenetta and his peers, reaches a token discretion, he renounces at once the role of romantic lover and his "Sweete smoke of Rhetorike" (III. 832) by declaring "I breath free *breath*" (IVb. 2680). Once again the "breath" image signifies at once life and speech. Freed from the inflexible structures of rhetoric and poetic convention, both found in dead letters, the one who turned sonnet turns back to "the converse of breath".

Penned speech implicates Mercury not only as the inventor of letters but also as patron of orators and merchants, two groups connected by the association of rhetoric and selling in the imagery of *Love's Labour's Lost*.[42] The final irony is that the words of Mercury have failed to either sell or communicate anything. When the Princess, newly informed of her father's

death, states her intention of returning to France, Ferdinand
and Berowne again declare the love which has been their sole
concern during the latter part of the play. In response to their
artifice the Princess protests "I understand you not, my
greefes are double" (IVb. 2710). In the end she, no less than
Dull, has been excluded from the rites of paper and ink and
is left, like the constable, in the dark. Berowne makes
another rhetorical attempt to persuade her, and the Princess
explains at greater length that the letters, sonnets and rhetoric have all seemed only "bumbast and as lining to the time"
(2739), a line in which the text, as in all its clothing
imagery, implies insulation against time's fleeting "present
breath".

If the opening scene of *Love's Labour's Lost* is an initiation
into the world of reading and writing, the penances that
conclude the play are an induction into the order of speech.
Marriage must be postponed for at least a year. Vows can
mean little to those who regard them as nothing but breath,
and breath as only a vapour. The Princess tells Ferdinand she
will not trust his oath, and Berowne too lacks the scruple
essential to the *decorum* of conversation. His, says Rosaline, is
"a gibing spirit,/Whose influence is begot of that loose
grace,/Which shallow laughing hearers give to fooles"
(2819–21), his wit being the antithesis of the formal reciprocal 'sets' played by the women. Berowne's penance is a course
in attention to the hearer and in reciprocation. After a year of
visiting the "speechless sicke" and forcing the "pained
impotent to smile", he will know that "A jests prosperities,
lies in the eare/Of him that heares it, never in the tongue/Of
him that makes it" (2811–24). Like Ferdinand, he is to be
divested of a protective cloak of rhetoric and compelled to feel
the "frosts" and "hard lodging" of the world through "thin
weeds" (2761). After a year, their boyish pursuit of book-
learning and word games over, the four young men may be
reconsidered as potential husbands. To this end, Katherine
wishes Dumaine "a beard" (2784) before all else. This
project, "too long for a play" (2840), may fit Ferdinand,
Dumaine, Berowne and Longaville for the 'breath' of life and
conversation, heralding the final triumph of speech over
writing.

Mercury versus Apollo

It is quite possible to read out of *Love's Labour's Lost* a symmetrical production of a diversity of sixtenth-century ideological materials associated with speech and writing. Initiations at the beginning and the end recapture a central structural opposition emphasized throughout in the relationship between two levels of action, courtly and low-comic. While the courtiers prepare to immerse themselves in books, Armado's rhetoric and infatuation anticipate the scenes that follow the collapse of the Academe. The late entry of Holofernes and Nathaniel, in the middle of Act 4, keeps learning and its bearing on penned speech in the foreground after the young men have abandoned their studies. Ferdinand's preoccupation with fame at the outset is recapitulated in the Show of the Nine Worthies, cut short by the climactic entrance of Marcade. In this pageant, a play within the play, all of these considerations are focused on the performance in hand. The men disrupt the Show, insisting on a narcissistic display of wit and proclaiming that the actors are not really who they pretend to be. The women observe *decorum*, attending to time, place and persons, encouraging the actors and accepting the conventions of dramatic illusion. Here the performance, a social ritual which formalizes the reciprocal pattern of speaking and listening in the relationship of stage and audience, is a testing ground for and a reaffirmation of the "converse of breath". Unlike the performances of the courtiers, acting which passes itself off as 'real' and aims to enchant, the theatrical illusion discloses itself as such and may purge speech, in some ways, of the interventions of the written. At this moment of theatrical self-consciousness the audience is again on the stage. In *Love's Labour's Lost*, as later in *The Tempest*, there is an open acknowledgment of the transaction and, in the Globe Theatre, no darkened auditorium, no sustained naturalism and no empathic escape into a fictive world.

This utopian image of the text's mode of production calls for further analysis in terms of what it represses, and the 'characters' and 'themes' that constitute the play's "converse of breath" on the level of its action continually face back into the repetitions and excesses of the 'letter' apparent in the densely patterned language and choreographed movements of the actors. But even a conventional thematic reading brings out a major contradiction in the historical transformation of the text into 'literature'. Only in the Elizabethan theatre, an institution of a still predominantly oral society, is *Love's Labour's Lost* "fitted to time, place and persons", and here writing takes on its full obstructive strangeness. This is inevitably lost, or trivialized, in the modern encounter with the play in books or the canonical text's *mise en scène* in a brightly lit space in the bourgeois theatre. Dogberry's "to write, and reade, comes by Nature" has largely lost its force for cultures to which literacy is at least second-nature and in which the dominant institutional practices of reading anxiously erase their theoretical assumptions to make it all seem as natural as possible. Implicit in Costard's weighing of Berowne's "guerdon" against Armado's "remuneration" in terms of a shilling as opposed to three-farthings (III. 936–8) is the assumption that language, uncontaminated by the communion of paper and ink, should be a currency. It is therefore ironic that *Love's Labour's Lost* now constitutes part of the linguistic and cultural capital by which the 'cultivated' set themselves apart from the dull. "Taffata phrases, silken tearmes precise,/Three-pil'd Hyperboles" (IVb. 2338–9) are no longer necessary, 'literature' having expanded with the contraction of the study of rhetoric. "The English working classes", as George Orwell wrote, "are branded on the tongue". The words of Mercury are harsh after the songs of Apollo.

The Quarto presentation gives Mercury and Apollo their proper weight as a postscript. In print *Love's Labour's Lost* is a self-contradiction which falls foul of the Socratic warning that anyone who writes or picks up a book "on the supposition that such writing will provide something reliable and permanent" must be "exceedingly simple-minded" (Plato, p. 157). This note about Mercury and Apollo renews that warning. Such comments on printed play-texts are not unusual in the period. A number of bemused reactions survive to Jonson's pretensions in publishing ephemeral plays as "Works".[43] Marston, in his preface to *The Malcontent*, regrets that what is essentially oral should be printed, and reminds readers of *The Fawne* that comedies in particular are produced to be spoken not read—"the life of these things consists in action" (Marston, 1934–39, I, p. 139; II, p. 144). There is at least an intriguing possibility that the prominent remark on Mercury and Apollo at the end of *Love's Labour's Lost* was added to Shakespeare's foul-papers on the way to the printer.[44] Its enigmatic quality might have served, like Berowne's "rime", to interrupt the trance, cut across the beam of print and throw the reader back into the world of Apollo. Perhaps people on three-year ventures into book-learning who read books like *Love's Labour's Lost* on the futility of such projects deserve to be confused. Then there is the scope Mercury and Apollo might provide for some future academician to travel back and materialize inside the text, assist it in delivering the spirit from the letter, police the traffic of other texts where it crosses at key points, and reaffirm a critical discourse inscribed in assumptions about the written tradition not unlike Ferdinand's. Edward Harrison's class on *Love's Labour's Lost* might well have ended with the observation that as we take our place in a great tradition to praise him, a dark whisper—swelled, one suspects, by the breath of Shakespeare himself—urges us to bury him.

Notes

1. In 1533 Thomas More estimated that sixty per cent of the population could read the English Bible (More, 1557, p. 850). Lawrence Stone dismisses this as Roman Catholic propaganda, "alarmist nonsense" based on a fear of the heresies that might arise from the availability of vernacular Bibles, but estimates that by the 1630s More's estimate might well have become a reality (Stone, 1964, p. 42). More recent research shows, however, that by the mid seventeenth century the majority of English men and women were still unable to sign their names (Cressy, 1981, p. 73; Spufford, 1981, p. 22). Shakespeare's father was probably illiterate (Schoenbaum, 1975, pp. 30–8; Cressy, 1981, pp. 57–8). On the problems of assessing the extent of literacy in pre-industrial England, *see* Schofield, 1968.
2. Baldwin, 1939, p. 4.
3. Chemnitz, 1582, p. 51.
4. Cf. Guevara, 1575, p. 164 and Huarte Navarro, 1590, p. 135.
5. Fulke, 1579, pp. 4, 23; Deanesly, 1920, pp. 452–3; Bainton, 1951, p. 250. Cf. Cressy, 1980, pp. 2, 44.

6. *See* Cohen, 1954.
7. Cf. Guevara, p. 164.
8. Martin Luther, *cit*. Ebeling, 1970, p. 132.
9. Bainton, 1963, p. 5; Grant, 1963, p. 102f.; Dickens, 1964, pp. 59–63; Jedin, 1961, II, pp. 56, 308.
10. Cipolla, 1969, pp. 41–2; Stone, 1965, p. 672f.; Simon, 1966; Charlton, 1965.
11. *See*: Cohn, 1970, pp. 108–9, 155, 170–1, 180–5, 213; Morton, 1970, pp. 71–92.
12. Coppe, 1649, I, p. 10; II, pp. 2, 12, 15.
13. *See* Kermode, 1954, pp. xxx to xxxviii.
14. Wilson, 1945, p. 89; Bentley, 1964, pp. 3–4; Brown, 1964, p. 212.
15. Brown, 1964, pp. 205–8.
16. For the use of Freud's theory of dream in Marxist criticism, *see* Macherey, 1978, pp. 150–1 and Eagleton, 1976, pp. 90f. On the 'political unconscious' of the text, *see* Jameson, 1981, *passim*.
17. *Cit*. Hulme, 1981, p. 75.
18. Hill, 1961, pp. 21, 151–6.
19. *See* Engels, 1892, p. 395 and *passim*.
20. Arnold, 1962, III, p. 271.
21. The Folio text has two consecutive fourth acts, here designated IVa and IVb.
22. Hart, 1906, p. 183; Arthos, 1965, p. 146.
23. Yates, 1947, pp. 2, 8, 123, 264.
24. Montaigne, 1892, I, p. 136.
25. Rice, 1958, pp. 46, 153; Nashe, 1904–10, III, p. 274.
26. Raggio, 1958, pp. 55–6.
27. Wilkins, 1641, p. 7; Starnes and Talbert, 1955, pp. 156–7; Raggio, 1958, pp. 53–5; Yates, 1964, p. 2.
28. Benjamin, 1958, p. 64.
29. "You are not ignorant all-telling fame/Doth noyse abroad Navar hath made a vow,/Till painefull studie shall out-weare three yeares,/No woman may approach his silent Court" (II. 512–15).
30. Starnes and Talbert, pp. 94, 179.
31. *Ibid.*, p. 432.
32. Jonson, 1925–52, VIII, p. 625. Cf. Sadoleto, 1916, p. 46.
33. Jonson, *ibid.*, p. 620.
34. Della Casa, 1892, pp. 8, 16–17, 86f. 104–5; Castiglione, 1900, pp. 70, 123–4, 140; Guazzo, 1925, I, pp. 72, 78–9, 94, 150–1.
35. Cicero, 1913, pp. 55, 137.
36. *Ibid.*, pp. 101f.
37. *Ibid.*, p. 97.
38. *See* Stone, 1977, pp. 159–60, 253–7.
39. Cicero, *De Oratore*, I, 30–4.

40. *See* Bradbrook, 1964, *passim*.
41. Talbert, 1963, p. 281.
42. *See* IVa. 985f., 1588–9.
43. *See* Wells, 1970, pp. 39–49; Albright, 1927, pp. 207f.
44. Suggested privately by J. G. McManaway.

4
Master and Slave

With us islanders Shakespeare is a kind of established religion in poetry.   (Arthur Murphy, 1753)

The slave trade was a crime when the chiefs made war on each other for the sake of captives whom they could turn into money. In many instances, perhaps in most, it was innocent and even beneficent. Nature has made us unequal, and Acts of Parliament cannot make us equal. Some must lead and some must follow, and the question is only of degree and kind. For myself, I would rather be the slave of a Shakespeare or a Burghley than the slave of a majority in the House of Commons or the slave of my own folly. Slavery is gone, with all that belonged to it; but it will be an ill day for mankind if no one is to be compelled any more to obey those who are wiser than himself.

(J. A. Froude, 1887)

Prospero's Third

When Prospero frees Ferdinand from log-carrying and hands
over Miranda, he describes the exchange as a loss of one third of
his substance:

> If I have too austerely punish'd you,
> Your compensation makes amends, for I
> Have given you here a third of mine owne
>   life,
> Or that for which I live:
> <div align="right">(<i>The Tempest</i>, IV. i. 1652–5)</div>

Prospero's "third" has been explained in different ways—the
years devoted to his daughter's upbringing, Miranda as
opposed to Prospero and his dead wife, Miranda as opposed to
Prospero and Milan. Theobald conjectured "thread" ("*thrid*") as
more appropriate since Prospero, a widower, should regard
Miranda as *half* himself. To complicate the issue further, Frank
Kermode in the Arden edition notes these variations and allows
a possible pun on "thrid"/"third" which gives them all a
simultaneous presence (Kermode, 1954, p. 93).

This act of semantic largesse in the most influential modern
version of *The Tempest* is part of a larger rhetorical strategy in
which the editor's text alternates between complexity and a
pedagogically convenient simplication. By this point the reader
has already been armed with an introduction more prestigious
than most in the Arden series,[1] and told that such a guide can
only be "a simple diagram of an exquisitely complex structure"
(p. xxv). The guide concludes by gesturing again to the unique
and irreducible, those distant meanings wrapped in a numinous
haze "beyond the last analysis of criticism" (p. lxxxviii). But
between these celebrations of an elusive essence that offers, in
its complex invisibility, a guarantee of transcendent meaning is
an explanation of the text which is all too straightforward.
Prospero *represents* cultivation and Art in the broad sense of
power over the self and the world (pp. xxiv to v, xlviii, li).
Caliban, on the other hand, is Nature, the vile, sense without
intellect, a figure "born to slavery, not to freedom" (pp. xxiv to
xxv). Caliban's lust is set against the noble affections of
Ferdinand, his natural corruption against the sins of the noble

malefactors who, although capable of accepting grace, choose
evil and place themselves temporarily beneath even the slave
whose nature will not accept "any print of goodness" (p. 32).
But the noble are redeemable, and Prospero's "great achieve-
ment" in the play is to bring them to "self-conquest" and
"redemption" (pp. lxi to lxii). If Antonio is a defaulter, this is
where the simple structure bounces back again into its
renowned complexity. A world without his like would be "a
world without freedom" (p. lxii). Kermode allows some of
Antonio's "original brightness" (p. lxii) to shine through in the
final "brave new world" engineered for Miranda, which
momentarily threatens to redeem even the inherently brutal
nature of Caliban:

> I'll be wise here after,
> And seek for grace. What a thrice-double ass
> Was I, to take this drunkard for a god,
> And worship this dull fool!
>
> (p. 131)

In the Arden *Tempest* there is no suggestion here of guile,
evasion of further 'pinches' from Prospero, or another stage in
Caliban's developing rejection of would-be kings of his island.
There is at the end only the fraction of a possibility that the
uneducable slave may, after all, aspire to a fuller humanity by
yielding totally to the ethic of his oppressor (p. lxi).

It is only in this minute detail that the theory of slavery in
Kermode's *Tempest* differs from that of Aristotle, who claimed
in the *Politics* (1245 a–b) that some are born to be slaves and
others to rule over them, members of each category being fixed
in their unchanging natures. If the English student who reads
Love's Labour's Lost on a three-year course of book-learning is
placed in a contradictory position, the descendant of actual
slaves reading *The Tempest* under a post-colonial education
system is doubly enmeshed. What, for example, should a black
student who wishes to show a refined sensibility to the Oxford,
Cambridge or London GCE examining board do with this
formulation of the politics of the play according to Kermode:
"If Aristotle was right . . . then the black and mutilated
cannibal must be the natural slave of the European gentleman,
and, *a fortiori*, the salvage [*sic.*] and deformed Caliban of the

learned Prospero"? (p. xlii).[2] Discuss. Aristotle's proposition, although hedged here with an 'if', is the most basic affirmation in Kermode's version of the play. The author, named 'Shakespeare', cannot be called to account, not least because of the easy escape route through 'complexity'. Even as simple ideas and structures are expounded, Kermode claims that the play does *not* offer definitions "with the single-minded clarity of a philosophical proposition", and that this, like Shakespeare's "mature poetry" generally, has a "richly analytical approach to ideas which never reaches after a naked opinion of true or false" (p. xxviii). The rhetoric of complexity, maturity and exquisite riches clothes the nakedness and barbarism of the basic affirmation about masters and slaves being created by nature. Now you see it, now you don't. 'Shakespeare' is and is not an early apologist for slavery in the New World. Many of the sources, writes the editor, were devoted to the task "of persuading the public that exploration was an honourable and indeed sanctified activity" (p. xxxi). By implication the text and commentary, purged by the white magic of art and disinterested liberal scholarship, are involved in no such ideological work. In this privileged space of 'complexity' there is no persuasion, no point of view, and *The Tempest* that emerges can still endorse one of the most fundamental tenets of colonialism and fascism, safely distanced to Aristotle and the Athenian slave-state commonly regarded as the birthplace not only of the humane spirit of disinterested inquiry but also of Western democracy.

Kermode's *Tempest* is well suited to the classroom. It is the triumph of Prospero as "schoolmaster" or "tutor" (p. 20). The hero educates those who have the potential and keeps the incorrigible duffer and sneak in his place. Give or take a few ineffables, the Arden edition makes the play teachable in an hour or two while gesturing towards infinite riches to be explored in a brave new world free of such intractable facts of nature as examinations and the curriculum. Here the teacher becomes Shakespeare's 'superman'. In keeping with its structure and tone, this version is conservative in its critical ideology. 'Characters' are discrete and 'represent' specific 'ideas'. Ambiguities are resolved by appeal to the laws of genre (pp. xxiv, lv), so Aristotle rules in form as well as in the theory of slavery. The commentary as a whole is confirmed with

reference to Shakespeare's intentions (p. lxxxviii). Within this
framework the political is transformed into the personal, issues
of power into self-knowledge, redemption, and power over the
self. The play is *there* to be understood, like Macherey's rock
stripped of its incrustations, and this understanding, free of
prejudice and ideology, will constitute's the pupil's education
and mastery.

This version of the Arden *Tempest* is, inevitably, a simple
diagram of an exquisitely complex structure, rich in the sort of
historical detail and solidity of specification that led Edward
Harrison to ally most of the academic literary scholarship of his
day with the forces of darkness in *Macbeth*, which "tell us
truths, win us with honest trifles, to betray us in deepest
consequence" (Harrison, p. 59). It has colonized again the text
of *The Tempest* and left it safe for debate on the monumental
issues that so irritated Harrison, such as whether Prospero is
perfect from the outset or merely achieves perfection as the play
progresses. Between Harrsion's comment (1929) and the date
of the Arden Introduction (1954) falls a period of 'rare men' and
hero-worship which gives a special resonance to Aristotle's
theory about those born to be irrevocably either masters or
slaves, and to the information that Shakespeare's intention was
to construct a text which reproduces this theory at a fundamental level. At such a time it would seem advisable, especially
in the terms of liberal humanist criticism, to confront directly
the relationship between this proposition and the exquisite
complexity of an aesthetic structure which can somehow
embody it, yet make it transcendent to the point of no longer
being itself.

Kermode's work of disinterested elucidation is the classic
labour of Nietzsche's philologist, who struggles to keep books
that are held to be valuable in a condition in which they may
also be regarded as genuine and intelligible:

> It presupposes that the rare men are not lacking (though they
> may not be visible), who actually know how to use such
> valuable books . . . Philology presupposes a noble belief,—that
> for the benefit of some few who are always "to come," and are
> not there, a very great amount of painful, and even dirty labour
> has to be done beforehand.   (Nietzsche, 1960, p. 139)

The heroes Kermode's *Tempest* awaits might, at its particular historical moment, carry troubling connotations in excess of Nietzsche's intentions. But this play, if disturbing as a product of the post-war years, is more comprehensible in the context of an emerging African and later Caribbean threat to a dwindling imperial power. It belongs to the period when the exquisite complexities of Mau Mau and its legacy were being reduced in the propaganda of British politicians and the press to a simple diagram of Caliban's anarchic brutality. It is testimony to the labour of preservation by which Shakespeare criticism keeps cultural monuments intact that this version of the play should still be reprinted and remain, in its way, definitive. Long after Professor Kermode has achieved redemption as godfather of British 'structuralism', with its suspicion of character, intention and plain meaning, his *Tempest* lives on. Prospero remains eternally master and Caliban slave, each by nature, even though Kermode acknowledges that "poetry has a history; ideas-in-poetry (which are not the same as ideas) have a history too; and the historian's task is a delicate and creative one" (p. lxxxviii). The central theoretical issue is still being obscured (an effect of ideas-in-Shakespeare-criticism) by a discourse which deflects the question of the precise relationship between an exquisite complexity on the one hand, and on the other a proposition which rewrites historical relations of oppression as universal facts of nature. But when Kermode refers to the historian's task as "creative", his text breaks through the confines of its historical and philological discourse. Here "creative" entails more than the flaccid jargon of humanist criticism, the register of the 'imaginative', the 'complex' and the 'exquisite'. The term reveals the historian's project of elucidation as a *production* of historical 'intentions' and 'facts' in the present. Here Kermode's work of clarification relocates itself, in Nietzsche's term, in the process by which any text kept alive in the institutions and rituals of ideology is severed from its source and, "no matter what its origin, is periodically reinterpreted by those in power in terms of fresh intentions" (Nietzsche, 1956, p. 201). *The Tempest* is unleashed.

Edward Harrison's cryptic note on Hegel's master–slave relation as a key to "*The Tempest* read on the island instead of at the blind heart of Empire" (p. 8) adds another dimension to the play of Prospero's "third". On the island Prospero controls three others, each in a particular relationship of subjection, each his to punish, liberate or exchange at will. In Hegelian terms these constitute and guarantee their master's identity, or what Prospero, when he hands Miranda to Ferdinand, calls "mine own life,/Or that for which I live". His very subjectivity is constructed in relation to his own subjects—Miranda, Ariel and Caliban, who also stands in for the other two: "For I am all the Subjects that you have,/Which first was mine owne King" (I. ii. 480–1). If *Love's Labour's Lost* reproduces the idea that knowledge of the self develops through mutual exchange, specifically in language as the "instrument of society", *The Tempest* rediscovers this network in a colonial context and goes beyond the free converse of already constructed 'individuals' into the production of the *subject* itself, in the double sense of individual identity and ideological subjection. Prospero's initial attention to Miranda as a listener—"I pray thee marke me", "Do'st thou heare?", "Heare a little further"—is inscribed at once in the earlier ethic of reciprocal *decorum* and in *The Tempest*'s transformations of master and slave. In Hegel's formulation, a theory which does more for the true complexity of the play than Aristotle's, the master–slave relation is not given by nature but produced as a condition of self-consciousness itself: "Self-consciousness exists in and for itself when, and by the fact that, it so exists for another; that is, it exists only in being acknowledged" (Hegel, 1977, p. 111).[3] I recognize myself through recognizing another recognizing me. By enslaving the other I overcome the threat to my identity posed by its dependence on her or his recognition. Prospero teaches Miranda who she is—"my daughter who/Art ignorant of what thou art, naught knowing/Of whence I am" (I. ii. 101–3)—by affirming his own identity and her relationship to it. This finds him in a characteristic process of constructing and maintaining 'Prospero' which he also pursues with his other two "thirds", Ariel and Caliban, both of whom forget or resist his definitions.

Prospero is only safely himself in relation to those who are his—daughter, minister and slave. When Miranda marries Ferdinand he is diminished by a third. But the fact that the gift can be transferred intact points to the contradiction in this ceremonial sacrifice of his own life. Miranda, like Ariel and

Caliban, poses a threat over and above her initial confirmation of Prospero's self-consciousness. The Hegelian
master, having stabilized his identity by the subjection of
the other, has only raised the original uncertainty to a higher
level by instituting his own fear of the developing self-
consciousness, and eventual revolt, of the slave. Prospero is
characterized by a constant preoccupation with the potential
disobedience of his daughter, no less than Ariel and Caliban,
or the extent to which each may aspire to the proper name
which signifies the subject as agent rather than mere subjected object.

Caliban, who strives against domination, suffers the "pens"
and "pinches" of unending constriction. Even Ariel, the
'good native', is constantly reminded of the myth of his
origin, enmired in nature and black magic, trapped in "a
cloven Pyne" (I. ii. 404) and then freed into slavery by the
benevolent Prospero. In spite of his services, Ariel still hears
that he is essentially a liar and a "malignant thing" whose
identity will be reimposed again and again by his lord: "I
must/Once a moneth recount what thou has bin,/Which thou
forgetst" (389–91). Prospero's squirming unease, a token of
perfection only in the culture of the queen's Christmas broadcast and the stiff upper-lip, is the classic predicament of the
Hegelian master's making. To secure recognition he has
transformed the slave into a beast or an object, which can no
longer satisfy him as a source of the recognition he craves.
The relationship of father and daughter is marked by the same
tormented concern with place, identity and forgetfulness.
Miranda's imaginary yielding to the desire of a Caliban always
clouds Prospero's view of her dalliance with Ferdinand, the
other "patient Logge-man" prepared to "slave to it" (III. i.
1312–12) for her pleasure. In love, she is to her father the
"poor worme" which is the source and site of infection
(1272). The threat of plague, "barren hate", "Sower-ey'd
disdaine" and weeds bestrewing the "union of your bed" (IV.
i. 1672–3) remains until the contract is fulfilled and Prospero
is diminished by a third. At this moment the 'character' fades
into the function of stage-manager at the wedding masque
and becomes collected only when the master recalls his need
to control and punish:

> I had forgot that foule conspiracy
> Of the beast *Calliban*, and his confederates
> Against my life: the minute of their plot
> Is almost come
>
>   (IV. i. 1809–12)

Prospero is himself again.

The Hegelian dialectic embraces the contradictions flattened out by Aristotle and Kermode. The master's own certainty is doomed to be mediated by the recognition of one unworthy of recognizing him. His superiority over nature is also mediated by the work of the slave (Ariel, Caliban, temporarily Ferdinand), who transforms the given conditions so that they conform to the master's requirements. While the master is served by nature without having to serve nature in return, the slave, put to work, becomes a master of nature who may come to rule in a world transformed by his work. The slave's labour, which changes the world, may also contribute to his recognition of his place in it—a recognition founded on a political will and consciousness rather than the static 'self-knowledge' of the master, which resolves itself into the tautologous formula "I am I".[4] While the master is slave to the contradictions in his own position, the slave can become, and is always in a sense, master.[5] The Caliban who remains on the island will never again be the willing dupe of a Prospero, a Trinculo or a Stephano. Already in his revelry, shared with the butler and jester, there are hints of an advance from the native who welcomed Prospero and showed him "all the qualities o' th' Isle" (I. ii. 476). These scenes of riot and political topsy-turvydom are firmly in the tradition of popular utopianism and the Land of Cockaygne, offering a carnivalesque release from designated role and identity—a release which goes beyond festivity's immediate conservative function as an ideological safety valve. The inversion of customary rule and normal good sense offers a glimpse of their conventional, finite quality as constructions given by law and history, not by nature. The relation of master and slave, in which identity itself is inscribed, is at least reversible.[6]

In the reading from the island, the Hegelian account suggested by Edward Harrison, Miranda's "brave new world"

(V. i. 2159), the exquisite climax of the Arden version, becomes a foil to Caliban's silent repossession of his island, all of the play's platitudes of mastery in a *reductio ad. absurdum* spoken by its true, willing slave as she passes from one master to the next. Harrison's reading does not banish the more orthodox version but shadows it throughout. Kermode adopts the informal empirical approach which means, as always, that undisclosed theories inform the reading in oblique, unsystematic ways, and at one point Hegel sits anonymously and uneasily beside Aristotle. Kermode presents the Renaissance sources on the inhabitants of the New World in terms of a conflict between the 'noble savage' thesis and the antithetical view of 'savages' as products of a corrupt nature in need of cultivation (pp. xxxiv to xxxviii). His *Tempest* is put forward as a synthesis but one which, by juggling aesthetic complexity and the slippery category of "ideas-in-poetry", banishes the contradictions accepted by Harrison and recognized in Hegel's dialectic as perpetually raging beneath the calm, empirical surface of things. While Kermode's play is empirically and innocently itself, an entity which may be encountered without incrustation or appropriation, Harrison's version, the Aristotle/Kermode *Tempest* rewritten to incorporate its own negation and the material history of its mastery, is already, at the moment of reading, consciously inserted into a system of discourses and political intentions.

The Arden *Tempest*, at heart a neo-Aristotelian morality play on master, slave and the value of what Kermode calls "self-conquest" (p. lxi), deals with characters, their natural strengths and shortcomings, the nurturing of the self and a mimetic concept of drama from which the commentary, endorsed by Shakespeare's intentions, derives the unspoken paternal assumptions of empire. On his island Harrison is better placed to read these assumptions out of *The Tempest*, to reveal the contradictions in Prospero's incessant hectoring of his subjects, the intricacy of the master–slave dialectic, and a Nietzschean vision of the will to power which negates self-conquest depoliticized and re-presented as an absolute virtue:

> Certain individuals have such a great need of exercising their power and love of ruling that, in default of other objects, or

because they have never succeeded otherwise, they finally excogitate the idea of tyrannizing over certain parts of their own nature, portions or degrees of themselves . . . In every ascetic morality man worships a part of himself as God and finds that he needs to diabolize the other part.

(Nietzsche, 1910, p. 159)

This dismantling of thematic 'content' is accompanied by a questioning of mimetic form. In his concern with the *production* of individual identity in relation to the other, Harrison dislodges the position Kermode offers his reader as a given unified subject. He also undermines this subject's textual confirmation in the category of character. In line with Nietzsche's formulation of self-conquest, Prospero begins by protesting that Caliban is a "poysonous slave, got by the divell himselfe" (I. ii. 457) and ends with a recognition that signifies both property and identity: "this Thinge of Darkenesse, I/Acknowledge mine" (V. i. 2270–1). An excess in the language that constitutes the 'nature' of this diabolic darkness, and which has taught Caliban nothing but "how to curse" (I. ii. 505), here discharges the knowledge that Caliban and Prospero, each a space of heterogeneous connotations, are also in a sense one and the same. This excess is precisely what Kermode's *Tempest* suppresses, reinforcing Arnold's concept of literature as a safe repository of cultural values, a humanizing force which assumes the civilizing function of religion but none of its potentially disruptive fervour and irrationalism. The play it produces subscribes to what Nietzsche called the Apollonian dimension of classicism, summed up in "Know thyself" and "Nothing in excess" (Nietzsche, 1956, p. 34). As such it holds a particular attraction for bourgeois morality, "a mere fabrication for purposes of gulling; at best, an artistic fiction, at worst, an outrageous imposture", and absorbs the secular remnants of a Christian tradition which represents the "most sinister form of the will to destruction" (Nietzsche, 1956, pp. 10–11).

This will to destruction, related to what Kermode calls "providence" (p. xxxix) and to Hegel's Master–God who offers the comforts of slavery to all,[7] reappears at the end of *The Tempest* with the return of Prospero's "third". In his penulti-

mate speech he gives his noble prisoners the programme for
tomorrow and the days to come:

> And in the morne
> I'le bring you to your ship, and so to *Naples*,
> Where I have hope to see the nuptiall
> Of these deer-belov'd, solemnized,
> And thence retire me to my *Millaine*, where
> Every third thought shall be my grave.
>
> (V. i. 2304–9)

Here the "third" resumes and extends its play. The part of
Prospero no longer stabilized by the subjection of Miranda may
turn towards his grave. Alternatively this may be the third
which returns to the elements with Ariel, or that left on the
island with Caliban. Of the three parts devoted to the deathly
stasis that is the Hegelian master's goal of identity and power,
any one may become Prospero's grave without essential transformation. The other two can operate unchanged in the rule of
the restored 'legitimate' master of Milan. In the Jacobean
theatre the Epilogue requests that the audience dissolve this
'Prospero' and set him free with their breath. In the classroom,
students open their books and wait for the master whose first
words are always: "Be collected,/No more amazement".

Particularities of Time Past

In his entry for the 12 May 1930, written on the island of
Spanish Wells in the Bahamas, an exclusively white settlement
inhabited by the descendants of six puritan families shipwrecked on their way to the American mainland, Edward
Harrison observes that Prospero merits an earlier, violent
death, "an Antigonus death, the corpse left to rot on the strand;
seasoned by the spindrift, carrion for scavengers of the land, sea
and air" (p. 39). He notes that Prospero's protection is "only his
book—Shakespeare's book, now my own", and misquotes
Caliban's advice to his confederates: "After first seizing his
book, with a log batter his skull, or paunch him with a stake, or
cut his wezand with a knife. But remember first to possess his
book" (p. 40).[8]

The early sources on colonization bear out this threat of writing and print. In *A briefe and true report of the new found land of Virginia* (1588) Thomas Harriot describes the native Americans as having "no letters nor other such meanes as we to keep records of the particularities of times past" (Quinn and Quinn, 1973, p. 69). When the Bible is explained to them as the writing of the one who is behind letters as well as guns, fireworks and magnifying glasses, they scramble "to touche it, to embrace it, to kisse it, to holde it to their breastes and heades, and stroke over all their body with it" (Quinn and Quinn, p. 71). Fifty years later, John Wilkins records another tale from the New World on the power of writing:

> There is a pretty relation . . . concerning an Indian slave, who being sent by his Master, with a basket of figs and a letter, did by the way eat a great part of his carryage, conveying the remainder unto the person to whom he was directed, who when he read the letter, and not finding the quantity of figs answerable to what was there spoken of; he accuses the slave of eating them, telling him what the letter said against him.
>
> (Wilkins, 1641, pp. 6–7)

The slave denies the accusation, curses the paper and fails to learn his lesson. On his next trip he again eats the figs but takes the precaution of hiding the letter under a large stone, "assuring himselfe, that if it did not see him eate the figges, it could never tell of him". But now, "being more strongly accused than before, he confesses the fault, admiring the divinity of the paper, and for the future doe's promise his best fidelity in every employment" (Wilkins, p. 7).

Wilkins's book, entitled *Mercury* in celebration of the inventor of letters, recapitulates the virtues traditionally associated with writing. Those without letters lack history in the sense of an objective record of what Harriot calls "particularities of times past", a means of communicating across space, and a key instrument for "the promoting of humane society" and "the perpetuating of our names unto following times" (Wilkins, p. 5). In comparison with these central functions the "pretty relation" about controlling the slave seems incidental, a fringe benefit of literate culture which, in Wilkins's terms, even benefits the Indian by raising him to a basic standard of honesty and decency. But Claude Lévi-Strauss has argued that the *main* historical function of writing has been to establish and sustain the relations of master and slave. Historically, the cultural assimilation of letters, he maintains in *Tristes Tropiques*, has gone hand in hand with the formation of cities and empires and the integration into a political system of large numbers of individuals, distributed into hierarchies, castes and classes. The primary function of writing has been to "facilitate the enslavement of other human beings" (Lévi-Strauss, 1961, p. 292), the 'disinterested' pursuit of science and the arts being secondary features which support and mystify the main objective. This principle, at work in the ancient civilizations of Egypt and China as well as in the European colonization of the Americas, is projected forward by Lévi-Strauss to more recent times. The apparent benefits of compulsory education, instituted throughout Europe in the nineteenth century, were subsidiary to its role in the extension of military service and a general tightening of control over the proletariat:

> The struggle against illiteracy is indistinguishable, at times, from the increased power exerted over the individual citizen by the central authority. For it is only when everyone can read and write that Authority can decree that 'ignorance of the law is no defence'.   (Lévi-Strauss, 1961, p. 292)

Here writing is again represented as primarily a means of enslavement, but Lévi-Strauss does not naively turn back against writing the empirical "particularities of times past" left in written form. The bourgeois historian's 'spirit of disinterested inquiry' is itself one of the elaborate diversionary fictions of writing, and in *The Savage Mind* (1966) Lévi-Strauss analyses this as one of the key mythic constructs embedded in the literate culture's 'rational' and 'empirical' discourses, supposedly distinct from myth. Ostensibly disinterested historical analysis, confronting the innumerable psychological, cerebral and hormonal events that constitute each moment of 'what actually happened', is an abstraction of 'facts' accomplished through selection, massive exclusion, and a repetition of ideological codes and narrative practices that serve specific ends in the present.[9] "History", for Lévi-Strauss, "is therefore never history, but history-for" (1966, p. 257). His history of writing challenges the concepts of history and writing implicit in the work of historians who disclose the 'creative' aspects of their discourse only in the *aporia* or the marginal indiscretion.

Apart from the Bible and Shakespeare

There is a science fiction story, by Isaac Asimov, in which William Shakespeare travels through time to the twentieth century, takes an English course, and fails his Shakespeare paper because he has not read enough criticism.[10] In the circumstances Shakespeare should have had a word with Matthew Arnold, who persuaded the examiners that literary criticism is "a disinterested endeavour to learn and propagate the best that is known and thought in the world" and that the function of the critic is "to see the object as in itself it really is" (Arnold, 1962, III, pp. 258, 282). Waiting in the background too is T. S. Eliot, for whom criticism was "an intuitive activity of the civilized mind" in which "there is no method except to be very intelligent".[11] Having attempted one question on arcane matters of generic classification and responded to an invitation to discuss an unattributed quotation which offers a simple-minded interpretation of one of the plays, is W. Shakespeare to read beside the "Fail" a marginal note indicating that he has not seen the object in itself or shown evidence of a civilized mind? Or should the information be made available that the 'questions' are coded stimuli for a very narrow range of ideological productions in an idiom which, like any technical language, requires more and less than intelligence and intuition to operate it.[12]

But the irony in Asimov's fable is based partly on a misconception. It takes the claims of Arnold, Eliot and their critical legacy as a norm from which to gauge the performance of the educational institution as a decline from the spirit of the creative text to the letter of its secondary, parasitic accretions. The trouble with Asimov's 'Immortal Bard' is, in fact, that he has not read enough Shakespeare, insofar as the latter is not a transcendent 'spirit' that haunts the text but a cultural signifier constituted in the history of the author's printed plays and poems and their reproduction within the institutions and practices of ideology. There is no such thing as the object as in itself it really is. As soon as the play is printed it becomes, in the terms of *The Tempest* and *Love's Labour's Lost*, radically other than itself, and the 'breath' of the original performances is available only as the construction of a "history-for" directed towards its own present ends.

In spite of the text's biases towards the 'breath' of speech, the later construction of Shakespeare and his work is the triumph of writing. In the First Folio of 1623, when the plays were addressed not to an audience but "To the great Variety of Readers", there are already intimations of the cultural myth of the writer-as-hero examined by Asimov in the strange encounter of Shakespeare with himself, shaped by the rituals of twentieth-century English Literature. Ben Jonson's valedictory verses described the "Sweet Swan of *Avon*" as one who "like *Apollo* . . . came forth to warme/Our eares, or like a *Mercury* to charme", now transformed into a "Moniment, without a tombe". The play on "Moniment" anticipates at once the 'monumental' status of the Bard as a cultural signifier and the untombed 'money-mint' that Shakespeare's former colleagues turned literary editors, John Hemings and Henry Condell, refuse to let lie in peace and dignity. The fame and immortality sought by Ferdinand and his friends in *Love's Labour's Lost* now comes to burden the memory of the author, "alive still, while thy Booke doth live" (Hinman, 1968, pp. 9–10).

The conventions of eulogy proved prophetic in this case as Shakespeare's book assumed the power of the Book Harriot's Indians rubbed on their heads and bodies. As early as 1753, Arthur Murphy wrote that "With us islanders Shakespeare is a kind of established religion in poetry" (Vickers, 1974–81, IV, p. 93), while Francis Gentleman, in 1774, looked back on the exegesis of the last fifty years and concluded that Shakespeare "has been almost as much traded upon, and as viley interpreted as the Bible" (Vickers, VI, p. 107). At last, in 1796, the deified Bard becomes Prospero himself, who encounters Ovid, Ariosto, Aeschylus and Dante on the "Island of Fancy", to finally stand on a "mass of rock", alone on "the topmost height", waving aloft the effete phallus of high culture:

On the regal throne
Of this romantic realm, stood Avon's bard alone.
Above stood he—for there was none but he
On such a fearful precipice could stand;
Careless he stood, from fear and danger free,
And wav'd with ease that more than magic wand.
(Alexander Thomson, *The Paradise of Taste*, canto 7)[13]

The island, at once at the centre and on the margins, is always a universal England, a construction which held true for one of the most popular institutions of BBC Radio, *Desert Island Discs*, where establishment castaways as distinguished as Princess Margaret or Paul MacCartney were shipwrecked with only a handful of gramophone records, one luxury and any book "apart from the Bible and Shakespeare". The latter was disqualified by the elect status of an island race which absorbs its spirit without so much as a quick rub-down with the *Complete Works*. "Shakespeare one gets acquainted with without knowing how", as Henry Crawford says in *Mansfield Park*. "It is part of an Englishman's constitution."

The evolving discourse on the Bard became part of the ideological construction of 'England' under capitalism, of its empire and its hegemonic notions of a national and universal culture. In 1616, the year of Shakespeare's death, theatrical performances were prohibited in Stratford-upon-Avon, and in 1622 the borough council awarded the King's Players six shillings for *not* acting in the town (Addenbrooke, 1974, p. 3). But later, particularly after David Garrick's lavish bicentenary celebrations at Stratford in 1764, the unwitting author and his books contributed to the creation of a pocket of 'tradition' and arrested time which, in one of the most industrialized and urbanized countries in the world, came to represent the 'typically English'. In Stratford the England of green fields and yeoman-farmers stands in for the realities of capitalist production and its class relations.

Shakespeare's work too came to affirm 'nature' at the expense of textual production and reproduction. Neoclassical reservations based on its failure to comply with the traditional rules of good writing gave way, in the later eighteenth and nineteenth centuries, to the romantic concept of an untutored genius whose outpourings scatter the dead letters of convention. As early as 1668, Dryden could acknowledge that Shakespeare "needed not the spectacles of books to read nature" (Dryden, 1668, p. 47), and in later sources this becomes his transcendent virtue:

> Taught by yourself alone to sing,
>   Sublime you soar on Nature's wing;
> How sweet and Strain! how bold the Flight!
>   Above the Rules
>   Of Critic Schools
> And cool correction of the Stagyrite.
>   (W. Havard, "To the Memory of
>   Shakespeare")[14]

As Dame Nature's favourite child in the late eighteenth century, Shakespeare has acquired without study Ferdinand's goal of things hid and barred from common sense:

> Of all her sweet Prattlers she lov'd Willy best;
> She nurs'd the young Smiler with Milk from her Breast:
> And as he grew older, she nothing conceal'd,
> But all, all her Secrets to Willy reveal'd.
>   ("J.R.", "Ode to Shakespeare")[15]

In the nineteenth century this knowledge became a major component of "the best that is known and thought in the world", the object of critical inquiry according to Matthew Arnold. In Arnold's early sonnet, Shakespeare is again "Self-school'd, self-scann'd, self-honour'd, self-secure" (Arnold, 1950, p. 3), the phoenix who, in Thomas Carlyle's terms, is the "Voice" and "free gift of Nature" (Carlyle, 1841, pp. 166, 174). As the text was absorbed into the increasingly literate culture, contributing to the hierarchy of taste and cultivation associated by Lévi-Strauss with the assimilation of writing, this dual construction of the birthplace and the Bard masked the relations of both general and textual production in the legitimizing presence of 'nature', and located the cultural and geographical heart of an enchanted isle, a mythical England, somewhere between Stratford and Oxford.

These relations, so powerfully suppressed in Arnold's idealism—which was to become the dominant theoretical strand in academic criticism during the first half of the twentieth century—are more apparent in Carlyle's aggressive and nationalistic variations on the Bard, nature, and the religion of culture. Shakespeare, to Carlyle, is "the hero as poet", the "poor Warwickshire peasant" who rose from deer-poaching to become "the greatest of Intellects" (Carlyle, 1841, p. 174). The apparent populism of this image is coupled with a contempt for the masses which has characterized the treatment of the Elizabethan theatre audience from Ben Jonson's dismissal of "the foamy praise that drops from common jaws" to the modern survivals of groundling-bashing at the lower echelons of the education system and occasionally in published criticism. For Carlyle moments of transience and barbarity, geared to the "Globe Playhouse", surround those "bursts of radiance" in the plays which make us exclaim: " 'That is *true*, spoken once and forever; wheresoever and whensoever there is an open human soul, that will be recognised as true!' " (Carlyle, 1841, p. 179). It is at these points when "his great soul" bursts through the material conditions, that Shakespeare becomes a conqueror and a prophet, or greater, indeed, than a prophet. Shakespeare will always speak to all races when Mahomet, for example, and the "prolix absurdity" of the Koran are silent:

> Even in Arabia, as I compute, Mahomet will have exhausted himself and become obsolete, while this Shakespeare. . .may still be young;—while this Shakespeare may still pretend to be a Priest of Mankind, of Arabia as of other places, for unlimited periods to come! (Carlyle, p. 181)

If Carlyle's rapture conjures images of turbanned and exotically named *ayatollahs*—Bradley, Dover Wilson, Muir—charging across the sands, bursting with radiance and chanting "The quality of mercy is not strained", "Oh, what a rogue and peasant slave am I" and "All the world's a stage", these are not altogether inappropriate. The notion of the text's eternal, universal truth is one aspect of the Bard as imperial hero of culture. This is also the Shakespeare of "Once more into the breach, dear friends" which, co-opted to the rhetoric of journalists and politicians, sends the English warrior into glorious battle. Carlyle's Shakespeare is characterized by "valour, candour, tolerance, truthfulness: his whole victorious strength and greatness". When his "noble Patriotism" manifests itself, "a true English heart breathes calm and strong through the whole business" (Carlyle, p. 178), and his triumph is that of the Anglo-Saxon peoples. The other example of "the hero as poet", Dante, turns out in the last analysis to be, for Carlyle, a typical Italian whose work is marred by a passive misery. Strength through joy, in contrast, is the mark of the English hero, whose "joyful tranquillity" makes him "greater than Dante, in that he fought truly, and did conquer" (Carlyle, p. 175). This Shakespeare is the "strongest of rallying-signs" for "a Saxondom covering great spaces of the Globe", from America to the Antipodes and the Indian Empire. He is "King Shakespeare", who shines "in crowned sovereignty, over us all" and lets us say to one another: " 'Yes, this Shakespeare is ours; we produced him, we speak and think by him; we are of one blood and kind with him' " (Carlyle, pp. 184–5).

Carlyle's rant, aptly described by Nietzsche as "a loquacity that comes from a pure satisfaction in noise and confusion of feelings" (Nietzsche, 1960, p. 130), suggests another science fiction story, an alternative history best written by Philip K. Dick, in which the Stratford Rallies, attracting Anglo-Saxons from all over the world, are organised by uniformed members of the International Shakespeare Association (henceforth designated by the initials ISA). But Nietzsche's comment is misleading in that Carlyle's discourse is no personal eccentricity but a remarkable articulation of the diversity of images that constitute 'Shakespeare' in the late eighteenth and nineteenth centuries. It is also the most condensed single source for constructions of the Bard administered in twentieth-century 'popular' culture. The exact status of this signifier became clear in the Gallup Poll's 'Cultural Olympics' of 1976, when Shakespeare was "correctly identified" by eighty-nine per cent of Americans and ninety-two per cent of the British sample, beaten into second place only by Columbus and soundly thrashing the likes of Beethoven, Napoleon, Aristotle, Freud and, in seventh place, Marx, who was recognized by only forty-one per cent of the United States contingent. This is the cultural king or father who invites the oedipal assaults of the rival claimants, always of higher birth than Shakespeare and, in the case of the Earl of Oxford, supported by Freud himself. The definitive answer to this, a major problem in the popular discourse on the Bard, is provided by Michel Pêcheux: "Shakespeare's works were not written by him, but by an unknown contemporary of the same name" (Pêcheux, 1982, p. 107).[16]

Although the academic Shakespeare industry would wash its hands of the vulgar excesses of bardolatry, it shares with this more popular discourse much of the theoretical ground common to Matthew Arnold and Carlyle. In both cases the book is a repository of abiding cultural values, emanating from the 'vision' and talent of a uniquely gifted individual and worthy of an exegetical and philological attention traditionally reserved for sacred texts. At the up-market and down-market ends of the business the works are assumed to have essential qualities, available without recourse to a careful theorizing of the relations of production both at the point where meanings are encoded and at the point of reading or hearing. The academic and the popular Shakespeares are both central to the reproduction of the concepts and practices of a national and a universal 'culture', and if the Bard and King Shakespeare are now decorously absent from the language of criticism, they are firmly ensconced in its economic and institutional base, in the most central compulsory component of the majority of English Literature courses. The apparent gulf in 'taste' or 'refinement' which crosses this theoretical continuum is central to the 'culture industry' as a whole and its role in the reproduction of a hegemonic relation of classes and ideologies.[17]

In spite of the self-proclaimed pluralism of Anglo-American Shakespeare criticism, there has until recently been little apart from the work of Harbage (1941), Bethell (1944) and Hawkes (1973) to challenge in any fundamental way this generally unspoken theoretical agenda. It is in historical analyses from Eastern Europe, by Robert Weimann (1978) and, more obliquely, Mikhail Bakhtin (1968) that the question of the text's relationship to ideology assumes the proportions of a direct threat to the idealist construction of Shakespeare and his place in culture. These have appeared in translation, and begun to take effect, in the context of a more general assault on traditional critical ideologies from contemporary Marxist and post-structuralist literary theory and, on the institutional level, the assimilation of this theory into the sociological and semiotic analysis of ideological forms in the emergent disciplines of

Cultural and Communication Studies. Jan Kott, the house deviant of Shakespeare criticism in the 1960s and early 1970s, described the bibliography on *Hamlet* alone as containing more entries than the Warsaw telephone directory. At a time when it is safe to assume that the *Hamlet* bibliography is expanding at the faster rate, it is dangerous to generalize about the whole output of Shakespeare criticism, and particularly contentious to relate it all back to a theory of culture and literary production formalized during the Victorian period. Here it will be more politic to establish a theoretical and institutional horizon at a mid-point, eight years before Edward Harrison leaves for British Honduras, and to let each commentary be judged in terms of the elements it reproduces, or challenges, from the clear system of norms and practices laid down for an emergent English Literature by the central educational apparatus of the British government.

Fish-Knives and Antimacassars

The report of Sir Henry Newbolt's committee to the British Board of Education on *The Teaching of English in England* (1921) subscribed explicitly to Matthew Arnold's concept of literary culture, expanded to incorporate the practice of teaching at all levels from the elementary school to the university. One of the founding texts of the discipline, it echoes with most of the central formulations of 'Shakespeare' in relation to 'culture', from Jonson's eulogy to Thomas Carlyle's. English Literature appears as a subject of recent invention, the first Chairs of English having been founded at Cambridge as late as 1878, and at Oxford in 1885. It is a discipline which still calls for some justification. According to the report, English universities should in future acknowledge "the immense importance of the native language for the purposes of humane culture" and recognize that the language and literature, "a great source of pride", could also become a great bond of English "national unity" (Newbolt, p. 202). For the strengthening of this bond books will be used not as ends in themselves but as "instruments through which we hear the voices of those who have known life better then ourselves" (p. 14). This "self-expression of great natures" (p. 21) or "record of the experiences of the greatest minds" (p. 149) is related to, but ultimately transcends, the historical or the sociological:

> All great literature has in it two elements, the contemporary and the eternal. On the one hand, Shakespeare and Pope can tell us what Englishmen were like at the beginning of the 17th and at the beginning of the 18th centuries. On the other hand they tell us what all men are like in all countries and at all times. To concentrate the study of literature mainly on the first aspect, to study it mainly as history, is to ignore its nobler, more eternal and universal element.   (Newbolt, p. 205)

The parting shot of this celebration of the timeless and universal is that great literature can never "depend for its importance upon historical considerations", yet this is stated in the context of a historical mission to make literature itself a central bond in the national culture. To this end the report must overcome radical working-class opposition to high culture, an issue summed up as "literature and the social problem" (p. 388). The problem, according to the committee's informants—there was no direct contact—is that "the working classes, especially those belonging to organised labour movements", are "antagonistic to, and contemptuous of, literature". They associate it with "antimacassars, fish-knives and other unintelligible and futile trivialities of 'middle-class culture'" and suspect academic literary studies to be an attempt "'to side-track the working-class movement'" (p. 252). Tolstoy's attack on Shakespeare is cited as an example of this attitude, "now prevalent in Bolshevist Russia" (p. 254). The answer, if the working-classes only knew it, lies in the power of literature itself to 'humanize' and 'civilize' them out of these beliefs, a matter which involves "grave national issues":

> For if literature be, as we believe, an embodiment of the best thoughts of the best minds, the most direct and lasting communication of experience by man to men, a fellowship which "binds together by passion and knowledge the vast empire of human society, as it spreads over the whole earth, and over all time", then the nation of which a considerable

portion rejects this means of grace, and despises this great
spiritual influence, must assuredly be heading to disaster.

(Newbolt, p. 252)

For those who seek grace, Shakespeare is "open to all the
world", while "the literature of England belongs to all
England, not to the universities or to any *coterie* of the literary or
the learned: and all may enjoy it who will" (p. 204). Meanwhile, in another part of the text and on the subject of teaching
correct English in elementary schools, the humanists and
democrats who make up the committee are pleased to announce
that, according to the Divisional Inspector of schools, the
teachers of phonetics and voice production "have gone some
way towards getting rid of undesirable forms of London speech"
(p. 65). If Caliban is recalcitrant at the prospect of grace, there
is at least hope for his offspring as they move closer to Prospero's
language.

As the first set text to be studied, Newbolt's *The Teaching of
English in England* would be particularly useful in clarifying the
aims and ideological basis of any English course, particularly
one that sets out to do something in the order of "refining the
sensibilities" or "enhancing the critical awareness". The most
enhanced critical awareness in the text seem in fact to be those
of the representatives of organized labour who recognize more
enduring divisions of interest and relations of exploitation
beneath the homogeneity of this construction of the nation and
its culture. A decade before the Newbolt Report, Robert
Bridges condemned "those wretched beings", the proverbial
groundlings in Shakespeare's audience, who could be held
responsible for his artistic shortcomings (Bridges, 1927–35, I,
pp. 28–9). Ten years after Newbolt, L. C. Knights defended
the Elizabethan audience at the expense of the corrupt taste of
modern cinema-goers (Knights, 1931–32, p. 619). The next
text in this sequence will celebrate the cinema audiences of the
1920s and early 1930s at the expense of the contemporary
television viewer, and the Arnold/Newbolt theory of culture
allows scope for canonized television programmes, in turn, to
be assimilated to 'high culture' once their moment of popular
currency is safely distant, and to be reproduced in the contradictory process of a hegemony which constitutes, in one

movement, both 'unity' and a discrimination based on hierarchical division. If Arnold is Newbolt's "apostle of culture"
(p. 259), the question remains "Whose culture?" The answer
for the colonial subject, the working classes who set themselves
apart from the grace which binds Newbolt's "vast empire of
human society" and—to cite the more marginal instance which
so obsessed Edward Harrison—for Welsh school-children
under Arnold's inspectorate, is in Walter Benjamin's recognition that "there has never been a document of culture which was
not at one and the same time a document of barabarism". [18]

Fulfilling the demands of a humane pluralism and the liberal
doctrine of balance, the other basic text beside the Newbolt
Report on our revised English syllabus might well be Althusser's "Ideology and the Ideological State Apparatuses", which
provides a model for placing the history of the Bard, the
construction of a literary culture and the institutional refining
of sensibilities in a larger context. In Althusser's formulation,
all forms of textual production and reproduction would be seen
to take place in specific Ideological State Apparatuses (ISAs) of
which the *cultural*—which would include Arts Council subsi-
dies and the 'legitimate' theatre—and the *educational* are
examples. The ISAs work in the social formation to reproduce
the class relations of the dominant mode of production, thus
contributing to its perpetuation. Any interference in this
process will ultimately draw a response from the Repressive
State Apparatus (RSA), which includes the law, the police and
the military, but in normal circumstances this work is accomplished without direct violence in the ISAs. The religious and
family apparatuses were, according to Althusser, dominant
under feudalism and, under capitalism, this dominance
belongs to the family and the educational ISAs, although any
revision of this model would have to take into account the
emergence of the communications apparatus as a third major
force. In the British education system after the Newbolt Report
English took on a particularly influential role, expanding to fill
a vacuum left in the humanities and social sciences by the
failure of Philosophy and Sociology to develop as disciplines in
any way central or critical in the arena of ideological conflict
and social change. [19] This failure also weakened what could have
been an important institutional check on the pretensions of

English Literature, which in the event advanced as the least disciplined of the academic disciplines, a loosely-theorized assembly of ideological practices which ranged from imposing a middle-class standard of 'correctness' on the language in schools to upholding the 'great works' of the literary tradition and claiming for the university English School a uniquely privileged position for the defence and nurture of 'human values'.[20] These practices were all based on nominally apolitical concepts of the nation, culture and the life of the individual.

Even in the most unwordly of English Literature courses, devoted to consuming the body of culture neatly butchered into authors and periods, the time comes when humane letters and the sanctity of the unique individual response have to be put to one side. The examinations follow in their season, like an inexorable force of nature, and the stamps are primed for the foreheads of the A, B, C and D people. As Althusser points out, this reproduction of the relations of production in education systems is accompanied by the administration of an appropriate level and amount of " 'know-how' wrapped in the ruling ideology" to "each mass ejected *en route*" who occupy a particular class position beneath those who reach the summit:

> either to fall into intellectual semi-employment, or to pro-
> vide. . .the agents of exploitation (capitalists, managers), the
> agents of repression (soldiers, policemen, politicians, admini-
> strators, etc.) and the professional ideologists (priests of all
> sorts, most of whom are convinced 'laymen').
>
> (Althusser, 1971, p. 155)

With regard to the educational re-presentation of Shakespeare, popular culture of the Elizabethan and Jacobean period, those who leave school around sixteen will be generally averse to it,[21] and disenfranchised from this degree of 'culture' and 'creativity'. Their "know-how", nevertheless, should extend to the point made by Newbolt that Shakespeare is, in a sense, "open to all the world". Those who get closer to the summit, particularly through courses which acknowledge pluralism and balance by ignoring or maginalizing the more challenging aspects of contemporary critical theory, know that the text is valuable, an object in itself, and for all time. This knowledge may be absorbed from the air without recourse to the poor taste of bardolatry or even the more embarrassing formulations of Newbolt, Eliot or Arnold. At each level the knowledge produced will remove all traces of its own conditions of production in the ISA, or fly the banner of popular education and cultivation available to all. In this construction 'literature' is *there*, Arnold's mythical "object as in itself it really is", displacing the production in pedagogic discourse of "a special language which is both *different* from the common language and *within* it" (Macherey and Balibar, 1978, p. 9) and which repeats the process of division masked as unity evident in Newbolt's 'culture'. This 'literary' language, experienced by the bourgeoisie as its own and by members of the subordinate classes propelled out of the education system at an early stage as an exclusion from and within language itself, incorporates a range of texts and signifying practices—poems, novels, texts once regarded as transient productions of the popular theatre, some sermons, essays, political or philosophical treatises but not others.[22] The criterion for selection is the elusive *essence* of the literary, grasped by intuition as much as anything else, which stands in for the cultural and lingusitic capital available to those who are given full access to its codes and reinterpreted by the lay 'priests' at the summit as the 'canon' or, until relatively recently, 'culture' itself.

In reproducing class relations and the dominant ideology the educational apparatus works in tandem with others. Productions of Shakespeare in British theatres, where the price of entry will be paid in part by the extraction of funds from sections of the population who have no interest in attending, take place at a time when, because of television, and probably for the first time ever, most people spend more time watching drama than in preparing and consuming food (Williams, 1974, pp. 59–60).[23] In 1964 at the end of the first season of the English National Theatre, an institution as exclusive as the 'national culture' celebrated by Newbolt, survey figures showed that only 0.3 per cent of its audience came from the class of manual labourers.[24] The Shakespearean text, which presents itself in its own theatrical context as a 'converse', an integrative rite of its society, is inserted in the modern theatre, as in the classroom, into rites of selection and separation. This too has its more idealist interpretation. Most audiences are "multiplicitly various", writes an editor of *Love's Labour's Lost* and historian of the Royal Shakespeare Company who has spent many hours in the dark, and the art of the theatre "is essentially democratic, for it is practised by the people, about the people, and to the people" (David, 1978, pp. 15–16). The groundlings who crack nuts and banter with the Fool at modern RSC and National Theatre productions will, no doubt, be glad to hear this and to praise Matthew Arnold, a pioneer of the movement towards founding a national centre for drama, and his more sinewy disciple Leavis, to whom both Peter Hall and Trevor Nunn, theatre directors and Cambridge English graduates, pay homage. [25]

Those who practise it rarely live by Shakespeare criticism alone, but apart from acknowledgments, footnotes that credit the unpublished work of research students, and occasional anecdotes to lighten the tone, the material conditions that determine such work are rarely brought into the text. In this the criticism departs from the reflexive dimension present in most of the plays. In one exception to this generally detached, disinterested approach, John Dover Wilson, a member of the Newbolt Committee, looked back at the end of his career on his experiences as an Inspector of Schools. Observing an English lesson, he notices that the class is studying *As You Like It* and that they are, as is generally the case, "frankly bored with it" (Wilson, 1962, p. 141). The boys enjoy the wrestling and the girls some of the songs—"but for the rest, well, whatever *was* it all about?" (p. 141). Secretly appalled on Shakespeare's behalf that this play should be studied for examinations at all, Dover Wilson banishes the teacher from the classroom and proceeds to offer the pupils, and the reader, an avuncular explanation of "what the Elizabethans thought it was all about" (p. 142). What follows is as depressing as the title of the book, *Shakespeare's Happy Comedies*. Dover Wilson writes about the apprentice boys in the audience and the appeal to them of songs, the wrestling match, Touchstone's jokes, and an elaborate visual scene, covering only twenty lines in the text, in which the hunters return with the body of a deer. "There was then", he concludes, "plenty to attract and please the groundlings in *As You Like It*", although some of the apprentices might have "despised the antics of the boy-players as effeminate" (p. 145). He goes on to outline another, better, play housed in the same text, "written not for the groundlings (though Shakespeare never forgot them) but for the young gentlemen in the audience". This one is "an exquisite essay in the pastoral manner, and a sly criticism of it" (p. 146).

The word 'exquisite' brings to mind again Kermode's *Tempest* and what the home-grown Calibans of the Newbolt Report refer to as the "unintelligible and futile trivialities of 'middle-class culture'." But Dover Wilson's reading of *As You Like It* reveals a clearly intelligible political dimension. The text, like Newbolt's 'culture', is at once a unity and a space divided between the cultivated class and the manual worker, who is oblivious of such sophisticated matters as genre, capable only of grasping dumbshows and noise. The analysis relocates it own material conditions in the text. The pupils begin in the position of the groundlings and by the end those who have not fidgeted and who are earmarked for redemption behold the full text, stripped of its accretions and propelled back to a solid, empirical site in English history which, by being so much like the classroom, goes to show that boys will be boys and human nature never changes.

Dover Wilson's *As You Like It*, like Kermode's *Tempest*, is engagingly frank in supplying materials that can be used to reveal its political agenda and the determinate relations of academic production its discourse strains to obscure, in this particular case at the moment of naming them. To some extent this discourse of 'groundlings', 'high culture' and the 'exquis-ite' is already beginning to assume a mainly antiquarian interest. It would be reductive in the extreme to lump all modern Shakespeare criticism and teaching under this banner, an exercise in a crude functionalism or vulgar Marxism incom-patible with Althusser's crucial emphasis on the "relative autonomy" of ideology and the "reciprocal action" of the superstructure on the economic base (Althusser, 1971, p. 135). To avoid turning this autonomy back into a traditional liberal pluralism, however, it is important to recognise that even the most scholarly and ostensibly objective texts carry their ideo-logical payload. The 'scientific' bibliographical studies that have flourished this century posit a stable 'original' Shakespearean text which may comply with the literary culture's notion of the author and his works but not necessarily with the practices of an acting company which may have adapted a play to the demands of different performances with no concept of an ideal point at which it becomes properly itself.[26] The prevalence of modern-spelling editions makes the text and its language *present* at the expense of the inevitable 'strangeness' of the early printed versions, working with Newbolt's assumption that the work's eternal and universal aspects take priority over its status as a historical document, and removing the obstructions posed by the 'letter' to a discovery in Shakespeare of what Leavis called "the very spirit of the language", formed in rural England and still carrying the force of a moral norm by which to assess the draining of 'life' from modern linguistic practices (Leavis, 1982, pp. 126–7). This transformed text, made as definitive as possible by the 'new bibliography', takes its place in a 'unified' national language and culture two hundred and fifty years after commentators on the earlier texts, only a century after Shakespeare's death, attributed their 'obscurity' to the fact that the English language had already changed immeasurably.[27] This historical difference is further resolved into an abiding presence by the explanatory footnotes that patrol the plays. Through these the *Complete Works*, already considered to be "refrigerated" and swollen to "the burden of many camels" by the end of the eighteenth century, (Vickers, VI, p. 49) remain a stable container for a central unifying purpose, spiced by the exquisite complexity of fruitful ambiguities, cross-references and wordplays usually limited to a decorous maximum of three or four permutations of meaning per item.

Without the scholarship that illuminates "things hid & bard from common sense" it would, of course, be impossible to turn the text back on the construction of 'Shakespeare' as a cultural monument. But without it, equally, such work would be unnecessary. Under the democratic ideology of a liberal education any attempt, however well intentioned, to make Shakespeare "open to all the world" will be marked by contradictions. Historical studies that are not openly 'history-for', interpretations that chase the essential meanings of the text and purely formalist descriptions of linguistic, generic or dramatic effects—in the wake of the New Criticism[28]—will always work to either sustain or confront theoretical positions already in place and operating in specific ideological apparatuses. Every work of Shakespeare criticism is a work of critical theory and a form of ideological practice.

Ideological affiliations should be scrutinized and declared in advance, claim the authors of *The Practical Criticism of Poetry*, and the enemies of free democratic discussion are "those who are totalitarian at heart, and believe in education as indoctrination" (Cox and Dyson, 1965, pp. 29–30). Declaring no such interest of their own, Cox and Dyson show that 'culture' and ideology are never far apart by describing the good teacher and critic in the most undemocratic of analogies. Those best equipped to stem the tide of indoctrination are comparable to the connoisseur, of wine for example, or the conductor, not of buses but of classical music (1965, pp. 18–22). The critic will sample the vintage of the tradition or interpret the score of the text, bringing the dead letter to life. If the underwear of much democratic and open-minded criticism is still patterned with fish-knives and antimacassars, wine-tasters and Toscaninis, it is rarely revealed with such allure. The text, as Roland Barthes points out, is always most erotic "where the garment gapes" (Barthes, 1976, p. 9). Such candour is hard to come by but 'disinterestedness' is always, at best, an ideological flag of convenience.

Rewriting Writing

There was a proverb, about a cat that wanted fish but was unwilling to get its feet wet, which was sufficiently well known in 1606 to be referred to metonymically in the popular theatre. Lady Macbeth, goading her husband to murder Duncan, asks:

> Would'st thou have that
> Which thou esteem'st the Ornament of Life,
> And live a Coward in thine owne Esteeme?
> Letting I dare not, wait upon I would,
> Like the poore Cat i' th' Addage.
>   (*Macbeth*, I. vii. 518–22)

In Shakespeare's plays proverbs and *sententiae* usually express, or conceal, a devious or misguided purpose, received wisdom being generally treacherous in one way or another.[29] But such implicit warnings do little to deter the modern discourse that mines the Shakespearean text for adages and verbal gems to be recycled as proverbial wisdom doubly validated by the mark of that most potent of cultural signifiers, the Bard. This is the work of the "collective and anonymous voice originating in traditional human experience" that Roland Barthes called the *doxa* or, more specifically, the Gnomic Code, the distillate of discourses wherein 'Life', seen as the transcendent reality to which all language refers, is concocted from the detritus of language itself—"a nauseating mixture of common opinions, a smothering layer of received ideas" (Barthes, 1974, pp. 18, 206). As regards Shakespeare its products can be sometimes disconcerting. Visitors to the Exxon/Folger Shakespeare Library exhibition which toured the United States in 1980 were sprayed with a prophylactic shower of adages emanating from speakers concealed at the entrance before proceeding to the mandatory model of the Globe Theatre, the costumes, Elizabethan printed books and other cult objects housed in the sacred space within. But even this onslaught of roses by any other name glistering in the winter of our discontent pales beside *A Shakespeare Birthday Book*, compiled by the Reverend A. E. Sims. This volume comprises 365 eternal verities and moral injunctions culled from the plays and poems, each headed by a day of the year, with ornamental borders and colour plates commemorating such figures as Falstaff and Mistress Quickly, Romeo and Juliet, Shylock and Jessica, Perdita, and Lady Macbeth herself. The improving sentiment it offers Christian boys and girls born on 15 March, in a bizarre transformation of something like 'he who hesitates is lost', is—complete with the poor cat—Lady Macbeth's incitement to regicide.

At first glance the Shakespeare of the Reverend Sims, like that of the Exxon Corporation, appears to be located in the discourse that spans calendars, dictionaries of quotations, BBC radio programmes in celebration of the Bard's birthday and ashtrays on sale at Stratford-upon-Avon. But the 15th *is* the Ides of March and this, combined with the choice of quotation, interrupts the 'finish' of the appropriation which acts as an ideological commentary on the texts. This is the fissure that reveals beneath the hallmarked platitudes a shadow-text of cabbalism, conspiracy and assassination. Even the ontological comfort of an author is denied as 'A. E. Sims' becomes the function of the *Birthday Book* that fractures and diffuses its anagram 'is same' to deny the text its univocity, identity and self-presence. The publisher's imprint gives no date but one would imagine Sims a contemporary of Borges, Pynchon and Barthes himself, for whom "the work of the commentary, once it is separated from any ideology of totality", consists "precisely in *manhandling* [*malmener*] the text and *interrupting* it", thereby denying not "the *quality* of the text . . . but its 'naturalness'" (Barthes, 1974, p. 15).

The work of the Reverend Sims spans a moribund humanist criticism and the art of the *aporia*. His text is at once Arnold's "best that is known and thought in the world"—a dutiful uncovering of "Shakespeare's insights into the human condition"[30]—and a sortie into the "galaxy of signifiers" envisaged by Barthes, in which the function of interpretation is not to give the work "a (more or less justified, more or less free) meaning, but on the contrary to appreciate what *plural* constitutes it. . .unimpoverished by any constraint of representation (of imitation)" (Barthes, 1974, p. 5). Here 'Shakespeare' embraces both the phonocentrism of the Newbolt tradition, where books are "instruments through which we hear the voices of those who have known life better than ourselves", (Newbolt, p. 14) and the play of a post-structuralist *écriture*, the space in which the social codes of 'communicative' language break down and the 'natural' closures of the humanist subject and sign are thrown back into crisis and heterogeneity.[31] And if the triumph of one view of writing, directly opposed to that in *Love's Labour's Lost* and *The Tempest*, accompanied the production of the national and universal poet-hero who was simultaneously a voice of nature and a law of hegemonic culture, another view, which may be associated primarily with the writing of Barthes, Derrida and Kristeva, offers the possibility of dismantling this construction *through* the Shakespearean text, and of beginning to clean up after it. What might now be called the 'textuality' of Shakespeare's plays, the linguistic and semiotic *excess* which has been the occasion of innumerable interpretations, each performing its particular ideological closures under the stamp of an originary intention and authority, can be unravelled outside the theory which takes as axiomatic a voice speaking monumental and incomparably elegant truths that echo through eternity. This voice is what was always already lost, for Nietzsche, in the business of the institutional re-presentation of texts and both Barthes and Derrida elaborate, from this absent centre, a different practice of reading. In this Nietzschean 'interpretation', a "triumphant plural" or "galaxy of signifiers" takes the place of the traditional "structure of signifieds" (Barthes, 1974, p. 5) and the text becomes "the affirmation of a world of signs which has no truth, no origin, no nostalgic guilt, and is proffered for active interpretation" (Derrida, 1978, p. 292).

The Newbolt view of writing, as a means to prolong the resonance of the voice, is in a sense directly opposed to the books castigated by Berowne and finally drowned by Prospero. The two concepts do, however, share assumptions about the primacy of speech over a material letter which is at best merely instrumental and at worst oblivious and opaque. But in *écriture* this 'letter' assumes priority as the signifier which continually refracts and dismantles the expected mimetic reference, resisting the closures of a transcendent 'truth'. Its insistence in the Shakespearean text is inescapable. In Lady Macbeth's call to regicide, for example, the materials of language itself ("I dare not", "I would", "adage") replace the 'concrete' register of the proverb ("cat", "fish", "wet feet") to cut loose and *make present* the discourse rendered transparent by a characteristically self-naturalizing and 'given' idiom. The adage, always 'what goes without saying', is visibly said in *Macbeth* and, in the same gesture, unspoken as a *writing*, an inscription the signified is no longer sufficiently composed to erase.

In *Love's Labour's Lost* the moment of speech's triumph is swamped in an excess of the letter which renders the text at once barely intelligible and open to being deciphered in too many ways. Read with a view to discovering its thematic centre or true meaning, the play may become a *locus classicus* of the metaphysical tradition outlined by Derrida in *Of Grammatology*, a tradition in which the priority of 'breath' over the letter always implies the existence, beyond the play of inscriptions, of a transcendent *presence* to which speech is closer and more responsive than writing. But to reach this presence, in the special sense of the essential meaning of *Love's Labour's Lost*, is to write off an irreducible materiality which confirms, even in the performance's own "present breath", the constitutive and disintegrative work of a writing that can never be fully dissolved in speech and presence. In the criticism this appears as the text's "linguistic doodlings" which insist that words "not only mean but are", as the indulgence in a "sensuous enchantment with language" or a punning fascination with "light" words that illuminate their own emptiness and unchastity,[32] and as the foregrounding of "sight and sound" at the expense of what they may signify in terms of "story and character".[33] When Moth says of the pedants that "They have beene at a great feast of Languages, and stolne and scraps" (IVb. 1776–7), his words recapture the fragmentation of the text at large, in which a mimetic referent is continually dispersed by an exuberant jamming of denotation—in coinings, pedantic obscurities, barbarisms, metrical experiments and multiple puns.[34]

This obtrusiveness of language is matched by a self-conscious concern with the stage which, while straining towards a metalanguage concerned with the place of drama in a larger, social "converse of breath", sustains a barrier at the level of the theatrical signifier, a residue which impedes representation, turning characters back into illegible hieroglyphs or signs[35] and superimposing on the dramatic action a densely patterned movement of bodies, costumes and objects on the stage. The net effect is radically incompatible with a tradition of interpretation which follows biblical exegesis in attempting to recover the 'spirit' from the letter of the sacred text, a hermeneutic which turned *Love's Labour's Lost* into what the *New Cambridge* editors describe as "a happy hunting-ground for the unbridled theorist and the crank" (Quiller-Couch and Wilson, 1923, p. xvi). But in *The Tempest* too the play of linguistic and theatrical signifiers constitutes a density which can accommodate constructions of its 'presence' or truth as different as those of Kermode and Harrison while exceeding and undermining all such single-minded readings, along with its own production of an immediate 'breath' that binds Prospero to Miranda and also to the audience, which must finally fill his sails to release him from illusion. All those who taste the "subtleties o' th' Isle, that

will not let you/Beleeve things certaine" (V. i. 2086–7) are subject
to the syntactical ambiguity in which the island, also the
theatre, projects both a "certaine" truth to be grasped once the
present confusion is dispelled, and the impossibility of ever
acceding again to such certainty.

In this 'textuality', the plain truth of idealism and empiricism loses its unmediated innocence and self-presence to be
precipitated again only as a more subtle and devious species of
text. Writing no longer *contains* speech, serving as its husk, but
is trapped and deleted by speech until the text's undoing of
'natural', purely communicative language and its subjects
discloses the metaphysical and ideological inscriptions that
precede the spontaneous life of 'breath'. So another ideology of
writing displaces that of the Arnold/Newbolt tradition in
which great writers speak on,[36] and as *écriture* the text maps the
contradictory ground from which the earlier critical practice
could say what the work was *really* all about but also affirm its
inexhaustibility as an 'art' which transcends such ideological
closures.

The post-structuralist text, for all its contemporaneity and
its recognition of 'active' reading, also marks a return to an
impossible source in the *historical* duplicity and fragmentation
always resolved into a unity or held only in peripheral vision by
traditional exegesis. This division and heterogeneity was partially acknowledged by Allardyce Nicoll, for whom Shakespeare's "tragic art" was a land "where contraries are true", and
where contradiction had to be "reasoned away" if character was
to remain coherent.[37] A. P. Rossiter described the same process
as a "two-eyedness' or "constant Doubleness of the Shakespearean vision" (1961, pp. 52, 63) and Robert Weimann,
pre-eminently, has accounted for it in historical terms through
an analysis of the relationship of 'naturalistic' and 'conventional' modes in Shakespeare's plays, an interplay founded in
part on a division of the acting space—between an area
associated with dominant ideological forms and dramatic
illusion (*locus*), and another allowing scope for burlesque,
topsy-turvydom, direct contact with the audience and an
interrogation of social and theatrical representations (*platea*).[38]
Where Weimann speaks of a coexistence in the popular
tradition of "dramatic enchantment and disenchantment"

(1978, p. 247), it is not altogether ahistorical or anachronistic
to discover in the Shakespearean text a *deconstructive* mode which
acts on mimesis.

This division and 'doubleness', constituted in specific festive
and dramatic traditions, is also related to a broader historical
crisis in representation, the break-up of concepts of language as
woven into the correspondences and harmonies of what was
once called the 'Elizabethan World Picture' and the emergence
of more instrumentalist theories of signs based on 'mathematical plainness' and the subjection of words to empirical
'things'.[39] Michel Foucault has argued that a sixteenth-century
view of language as an opaque "thing in nature", a cipher but
one tautologously folded back into the grammar of existence
itself, gives way in the seventeenth century to analyses of
'representation' in a much more neutral and transparent sense,
no longer solid and "inscribed in the fabric of the world" but
having value *"only* as discourse".[40] In the gap between these
two systems, or in the excess and dislocation brought about by a
conflict of the two, there appeared, in Foucault's terms, a type
of text in which resemblance and illusion are at play and, in the
early seventeenth century, "the privileged age of *trompe-l'oeil*
painting, of the comic illusion, of the play that duplicates itself
by presenting another play, of the *quid pro quo*, of dreams and
visions" (Foucault, 1970, p. 51). Here it is possible to redis-
cover, inscribed in specific historical crises, a Shakespearean
text in which the social code breaks down through the process
of what Kristeva calls a "heteregeneousness to meaning and
signification" (1980, pp. 132–3).

Elizabethan literary theory puts only a contradictory harness
on this process, claiming that poetry is both an untrammelled
making from 'nothing' and a faithful representation of what is, a
rhetoric which instructs while pleasing but which, equally,
affirms nothing.[41] The theory which does impose a clear limit is
that of the Arnold-Newbolt tradition, intent on a 'human'
truth and value which can sustain a nominally depoliticized
'culture' and personal refinement as "the best that is known and
thought in the world". This ideal knowledge, which post-
structuralism collapses back into the order of *writing* or the
signifier, is already in crisis in the text, however heavily
patrolled by the uniformities of modern spelling, footnoting

and commentary. In the wake of a phonocentrism which assumed that the work must be *saying* something, however qualified by an inexhaustible aesthetic complexity, the "galaxy of signifiers" and "triumphant plural" find other ways of making it signify as much and as little as possible, and their strategies suggest new uses for those disintegrative features of the 'letter' limited and contained by exegesis. Where heterogeneity and contradiction take precedence over unity and presence, a more positive use, in disseminating rather than consolidating meaning, may be found for textual variants, orthographical vagaries, ambiguities of grammar and syntax, and the pandemic indeterminacies of meaning, all held in the silent 'l' which, in Elizabethan pronunciation, allowed a continuous play of identity and difference between the 'word' and the 'world'.[42]

The Elizabethans, we are told in an authoritative account of Shakespeare's language, "preferred vigour to logic" (Brook, 1976, p. 65), a judgment which underwrites the modern critic's role, in the maturity of the culture, of affirming the priority of logic while preserving and stabilizing the exhuberant energies of the past. For David Hume the "glaring figures of discourse", "unnatural conceits" and "jingle of words" that characterized Elizabethan and Jacobean writing constituted a linguistic affront to empiricism and its concept of representation.[43] But the organicist view of culture, which patronizes the vigour of youth, redeems the signifier for empiricism and recuperates the rhetorical sophistication of these texts for the unequivocal notion of truth they in fact render problematic— through the insistence of a frayed, unravelled sign which defers the presence of any signified that can finally escape the order of rhetoric and its strategic disarray.[44]

So Shakespeare, already rewritten *ad nauseam*, waits to be written again, not only on the level of academic criticism but also that of the *doxa*. Here the birthday book is as good a place to start as any in restocking 'the wisdom of the Bard' with proverbs of the signifier rather than the signified—like "nothing is, but what is not" (*Macbeth*, I. iii. 253); "the truest poetry is the most faining" (*As You Like It*, III. iii. 1630); the immortal words of the old hermit of Prague, who "never saw pen and inke", to a niece of King Gorboduc: "that that is is. . .for what is that, but that? and is, but is?". (*Twelfth Night*, IV. ii. 1999–2001); "*Richard* loves *Richard*, that is, I am I" (*Richard III*, V. 3645); "Comparisons are odorous" (*Much Ado About Nothing*, III. 1611); "Boskos thromuldo boskos", "Oscorbidulchos volivorco" and "Throca movousus, cargo cargo, cargo" (*All's Well That End's Well*, IV. 1978–94); "Pillicock sat on Pillicock hill, alow: alow loo loo" (*King Lear*, III. iv. 1856); "Nothing that is so, is so" (*Twelfth Night*, IV. i. 1926); and, for those born on 15 March, Hymen's "*If* truth holds true contents" (*As You Like It*, V. iv. 2703).

In all this it is best to retain the characteristic humility and self-knowledge of humanist criticism. To say anything of these matters may, after all, be self-defeating—a perpetuation, however inverted, of the poet-hero at the heart of a hegemonic 'culture'. Edward Harrison seems to have eventually turned his back on it altogether, concluding that any attempt to undo the damage could be no more than, as he puts it, "pissing into the wind" (Harrison, p. 33). After Placencia even the word 'Shake-speare', with its connotations of an imperial tumescence, fades out to be replaced only by passing references to "the barred" or a colloquially unmanned "Willy" (Harrison, pp. 42, 58, 79). His mission to civilize is now restricted to some speculative transportation of merchandise from the Belize ice factory. Harrison's disappearance in April 1933, in the course of an eccentric scheme to carry ice, by dory, from Punta Gorda up the Sarstoon River to the Indians and *chicleros* of the Peten rain-forests, bears only the faintest trace of any earlier desire for critical immortality.[45] His boat, named the *Patricia Herbert* on the bill of sale, appears in the journal only as the "Sweet Willy O", Garrick's name for Shakespeare coined during the bicente-nary celebrations at Stratford in 1764 and one which, surpris-ingly, never quite caught on.[46]

Notes

1. "Kermode's discussion of the significance of Art and Nature as controlling concepts in the play. . .has established itself as a standard approach" (Palmer, 1968, p. 22).
2. *See* Searle, 1973, pp. 42–8, *passim*.

3. On the master–slave relationship, *see*: Hegel, *Phenomenology of Spirit*, 178–96; Norman, 1976, pp. 46–55; Hyppolite, 1974, pp. 170–6; Kojève, 1980, pp. 8–64.

4. Hyppolite, pp. 158–9, 171.

5. *See* Kojève, pp. 23–4, 42, 52.

6. *The Tempest*, II. ii. 1222–3. *See*: Weimann, 1978, pp. 20f.; Boss, 1972.

7. *See* Kojève, p. 56.

8. *The Tempest*, III. ii. 1441–5.

9. *See also*: Eagleton, 1981, p. 51; White, 1973.

10. Asimov, 1960.

11. Eliot, 1965, p. 19; Hawkes, 1977, p. 152.

12. On English examination questions, *see* Belsey, 1983, p. 18.

13. Vickers, 1974–81, VI, p. 3.

14. *Ibid.*, IV, p. 290.

15. *Ibid.*, V, p. 421.

16. For the results of the Cultural Olympics, see *The Gallup Opinion Index*, February 1976. On the authorship question, Pepsi-Cola, publicizing its own experience with rival claimants, mounted a "Was Shakespeare Shakespeare?" exhibition in 1975. The main feature of the event, which was hosted by Joan Crawford and included a display of "Folios, Quartos, a model of the Globe Theatre, and other Shakespearean materials", was "a series of large boards written in quasi-Elizabethan script explaining the case for and against Shakespeare" (*Shakespeare Newsletter*, 15, 1965, p. 31).

17. *See* Adorno and Horkheimer, 1979, pp. 134f.

18. *Cit.* Jameson, 1981, p. 281. *See also* Baldick, 1983, pp. 89–107.

19. *See* Anderson, 1968, pp. 268–76, *passim*.

20. On the ideology of the Leavis tradition, *see* Eagleton, 1976, pp. 13–17; Mulhern, 1979.

21. "SKINHEAD VANDALISM IN STRATFORD" (*Shakespeare Newsletter*, September 1970, p. 28).

22. *See*: Macherey and E. Balibar, 1978, pp. 4–12; E. Balibar, 1974; Bennett, 1979, pp. 156–66; Eagleton, 1981, p. 123.

23. *See* the persuasive attack on subsidized productions of Shakespeare in Hawkes, 1973, pp. 226–9.

24. Elsom and Tomalin, 1978, p. 162.

25. *Ibid.*, pp. 19–21; Addenbrooke, 1974, p. 26.

26. *See*: Honigmann, 1965, pp. 2–5; Hawkes, 1971, p. 27.

27. Halliday, 1957, p. 34; Vickers, II, p. 7, 490 and V, p. 83.

28. On New Criticism and ideology, *see* Fekete, 1977, and Eagleton, 1983, pp. 46–52. For the particular limitations of New Criticism in relation to Shakespeare, *see* Weimann, pp. xix to xxii. My comment on 'history-for' also applies to the New Historicism.

29. *See* Lever, 1938, p. 173.
30. The proper business of Shakespeare criticism according to Richard David, 1978, p. 46.
31. Cf. Kristeva, pp. 132–3.
32. *See*: Calderwood, 1971, pp. 53, 56–7; David, 1951, p. xxxvii.
33. Granville-Barker, 1927–48, II, pp. 421–22.
34. David, 1951, p. 128; Powell, 1980, p. 25; Ellis, 1973, *passim*.
35. *See*: I. 319–62; IVb. 1926–33, 2407–8. According to Nathaniel "society (saith the text) is the happiness of life", to which Holofernes replies: "And certes the text most infallibly concludes it" (IVa. 1325–28). The letter, which kills, also always has the last word.
36. On other aspects of this tradition's phonocentrism, *see* Eagleton, 1981, pp. 6–10.
37. *Cit*. Rosenberg, 1978, p. 3.
38. Weimann, pp. 159, 247.
39. *See* Foucault, 1970, pp. 17f., 29–35.
40. My italics. Foucault, 1970, pp. 42–3.
41. Puttenham, 1589, pp. 1–2; Sidney, 1966, p. 52. For detailed accounts of these, and related paradoxes in sixteenth and early seventeenth century literary theory, see Colie, 1966; Kaiser, 1964; and Fish, 1972.
42. Hulme, 1962, p. 208.
43. Vickers, IV, p. 171.
44. Cf. Crewe, 1982.
45. "Writing is triumph. . .manic life-after-life insurance. That is what makes it unbearable. Essentially indiscreet and exhibitionistic. Even if we read no 'that's me there' in it. And the increase in discretion is only a surplus-value of triumph—enough to make you sick . . . " (Derrida, 1979, p. 123).
46. Cf. these lines from Garrick's song: "Untouch'd and sacred be thy shrine,/Avonian Willy, bard divine,/In studious posture leaning" (Halliday, p. 71).

5
The Tale Thickens

Words, words, words! That will be my device as long as I have
not been shown that our languages echo a transcendent reality.
(Jules Laforgue, *Hamlet*)

Unless I wish it, not a bird flies in this empire, not a leaf stirs on
the trees. (Atahualpa to Pizarro)

Imperfect Speakers

At the end of his first encounter with the "weyward sisters", Macbeth addresses them as "imperfect Speakers" (I.iii.170) and bids them to tell him more. On the order "Speake, I charge you" (179), they disappear like bubbles into the earth, leaving Macbeth and Banquo to doubt their own perceptions, and their language. When Banquo asks if they have "eaten on the insane Root", he also wonders about the reality of "such things . . . as we doe *speake* about" (185–6). The tentative moves of Macbeth and Banquo to verbally grasp what has happened are like an old song, a nursery game which recalls the doggerel of the sisters themselves:

> *Macb.* Your Children shall be Kings
> *Banq.* You shall be King
> *Macb.* And *Thane* of Cawdor too: wente it not
>   so?
> *Banq.* To th' selfe-same tune, and words:
>
> (188–91)

When Rosse, at this point, enters to deliver his report, it is clear that 'imperfect speaking' is not a disorder exclusive to the sisters or to those who have been in immediate contact with them:

> The King hath happily receiv'd, *Macbeth*,
> The newes of thy successe: and when he reades
> Thy personall Venture in the Rebels fight,
> His Wonders and his Prayses do contend,
> Which should be thine, or his: silenc'd with
>   that,
> In viewing o're the rest o' th' selfe-same day,
> He findes thee in the stout Norweyan Rankes,
> Nothing afeard of what thy selfe didst make
> Strange Images of death, as thick as Tale
> Can post with post, and every one did beare
> Thy prayses in his Kingdomes great defence,
> And powr'd them downe before him.
>
> (193–204)

The perplexing density of Rosse's report releases imperfections of its own, while repeating the haste and excitement of the

messengers and narratives it describes, which arrive headlong
and inarticulate, "as thick as Tale/Can post on post", leaving
Duncan amazed, silent, and finally awash in information. The
thickening of Rosse's account is a contagion caught from these
other reports or an indication, perhaps, of his own penchant
for the "Relation too nice" (IV.iii.2010) later criticized by
Macduff. There is a call here for a performance which incorporates at once a lack and an excess of rhetorical preparation, and
the information imparted reproduces this uneasy play of opposites. Verbal and syntactic ambiguities edge the heroic image
of Macbeth from the good to the evil cause—"Thy personall
venture in the Rebels fight", "He findes thee in the stout Norweyan Rankes". This shifting also applies to Duncan, drawn
into the narrative to the extent of occupying its protagonist's
position. "When he reades", the King becomes his subject,
Macbeth, mirroring in the contention of "Which should be
thine, or his" the usurpation that is imminent. The tale
thickens further as Macbeth becomes not only protagonist but
author, of "Strange Images of death", and reader, in place of
the king, of Rosse's narrative about narratives.

Any attempt to relate the content of narratives in the early
scenes of *Macbeth* has to negotiate a conflict between two basic
linguistic modes which results in a potentially baffling
opacity. On the one side is the attempt to construct an unequivocal idiom in which the theory of the divine right of kings
and its place in the Great Chain of Being is made one with
nature to the extent that the 'unnatural', constitutive operations of language itself are strenuously deleted. On the other
there is an inescapable undertow of negation, in which the
hurly-burly of language which precedes the construction of
these sealed hierarchical categories leaks back to interrupt the
'natural' quality their linguistic mode silently claims for itself.
In Rosse's speech the first mode, affirming a positive metaphysical 'order' which can somehow, magically, exist outside
language and ideology, appears in the attempt to conjure up a
grateful, generous king and his loyal, heroic subject. Its negation is the intractability of language, which intimates a more
deeply rooted disorder than the one that has just been quelled,
and a potentially unending circulation of subjects through
hierarchical positions that only *seem* to be fixed and

sovereign—of king and thane, of author, reader and protagonist.

The same 'thickening' of the tale and dispersal of clear ideological categories divides the language of the "bleeding Cap-
taine" at the beginning of the play. The captain's report of the
battle opens with a reference to the "choked Art" of spent
swimmers who cling together for support and ends with the
choking of his own voice and the cacophony of gashes that "cry
for helpe" (I.ii.63). The Arden editor argues that, under these
cicumstances, some incoherence might be expected (Muir,
1953, p. 8) but the form it takes is no different from that in
Rosse's tale. First there is the intention of affirming an ideal of
manhood and service validated by reference to natural hierarchies and centred on Banquo and Macbeth, whom the rebels
can dismay no more than "Sparrowes, Eagles/Or the Hare the
Lyon" (54–5). But the language of the narrative palters "in a
double sence" no less than that of the play's central and most
conscious "imperfect Speakers", the sisters, incorporating
their characteristic blend of confusion and prophecy. The
rebels, by the end of the speech, have been compared implicitly with the crucified Christ, and Macbeth and Banquo with
his torturers (60–1). In the interim, the narrative production
of a "brave *Macbeth* (well hee deserves that Name)" (35) has
already been thrown into crisis, if not by a graphic excess in
the description of 'legitimate' violence then at least by strategic ambiguities in the text. Seeking the rebel Macdonwald,
Macbeth:

> Disdayning Fortune, with his brandisht steele,
> Which smoak'd with bloody execution
> (Like Valours Minion) carv'd out his passage,
> Till hee fac'd the Slave:
> Which nev'r shooke hands, nor bade farewell to him,
> Till he unseam'd him from the Nave to th' Chops,
> And fix'd his Head upon our Battlements.
>
> (36–42)

The clause "Which nev'r shooke hands . . .", applying equally,
and in different senses, to Fortune, Macbeth, or the Slave, disturbs the balance of a complex syntactic structure, which
totters to the climactic image of an impaled rebellious head,

Macdonwald's but also, proleptically, already that of Macbeth, his own worst enemy.

Such instances of disruption to the harmonious, univocal discourse of Tudor and Stuart absolutism proliferate in the early scenes of *Macbeth*. Rosse's first report to the king anticipates some of the instabilities of his language when he later addressed Macbeth and Banquo. Here another ambiguous 'Macbeth' faces the treacherous thane of Cawdor, a title soon to be his own, confronting him "with selfe-comparisons,/Point against Point, rebellious Arme 'gainst Arme" (I.ii.80–1). Again too much, and too little, is stated with the result that the image of the defender of right merges into its opposite. Equivocation in these opening scenes is a condition of language, which moves constantly back from the articulated code to an anterior heterogeneity, melting, like the sisters after their encounter with Macbeth and Banquo, "as breath into the Winde" (I.iii.183). Macbeth's first words in the play, "So foule and faire a day I have not seene" (I.iii.137), establish his connection with the sisters before they have even met. But the motion of their "faire is foul, and foule is fair" (I.i.12), which L. C. Knights described as a "metaphysical pitch-and-toss" (1946, p. 18), extends not only to those who become directly implicated in what the language of metaphysics would describe as 'evil'. Even Duncan, the perfect, saintly king of *Macbeth* criticism, unintentionally equivocates himself into complicity with his own downfall, confusion's masterpiece, when he acknowledges to his general, "More is thy due than more than all can pay" (I.iv.304).

The crisis of the sign and unequivocal discourse in the play is paralleled by that of the unified subject. As Macbeth embarks on the passage from 'Glamis' to 'Cawdor' to 'King', the identity sustained in the hierarchical order is fractured. After the first meeting with the sisters, when the prospect of murder is still only "fantasticall", the thought still "Shakes so my single state of Man/That function is smother'd in surmise" (I.iii.252–3). By finally daring to do more than "may become a man" (I.vii.525), he ceases to be a coherent subject, either of Duncan or in the sense of an intact, self-present identity. *Macbeth*, as Catherine Belsey has pointed out, explores the relationship between crisis in the "state", or the social order, and disruption in the "single state" of the subject (1980, pp. 89–90). Once the structures of Duncan's kingdom are wrenched from their place in 'nature', Macbeth himself becomes a plurality, a process rather than a fixity. In the same movement the bonds between the state, the subject and the unequivocal linguistic mode of 'order' and 'nature', always suspended in 'imperfect speaking', are broken. Only the "weyward sisters" who inhabit the heath, outside the closures of the social formation, can properly perform "A deed without a name" (IV.i.1579). But after Duncan's murder Macduff can speak of a "horror" which "Tongue nor Heart cannot conceive, nor name" (II.iii.816–17), while Macbeth recognizes that "To know my deed,/'Twere best not know my selfe" (II.i.737–8). The semantic volatility of all the earlier narratives, the negative undertow which compromises the ordered, 'natural' discourse of ideology and its unified subjects, finally comes into its own in the "written troubles of the Braine" (V.iii.2264) that emanate from Lady Macbeth between sleep and waking, madness and reason, and, most crucially, in Macbeth's description of life as "a Tale/Told by an Ideot, full of sound and fury/Signifying nothing" (V.v.2347–9). The "nothing" signified is not merely an absence but a delirious plenitude of selves and meanings, always prior to, and in excess of, the self-naturalizing signs and subjects of the discourses it calls perpetually to account.

The Macbeths, with the sisters, spill over the limits of 'character' to constitute the text's 'nothing' which, in turn, constantly erodes and undermines the hierarchies of irreducible 'somethings' proposed by metaphysics. To define this space of 'nothing' quite simply as 'evil' is to reprocess the text through a moral discourse it renders problematic. Even in orthodox Christian doctrine, if 'nothing' is identifiable with sin or chaos it is also the ground of all creation,[1] and *Macbeth* also signifies nothing in this paradoxically positive sense. The unequivocal discourse of a metaphysically sanctioned absolutism, even when it succeeds in avoiding self-contradiction and the interpenetration of opposites is 'single' not only in the sense of 'unified' or 'unambiguous' but also in a second sense, exploited here as in other plays, of 'weak' or 'simple-minded'.[2] In the choric scene following the murder of Duncan, Rosse and the Old Man discuss the night which has "trifled former knowings"

(II.iv.928) in terms that permit these "former knowings" to reassert themselves with a vengeance.

The studied theatrical archaism of the scene sets off the credulous rhetoric of Rosse and the geriatric amazement of his interlocutor, who together reconstitute order in a reprise of the bloody Captain's bird and animal lore. The feudal norm is unequivocally reaffirmed in the outrage of Duncan's horses breaking from their stalls and proceeding to "eate each other", a fact the Old Man prefaces with the standard formula for this type of narrative, "'Tis said . . . " (945). The same system of 'natural' correspondences is at work in his image of a falcon, "by a Mowsing Owle hawkt at, and kill'd" (939), but the 'singleness' of this type of language always sits uneasily in the text. It marks the language of Duncan and Banquo when they first arrive at Macbeth's castle, hallowed in their minds by the presence of the birds who make each "Jutty frieze", "buttrice" and "Coigne of Vantage" the place for a "pendant bed, and procreant Cradle,/Where they must breed, and haunt" (I.vi.439–42). There is clearly a hint here of the 'life-themes' discovered by G. Wilson Knight (1951, p. 125f.), but the situational ironies also tend to strip the rhetoric away from its experiential and 'natural' base, revealing that the birds at least, if not Banquo and Duncan, are a little naive in their literal adherence to the 'Elizabethen World Picture'. There is a similar element of bathos in Macduff's first reaction to the murder of his "pretty chickens, and their Damme" by the "Hell-Kite" Macbeth (IV.iii.2066–7), particularly in the context of his desertion of his family. After his father's flight, in response to the question "How will you live?", the young Macduff replies "As Birds do, Mother" (IV.ii.1747–8), an answer in which echoes of the Shakespearean fool mark a limit to the pretensions of one of the text's most insistent images of 'order'—'Let them eat ideology'.

The choric exchange between Rosse and the Old Man ends, after the play's most sustained burst of 'singleness', with a benediction which is also a curse and which restores to the text its characteristic signification of 'nothing'. As he leaves, the Old Man bids "Gods benyson go with you, and with those/That would make good of bad, and Friends of Foes" (II.iv.1978–9). His blessing applies equally to those who speak of falcons, owls, eagles and sparrows and to the proponents of "faire is foule, and foule is faire" who bring, from the viewpoint of the bird-watchers, a curse to Scotland. No one makes "good of bad" more forcefully than the Macbeths, who harness the ambiguities of language in the process. Lady Macbeth, for whom the 'single' is the inadequate, courts 'doubleness' in its various senses. In response to Duncan's pedantic greeting to "our honor'd Hostesse", she affirms:

> All our service
> In every point twice done, and then done
>   double,
> Were poore, and single Businesse to contend
> Against those Honors deepe, and broad,
> Wherewith your Majestie loades our house
>   (I.vi.449–53)

The 'Honors' here connote titles already bestowed on Macbeth, the royal presence which now graces his castle, and the sinister opportunities for further advancement that presence affords. The service done 'double' implies not only the obvious numerical sense but also the involvement of 'strength' and 'duplicity'. Making good out of bad is, at one level, a definition of this type of hypocritical show, in which the sense directed to the naive 'single' hearer is enriched by the speaker's recognition of true intentions. In the case of Macbeth, his "single state" broken open, one utterance may disclose different levels of duplicity and delusion in the process of the same subject. When Duncan's murder is revealed, he announces:

> Had I but dy'd an houre before this chance,
> I had liv'd a blessed time: for from this instant,
> There's nothing serious in Mortalitie:
> All is but Toyes:
>   (II.iii.852–5)

While the regicide conceals his crime beneath an extravagant show of 'single' piety, unknown to him the Macbeth of "Tomorrow, and tomorrow, and tomorrow" is already, by indirection, speaking an unequivocal truth.

In summary, the density of the narratives that accumulate in the early scenes of *Macbeth* is produced by a conflict between two linguistic modes. The first, which attempts to suppress the constitutive role of language, is the 'single', unequivocal identification of the ideology of divine right with nature. It pertains, in its own terms, to the 'good characters' of the play and the birds. The second, most fully itself in the language of the sisters and the protagonists, is evident elsewhere whenever 'imperfect speaking' cuts into the first mode and restores to it a discordant element of linguistic materiality and heterogeneity. The two modes proceed side by side until the end of the play, never fully resolving themselves into a unity. When Malcolm finally assumes power, the restoration of 'single' discourse is announced in his description of the Macbeths as "this dead Butcher, and his Fiend-like Queene" (V.vii.2522), the most reductive and parsimonious of all possible definitions, the mark of a speaker whose sole foray into equivocation, in the testing of Macduff in Act 4, Scene 3, lacks altogether the Vice's theatrical panache inherited by his antagonist. In contrast to Macbeth's, his discourse 'knows' and 'sees' very little or, to put it another way, does not know 'nothing'. Malcolm's "single state" is ripe for an encounter with the sisters.[3]

There is an influential strand in *Macbeth* criticism, one particularly suited in the recent past to the practical exegetical requirements of students, which works with the text's unequivocal mode to deliver a clear account of it as a "morality play" (Farnham, 1950, p. 79), a "vision of evil" (Knight, 1949, pl. 40), a "statement of evil" (Knights, 1946, p. 18), or "the story of a noble and valiant man who is brought to his damnation, presented in such a way as to arouse our pity and terror" (Muir, 1953, p. lv). The pandemic 'pitch-and-toss' and 'imperfect speaking' which unseat metaphysics in the play clearly fail to reach out to the critical discourse which can so casually refurbish "morality", "evil" and "damnation". At heart this is still the 'Shakespeare' of the Reverend Sims, embellished with images, themes, characters and a story but directed to the statement of a central, transcendent 'truth' in the text. These secondary narratives, which purport to help the text along in delivering its essential meanings, do so by privileging, at their most fundamental level, its 'single' mode and ignoring, or banishing to the realms of 'evil' or 'exquisite

complexity', the 'unnatural' operations of language that divide
and 'thicken' narrative in the play itself, which is ultimately no
more an affirmation of metaphysical unity and order than a
contradictory "Tale/Told by an Ideot, full of sound and
fury/Signifying nothing".

Antonin Artaud regarded Shakespeare as the source of 400
years of dramatic "falsehood and illusion", of a "purely descrip-
tive and narrative theatre—storytelling psychology" in which
the stage is kept separate from the audience, and administers to
its public the dominant cultural and ideological forms (Artaud,
1958, p. 76). This may be true of the 'single' *Macbeth* sustained
by much modern criticism and theatrical production but not of
the other play which, by fissuring the 'natural' subjects and
signs that exist for and in ideology, achieves precisely what
Artaud denies a 'Shakespeare' who leaves his audience intact
"without setting off one image that will shake the organism to
its foundations and leave an ineffaceable scar" (Artaud, 1958,
pp. 76–7). But this latter play has much to contend with, quite
apart from the critical assumptions that transform ideology into
'human values' and recover from the Shakespearean text,
however complex, their suitably harmonious vehicle. A normative criticism will always affirm unity by marginalizing texts,
or parts of texts, where 'Shakespeare' is nodding or not speaking
perfectly. The Newbolt Report advised teachers to avoid
passages which were not "verbally inspired"; for example, "the
tediously protracted dialogue" between Malcolm and Macduff
in Act 4, Scene 3, of *Macbeth* (Newbolt, p. 314)—a point where
the 'singleness' of text and criticism is most at risk. Where
pedagogic or discursive exclusion is impossible, another available strategy is the theoretical splits, guaranteed to unseam any
commentator from nave to chops. So Kenneth Muir wishes
away the contradictory thickening of the bloody Captain's tale
by combining naturalism—the wounded man is exhausted and
therefore incoherent—with an extreme of conventional formalism in which the character "utters bombastic language, not
because he is himself bombastic, but because such language was
considered appropriate to epic narration" (Muir, 1953, pp. li,
88). Fair is foul and foul is fair, and in the last instance the text
can be recovered from its own imperfect speaking by forms of
rewriting and incrustation not dreamed of even in Macherey's

philosophy. In nearly all modern editions, Rosse's description of the messages that reach Duncan "as thick as Tale/Can post with post"—words "well within the normal language patterns of this time" (Hulme, 1962, p. 25)—has been excised. Rosse now delivers lines written by Nicholas Rowe in 1709, in which reports "As thick as *hail,/Came* post with post". And what could be more natural?

Wild and Hurling Words

Narratives in *Macbeth* select and organize their detail for specific purposes in the present. The report not only tells or conceals what has taken place, but does so in a way that confirms the relations of a social order into which it is itself inserted as a gift, a form of exchange, or an act of fealty. The narrative constitutes subject positions for a narrator and a receiver, and there are no 'facts', only interpretations conditioned by context. Thus Rosse's report to Duncan of the battle against the rebels and then his account, delivered to Macbeth and Banquo, of the king's reactions to this and other reports are at once confirmations of the proper relations of monarch and loyal subject, and acts of duty or homage. The disruption of a narrative also dislodges the subject-positions it proposes. Through the accounts of Macbeth's victory, Duncan is able in a sense to be present in battle—"In viewing o're the rest o' th' selfe-same day,/He findes thee in the stout Norweyan Rankes"—but their mode of arrival and delivery, both "as thick as Tale", leave him in some consternation. In this confusion Duncan, the only king in Shakespeare apart from the weak Henry VI who sends his forces into battle without being at their head, can only find himself in Macbeth and, in the contention of praise and wonder, experience the uncertainty of "Which should be thine, or his". Duncan, "when he reades", is divided from himself. In another reversal of positions, common in these early scenes, it is really Scotland's, not Norway's, king who finally "craves *composition*" (I.i.86), an *ordering* and *making whole* that apply equally to the discourse and the subject.

In *Hamlet*, too, narrative is in this sense a form of 'composition' and exchange. Improbably, and in contrast to the

story-tellers in Macbeth, one of the most cogent narrators in
Shakespeare is Ophelia. The account of Hamlet's assault on her
is a rhetorical *tour de force*:

> My Lord, as I was sowing in my Chamber,
> Lord *Hamlet* with his doublet all unbrac'd
> No hat upon his head, his stockings foul'd,
> Ungartred and downe gived to his Anckle,
> Pale as his shirt, his knees knocking each
>   other,
> And with a looke so pitious in purport,
> As if he had been loosed out of hell,
> To speake of horrors: he comes before me.
>   (II.i.973–80)

The hearer, Polonius, is arrested by the image of closeted
domesticity, the shocking intrusion of disorganized costume,
the display of maidenly compassion, and the climactic switch of
narrative tense. He is able to muster only open-mouthed,
monosyllabic reactions—"Mad for thy Love?" (981), "What
said he?" (983)—that propel Ophelia's description of a Hamlet
in "the very extasie of Love" (999) forward to its next phase.
There is no related dramatic action to verify this narrative, and
the answer to Hamlet's question in the nunnery scene, "Are you
honest?" (1758)[4] remains something of an enigma throughout
the play. But the subject-positions the report creates for speaker
and hearer, or its composition of Ophelia and Polonius, are
clear. Ophelia registers the reactions of the "greene Girle"
(I.iii.567) Polonius has told her she is during their first
exchange in the play, when he advises her "thinke your selfe a
Baby" (571) and warns her "You do not understand your selfe
so cleerely,/As it behoves my Daughter"(562–3). More firmly
placed in the position of 'daughter', Ophelia has now reversed
the pattern that holds in the earlier encounter, when all of the
passive reaction-shots are hers—"I do not know, my Lord, what
I should thinke", "I shall obey my Lord" (I.iii.570, 602)—but
only in the interest of placing Polonius more securely, and
unequivically, in the position of 'father'.

Ophelia's narrative puts back in place the family relations
thrown into a mild crisis in Act 1, Scene 3, by the anxieties of
Polonius and Laertes about the possibility of her opening her

"chast Treasure" to Hamlet's "unmastered importunity" (494–5). An act of obeisance in this context, it is also a gift which Polonius will put to work in the larger network of relations that constitute the state. The image of a Hamlet mad for love will do much to explain the prince's "antic disposition" and to recompose Claudius and Gertrude. It will also confirm the status, and usefulness, of Polonius as Councillor of State, a role he pursues with fastidious and sycophantic single-mindedness. As Hamlet eventually points out to the corpse he drags from behind the arras in Gertrude's chamber, "Thou find'st to be too busie, is some danger" (2415) and as soon as he has received Ophelia's report, Polonius is characteristically busy relaying it to his betters. But what Ophelia accomplishes with consummate skill and economy in twenty-two lines takes her father, with his sententious circumlocution, the better part of a scene:

> My Liege, and Madam, to expostulate
> What Majestie should be, what Dutie is,
> Why day is day; night, night; and time is
>   time,
> Were nothing but to waste Night, Day and
>   Time,
> Therefore, since Brevitie is the Soule of Wit,
> And tediousnesse, the limbes and outward
>   flourishes,
> I will be breefe. Your Noble Sonne is mad:
> Mad call I it; for to define true Madnesse,
> What is't, but to be nothing else but mad.
>   (II.ii.1113–21)

By making so explicit the subject positions and relations that Ophelia incorporates into the substance of her narrative, Polonius thickens the tale beyond the patience of his hearers. Gertrude immediately cries out "More matter, with less Art" (1123). But this 'art', for Polonius, is what reaffirms his position as councillor, father, bearer of the sententious wisdom of age. Some ninety lines after initiating his report he emphasizes these guarantees of his identity in his prologue to the empirical proof of Hamlet's madness, to be staged for Claudius in the nunnery scene:

> Be you and I behinde an Arras then,
> Marke the encounter: If he love her not,
> And be not from his reason falne thereon;
> Let me be no Assistant for a State,
> And keepe a Farme and Carters.
>
> (1197–201)

These compositions of the 'truth' behind Hamlet's show of madness trace the network that binds family and state in language, the "instrument of society" which is not so much for the use of its members as the very means by which they are constructed as subjects. This network, and its corruption in Denmark, is made graphically present in the play's most crucial narrative, the Ghost's account of poison poured in through the ear to course through the smooth body of the monarch and his state, leaving it covered with a "vile and loathsome crust" (I.iii.757). By this act, and doubly in its concealment, "the whole eare of Denmarke" is "rankly abus'd". (723–4). The poisoned ear, as Terence Hawkes has shown, is an image central to a pervasive corruption of the channels of communication in Denmark.[5] Normal patterns of speaking and listening are displaced by Claudius's "most painted words" (II.ii.1705), by the courtly obfuscations of Polonius and Osric, and by the pattern of strategic concealment, spying and overhearing Polonius calls "the traile of Policie" (II.ii.1071). In this context, even before the revelations of the Ghost, Hamlet is compelled to suffer in silence—"breake my hearte, for I must hold my tongue" (I.ii.342). Horatio is distinguished less by what he knows ("There are more things in Heaven and Earth", *etc.*) than by the very fact that Hamlet can talk to him. There is no one else.

The central image of corruption, and the network that radiates from it, make the operations of a self-naturalizing discourse much more obvious in *Hamlet* than in *Macbeth*. The hierarchy of subject positions confirmed by the narratives of Ophelia and Polonius shapes both Claudius's attempt to piece back together an unequivocal order he himself has broken open and Gertrude's desire to reconcile Hamlet to his father's death through the 'single', and ostensibly natural, truth of proverbial wisdom. But again 'single' discourse is compromised by the heterogeneous mode which refuses to delete the constitutive materiality of language, and which unravels all composition. This second mode is in evidence in the 'art' of Polonius's narrative, where the information to which all such messages are directed is blocked by an inept, and insistent, manifesting of the latent structures they keep in place. There is a revealing contradiction even in the cogency of Ophelia's description of a distracted Hamlet. Here, as in her earlier exchange with Laertes, a gap opens between the position of "baby" or "green girl" that her discourse constructs for the speaker and on the other hand, that discourse's inescapable rhetorical finesse.[6] The 'character' is a process in excess of the subject constituted in the family and the larger hierarchical scheme. Even in sanity she is already "Poore *Ophelia*/Divided from her selfe" (2821–2), whose "speech is nothing" (2752) in that it says more than can ever be crammed into the position made available to her by her father, brother and king. But the 'single' mode is least stable, and most open to the deconstructive interventions of Hamlet, in the language of Claudius and Gertrude. When Claudius addresses "our sometimes Sister, now our Queen" (I.ii.186) and "my Cosin *Hamlet*, and my Sonne" (244), the glib attempt to reconstitute 'order' by glossing over the very differences by which order is constituted becomes easy prey for Hamlet's riddling wordplay about being "too much i' th' Sun" (247), with the king "A little more than kin, and lesse then kinde" (245). Gertrude opens herself to a similar attack when she advises Hamlet not to think about his dead father: "Thou know'st 'tis common, all that lives must dye,/Passing through Nature, to Eternity" (252–3). Hamlet's response, "Madam, it is common" (254), confronts the single with the double, one mode of language with another, the unequivocal statement with its dispersal in a pun.

This ambiguity, and resistance of the 'single', is the keynote of Hamlet's language in a play which contains more quibbles than any of Shakespeare's tragedies (Mahood, 1957, p. 112). After his conversation with the Ghost, the prince begins to reveal what he has heard to his friends but diverts his account into a sequence of enigmas and broken proverbs that Horatio describes as "wild and hurling words" (I.iii.825). After the assumption of an "antic disposition", Hamlet's language becomes a vortext for all unequivocal discourse and the subject-positions it proposes, drawing them in and throwing them out again in fragments. At the heart of this disintegrative process are the "Unckle Father, and Aunt Mother" (II.ii.1422–3) to whom he returns time and again. Before departing for England, Hamlet bids Claudius "Farewell deere Mother" and, in response to the baffled reaction, explains: "Father and Mother is man and wife: man & wife in one flesh, and so my mother" (2713–17). In the context of a language already corrupt, Hamlet assumes a negating, complicating function comparable to that of the Fool in other plays, a part described by Feste in *Twelfth Night* as the "corrupter of words" (III.i.1248). The corrupt language of those in power is at once burlesqued and resisted. Like the 'nothing' of *Macbeth*, Hamlet's 'imperfect speaking' is, as Ophelia points out, "naught" (2014), but its strategic hurly-burly points to the finite, fictive quality of all discursive constuctions. Even "the King", as Hamlet points out to Guildenstern, is "a thing . . . Of nothing" (2257–9).

What Laertes says of Ophelia's language in madness, "This nothings more than matter" (2926), is equally true of Hamlet's. The two fundamental linguistic modes, of 'matter' and 'nothing', come into direct open conflict when Claudius initiates what should be a polite, ritual exchange with the question "How fares our Cosin *Hamlet?*" (1948). Hamlet takes "fares" in its unintended sense of 'eats', and his reply leaves Claudius, the commentators, and possibly left the Globe audience dumfounded with too much and too little meaning: "Excellent Ifaith, of the Camelions dish: I eate the Ayre promise-cramm'd, you cannot feed Capons so" (1949–50). In the best edition of the play to date, Harold Jenkins suggests that there may be an allusion here to Hamlet's unfulfilled hopes for Claudius's support in the succession, with a possible pun on 'Ayre'/'heir' designed to throw the king off the trail of the true cause of his melancholy. An embedded Elizabethan proverb about love, like the chameleon, being able to feed on air may also bring in Ophelia and her part in Hamlet's feigned madness (Jenkins, 1982, p. 293). The reference to the 'cramming' of the capon could imply that Claudius's polite concern is merely a way of fattening Hamlet up for impending slaughter. But the main impact, as Claudius recognizes, is again that of "wild and hurling words" which, in effect, make up a language different from his own: "I have nothing with this answer *Hamlet*, these words are not mine" (1951–2). Hamlet's reply, "No, nor mine" (1953) is a further refinement and elaboration of the productive "nothing" which is set against the discourse of the king. In one sense it is a confirmation of 'single' language, reproducing the proverb which states that words, once spoken, no longer belong to the speaker (Jenkins, 1982, p. 293). But the words are also not Hamlet's in that this linguistic mode of 'nothing' declines to produce unequivocal meanings for, or from, unified subjects. Because Claudius resists this as not his language, the words also fail to take their subversive toll. In addition to being the adjectival pronoun, "mine" is also the verb 'to undermine',[7] which is the design of Hamlet's 'nothing' on Claudius's ideological closures.

Language in Denmark is like the "vile and loathsome crust" that covers the body of the dead king poisoned through the ear. Hamlet's compounding of corruption, in his role as traditional "corrupter of words", adds to the density of language. Set against the initial corruption, there is a norm of clear speaking, disclosure and reciprocation, of language as an instrument of society in the ideal sense. This is implicit in the order of Old Hamlet. It reappears momentarily in Hamlet's conversations with Horatio, Claudius's private recognition of guilt, and Gertrude's vow of secrecy in the closet scene, where she swears "if words be made of breath,/And breath of life: I have no life to breath/What thou hast said to me" (2573–5).

But the incrustations of language finally overwhelm both "the converse of breath" and any notion of a free subject or a metaphysical certainty it might propose. The voice of metaphysical truth in the play, the Ghost, is itself deeply compromised. The injunction to revenge and its prospect of damnation, coupled with the Protestant view of purgatory as a popish invention, keeps open the possibility that this "Apparition" (I.i.37) or "Illusion" (127) is a "Goblin damn'd" (I.ii.624) which, like the sisters in *Macbeth*, tells us truths only to "betray's in deepest consequence" (I.iii.237).[8] Even if the prince is right in naming the Ghost—"I'le call thee *Hamlet*" (629)—its demands are marked by the dead king's own lack of perception. If its supplementary injunction, "nor let thy Soule contrive/Against thy Mother ought", poses certain difficulties,

the stipulation "Taint not thy mind" is, under the circumstances, preposterous (770–1). The fusty Senecan air that clings
to this figure is strongest in the closet scene, where the Ghost
enters "in his night gowne",[9] appropriately cued in by
Hamlet's "A vice of Kings" and "A King of shreds and patches"
(2483) to take his place in a disengaging family snapshot.
Indeterminacies of language extend from the mortal contor-
tions of the signifier to the transcendental signified from
beyond the grave, one whose only ultimate guarantee to the
text is to seal it off as the site of an imperfect speaking to which
neither Hamlet's language nor any other can offer a solution.

Maimed Rites/Signifying Nothing

In his seminar on *Hamlet*, Jacques Lacan observed that in all
instances of death and mourning in the play the appropriate
ritual is cut short or omitted (Lacan, 1977b, pp. 40–3). Old
Hamlet dies without confession or absolution, Gertrude's
mourning is interrupted by her remarriage, Claudius buries
Polonius "in hugger mugger" in fear of the suspicions of "the
people muddied,/Thicke and unwholesome in their thoughts,
and whispers" (2818–19) and the corpse of Ophelia is attended
only by the "maimed rites" (1.3408) appropriate to a possible
suicide. This breaking of customary forms in *Hamlet* is not,
however, exclusive to death and mourning. "Maimed rites" are
in evidence everywhere as the correlative of an incrusting and
deformation in language, another dimension of what is rotten
in the state of Denmark. The curtailment of Gertrude's
mourning after a month is also the disruption of her wedding
rites, conducted "with Dirge in Marriage" (I.ii.190), "the
Funerall Bakt-meats" coldly furnishing the table of festivity.
(369). Claudius's attempt to pray is another abortive rite, his
thoughts remaining below to free another "rapsidie of words"
(2431) into the text's 'nothing'. The play begins with what in
the theatre must have seemed for a moment to be an actor's
error—a changing of the guard in which Barnardo calls the
challenge and Francisco, the sentinel on duty, has to insist
"Nay answer *me*" (I.i.5). It ends with the duel, a noble test of
skill with blunted rapiers which, in the event, leaves the stage

littered with the bodies of all surviving members of the two main families. At the centre of *Hamlet* is another "maimed rite", the dramatic performance that ends abruptly when "The King rises" (2136).

In the final words of the play, the new social order headed by Fortinbras is announced with the promise of a completed ritual at last, the bearing of Hamlet "like a Soldier to the Stage" accompanied by "the Souldiours Musicke, and the rites of Warre' (3896–900). The 'stage' in question is a platform on the larger stage of the Globe. But the fact that Hamlet, at the end of the play, will be borne not *from* but *to* a stage is itself appropriate. Apart from the arrival of Fortinbras, the other key factor at the end is the survival of Horatio in the role of guardian of the narrative. His task, repeated by Hamlet at the point of death, is to "report me and my causes right/To the unsatisfied" (3823–4) and "in this harsh world" to "draw thy breath in paine./To tell my Storie" (3834–5). So Fortinbras's final words, which herald the first completed rite in the play, also complete *Hamlet*, in contrast to the 'maimed' play-within-the-play, as a 'rite' of Jacobean society. The rite of *Hamlet* begins just after it ends, with the eventual relaying of Horatio's story to actors— described by Hamlet himself as "the Abstracts and breefe Chronicles of the time" (II.ii.1565)—who will tell the prince's story and report his cause right, with all the contradictory 'nothings' that suspend unequivocal narrative, in "The Tragedie of Hamlet, Prince of Denmarke".

Hamlet ends, and begins again, with its tail in its mouth. Narrative time and mimetic action become aspects of a 'single' dramatic discourse, embedded in and mediated by an acknowledgment of the ritual exchange in the theatre and the subject positions it constructs. The meeting of a 'natural', ideologically complicit mode with the material heterogeneity of 'nothing' on the level of language is repeated in a semiotics of dramatic performance. The mimetic content of the 'fable' *is* the forms that mobilize it, *Hamlet* being as much 'about' its own linguistic and theatrical signifiers as anything else. In the text, Saussure's analogy of the signifier and signified as different but indivisible, like the opposite sides of a sheet of paper, is extended into a Möbius strip in which end and beginning, 'inside' and 'outside' are not finally distinguishable.

"Remember thee?" says Hamlet after the account of his father's murder, "I, thou poore Ghost, while memory holds a seate/In this distracted Globe" (I.iii.780–2). While there is memory in the world, or in the 'globe' of Hamlet's own skull, this narrative will not be forgotten. At the same moment, Richard Burbage scans the "distracted" faces around him in the Globe Theatre and, breaking the illusion only in the 'doubleness' of language and of his own divided presence as actor and protagonist, marks at once a key item in the advance of the narrative of *Hamlet* and the relationship of stage and audience within which it is articulated.

When the players arrive at Elsinore in Act 2, the audience is again reminded of the social transaction involved, and of the building in which its individual members stand or sit. The text's allusion to a 'war of the theatres', and the threat posed to the livelihood of adult actors by the popularity of boys' companies, makes the action of *Hamlet* momentarily contemporary with its performances in the first decade of the seventeenth century. "Do the Boyes carry it away?" asks Hamlet, to which Rosencrantz replies "I that they do, *Hercules* & his load too" (II.ii.1407–8). The Globe itself, borne by Hercules, survives only because the prosperity of the text, as Rosaline reminds Berowne in *Love's Labour's Lost*, lies in the ear of the hearer. At the end of the play, before Fortinbras's men bear Hamlet "to the Stage", the audience is again in the action. Hamlet's dying words extend once more from those assembled on stage to the whole 'distracted Globe':

> You that looke pale, and tremble at this
>   chance,
> That are but Mutes or audience to this acte:
> Had I but time (as this fell Sergeant Death
> Is strick'd in his Arrest) oh I could tell you.
> But let it be.
>
>   (3818–22)

Horatio resists his suicidal desire to play the "Antike Roman" (3826) with its play on 'antic'—'antique', 'theatrical', 'bur-lesque'—only in order to comply with Hamlet's last request, recapitulated in another allusion to the production in progress:

> Give order that these bodies
> High on a stage be placed to the view,
> And let me speake to th' yet unknowing world,
> How these things came about.
>
> (3873–7)

It is by now a commonplace of *Hamlet* criticism that the play is shot through with references, explicit and oblique, to plays and acting. Words like "act", "prologue", "theme", "antic", "play", "audience" and "stage" recur in the text in double senses, while "seems" always implies at once deception and display.[10] During 'The murder of Gonzago', the audience watches an audience watching a play, in a characteristic moment of thickening, and disclosure, of the materials and signifiers of drama. By continually accepting its own illusion, and alluding to the contract between stage and audience within which it is put to work, the performance becomes a form of true, unconcealed seeming which purges the false. Although this self-reflexive theatrical rite is 'maimed' in the interrupted performance of 'The Murder of Gonzago', its completion with the conclusion of *Hamlet* itself, as a rite of Jacobean society, signals again the triumph of an idealized reciprocal exchange between actors and audience in the theatre—the exchange which acts as a foil and a normative frame for the corruption of language and acting at Elsinore. The illusion *per se* (action, narrative), stripped of these reflexive elements, offers an unresolved confusion, a dark Saturnalia. But into this irredeemably corrupt world of the represented Elsinore comes a stabilizing factor—the very conditions of its representation as theatrical illusion (actors, the stage, performance), woven into the 'doubleness' of the play's language and periodically incorporated in much more explicit ways, through the play within the play, for example, or the references to the Globe itself and the war of theatres. The 'corruption' and 'nothing' that characterize language at Elsinore on the level of plot or the play's represented 'world', carry their own positive value in the larger context of the rite. They constitute a space of excess and, in a double sense, 'play' in the subject and the signifier—a mode of speech and performance which dislodges the unified characters and signs of mimesis and also of the unknowing and undis-

closed theatricals that take place in the world outside the
theatre. Before the ever-receding horizon of the real, the
'natural' subjects and signs of everyday life as reconstituted in
the text of *Hamlet* shimmer like mirages, or like actors on a
stage who half pretend to be people whose conversation strays
incessantly to the problem of acting.

    Macbeth too projects the mediations of 'doubleness' and
'nothing' from language to the theatre. Here again numerous
theatrical references emerge on the "bloody Stage" (II.iv.930)
of Scotland in the course of the play,[11] culminating in
Macbeth's speech on 'signifying nothing', which moves from an
image of the actor who speaks to its final delirium:

> Out, out, breefe Candle,
> Life's but a walking Shadow, a poore Player,
> That struts and frets his houre upon the Stage,
> And then is heard no more. It is a tale
> Told by an Ideot, full of sound and fury
> Signifying nothing.

(V.v.2344–9)

On the 'single' level of plot and character this may be read as a
statement of despair or, giving more credit to the protagonist, a
moment of self-awareness when, in the very act of confronting
such darkness, "personal life announces its virtue, and superbly
signifies itself".[12] For those who follow Nietzsche in believing
that such basically 'moral' readings dwarf Shakespeare's
imaginative concept, this speech becomes a central statement of
the meaningless of life, the metaphysical coin's existential
obverse, which depicts a Macbeth transported, complete with
garbage-can, from the Left Bank to the South Bank.[13] At the
limit of such 'single' interpretation, aimed at decoding the
'spirit' of the text and its characters, V. Y. Kantak argues that
Macbeth, in this "last moment of deep sentience", reaches for
the poor player as "a fitting symbol of what he has become", a
fact which "expresses character" in that the image reflects the
protagonists "poetic power" and "radiant self-knowledge"
(Kantak, 1963, pp. 51–2).

    What this analysis obscures, as it strains to hold on to the
category of character, is the 'double' quality of the theatrical
signifier itself and the fact that the actor is not just what

Macbeth has become but what he has been all along. In this, and other accounts of the speech that are geared to an unproblematic notion of representation, certain key constituents of 'life', transcendentally signified and beyond the play of signs, are recovered from language which, in fact, unravels any such absolute referent of mimesis. Here, as in Jaques's "All the world's a stage" speech in *As You Like It*, a medieval commonplace about the futility of life—the world is *merely* a play, men and women *merely* actors—is transformed by the fact that it is spoken from the stage by an actor. The actor who speaks, or at least the actor he acts—Macbeth dwarfed by the "borrowed Robes" of kingship—*is* the poor player whose mediations block any smooth passage to what is being represented and, like the mad language of the "Ideot", foregrounds the irreducible materials of signification in signifying nothing.

The stage, then, can in no way be simply the means for expressing this commonplace. In this context it negates itself. 'Shadows' cast no light except in a ritual where language is no longer permitted to function 'naturally', where "Faire is foule, and foule is faire" and "nothing is, but what is not" (I.iii.253). The stage itself, and the actor, enter into the density of 'imperfect speaking', the cauldron in which the syntax of 'nature' is disrupted and reconstituted— "Eye of Newt and Toe of Frogge,/Wooll of Bat, and Tongue of Dogge:/Adder's Forke ..." (IV.i.1540–3). As the "single state" of Macbeth is broken, along with the coherence of unequivocal language, so the character itself is placed under erasure. Crossed by the walking shadow of the poor player who struts and frets, it constructs for the audience subject-positions quite unlike those of a purely mimetic drama or a language that affects easy access to its signifieds. The material residue of actors, costumes, movements and characters is thrown into the cauldron of signifiers that will never be fully absorbed in symbolic meanings but remain the ground and negation of all ideological and metaphysical absolutes. It is from within the unperceived closures of the signified—sublime confidence in unshakeable truth—that the voice of kingship and symbolic order finally constricts the limitless transformations of 'nothing' into the "dead Butcher" and the "Fiend-like Queene". The 'character' reaffirmed here is not so much an absolute subjectivity as the literal sense of the term, an *inscription*—the mark of a limited discursive practice. "'Tis the Eye of Child-hood", Lady Macbeth points out, "That feares a painted Devill" (II.ii.713–14). While embodying this one aspect of the semiotic innocence of childhood, Malcolm's metaphysics of evil, always problematic in a text in which the ravelled sleeve of language is never conclusively knit, displays none of the child's pleasure in nonsense: "Double, double, toyle and trouble;/Fire burne, and Cauldron bubble" (IV.i.1537–8).

In both *Macbeth* and *Hamlet* naive notions of 'representation' in language and drama, and the given, unified subjects they propose are referred back to the constitutive, and deconstructive, *processes* of the subject and the sign, and the ritual and institutional structures in which these processes are inscribed and take effect. A broad range of Elizabethan sources, from works of literary theory to Puritan attacks on the theatre, allude to the ambiguous operations of 'double' and 'nothing'. Philip Stubbes attacks actors as "doble dealing ambodexters" (Stubbes, 1595, p. 102), pointing to the plurality which, in the theatre, combines with the poetic language described by Puttenham as exceeding "the limits of common utterance" and drawing speech "from plainnesse and simplicitie to a certaine *doublenesse*" (1589, p. 128), to confound the 'single' in all its manifestations. The juxtaposition of unequivocal statement and 'nothing' is also present in Sir Philip Sidney's defence of the poet, who *"nothing* affirms, and therefore never lieth"* (Sidney, 1966, p. 52).

Robert Weimann's work suggests that this 'double' linguistic and theatrical quality in Shakespeare's text is related to medieval popular staging, with its mixing of mimesis and ritual and its division of the action between the *locus* of the platform or the stage proper, where dominant ideological forms are held in 'single' language and sustained illusion, and the unlocalized space of the *platea*, where the social production of meaning, obscured in 'innocent' notions of representation, is excavated and displayed through popular forms of burlesque, nonsense, hocus-pocus, and direct contact between actors and audience. [14] In the traditional ritual role of fool as "corrupter of words", one part of Hamlet is always outside the action, occupying the downstage area which is the equivalent of the *platea* in the Jacobean theatre. From this position the actor/ protagonist takes the audience into his confidence and implicitly upstages the work of actors who pretend to be what they seem and whose language strives to keep the 'natural' signs and subjects of ideology in place. In this context the remarks on naturalistic acting, the Fool sticking to the script and the stupidity of the 'groundlings', all made by the *locus* Hamlet, become doubly ironic.[15] As a development of the Vice and the "painted Devill" of the moralities and interludes. Macbeth too is divided between mimetic action and the forms of popular ritual, which are also apparent in his doubling as a carnival king or lord of misrule.[16] When, after the murder of Duncan, he announces that "from this instant,/There's nothing serious in Mortalitie:/All is but Toyes", the triple signification, of 'good subject', hypocrite, and the genuinely despairing Macbeth who will eventually emerge in the *locus*, is set off by a fourth—the reveller who conducts the rites of 'nothing' from the *platea*. If the *locus* contains an action which is no more than a "statement of evil", or something of that order, the *platea* affirms the 'doubleness' of an orgiastic interregnum, which incorporates language, and the theatre itself, as the place where anything can happen. Attached to this is the utopianism of carnival,[17] where nothing is serious while, at the same time, the 'nothing' which banishes hierarchical constraints is pursued in all earnest. The king who presides is characterized by the traditional iconography of festivity—intoxication, an emblematic lechery (IV.iii.1881) and an appetite which will not be satisfied until he has "supt full" with horrors (V.v.2334).

"The purpose of Playing", says Hamlet, "is to hold as 'twer the Mirror up to Nature" (1868–70), an act which, once spoken of within the illusion, implies much more than a realistic representation. The critical discourse that cannot go beyond mimesis and its 'natural', intact subjects and signs will inevitably find its own assumptions reflected, and fail to theorize or even describe the text's deconstructive mode without finally pulling it back towards unity and metaphysics. It will also take this reflection to be the play itself in its totality rather than only one of its dimensions. The text, in contrast, manifests the presence of the mirror—surface, frame and illusion of depth—as many reflections as there are spectators, and, in the subject that composes itself for each in the specular image, an uneasy coalescence which is both a momentary reduction of a much more various process and something always other than itself.[18]

So *Hamlet*, like *Macbeth*, addresses the *processes* by which the subjects and signs taken as read by a drama (and criticism) of plot, theme and character are constructed. The post-structuralist and materialist methods that recover these textual operations do so in ways that accentuate the status of all reading as an intervention and a production rather than a simple decoding. After the academic maunderings of 'Is it really a tragedy?' and 'What is the central theme?' criticism, the promise of current literary theory is a transformed, contemporary Shakespeare. But the perspectives it opens up also have a historical specificity—confirmed by Foucault's work on the late sixteenth- and early seventeenth-century crisis in concepts of representation, the work of Weimann and, more recently, Hattaway (1982) on the popular theatre, and Jonathan Dollimore's account of a discontinuity and "irresolution" in English Renaissance drama—a manifestation of conflict between "residual, dominant and emergent conceptions of the real" which is accompanied by an interrogation of mimesis and by what Dollimore calls a "decentring of man".[19]

Any attempt to recover a 'transparent' representation from Shakespeare now has to contend not only with contemporary theory but with this growing body of historical study. So when A. D. Nuttall, for example, defends his programme for *A New Mimesis* (1983) by reference to Shakespeare's dramaturgy, he is able to sustain an argument only by disregarding the ways in which post-structuralism can remain responsive to historical considerations and by ignoring the work of Weimann and others on the popular dramatic tradition, crucial for any serious contemporary study of the plays of this period. Nuttall's doctrinaire attack on contemporary theory creates a straw opponent, the "radical formalist" or mechanically "opaque" critic, who serves as a convenient pretext for trotting out some of the central tenets of the 'great tradition' of English criticism. These are enshrined in the person of Nuttall's "transparent" critic who remains flexible, alive, open to the experiential domain of "people and things", and who is able to engage in a fruitful dialogue with the literary work (1983, pp. 77, 94, 125, 192). Nuttall's own text, secure in its grasp of which cultural practices are 'natural' and which 'artificial',[20] produces a version of Shakespeare in which an unmediated 'self' and 'experience' are shored up against the interventions of discourse and ideology or the fracturing of the unified subject and sign. Unlike the "opaque" adversary, a "transparent" reader runs no risk of imposing his or her theoretical or discursive frameworks on the plays because the text refuses to submit passively to analysis and, for those open to prompting, Shakespeare himself, like the Holy Spirit, "is for ever popping up at one's elbow with suggestions and insights"—insights which, astonishingly, happen to coincide with Nuttall's understanding of modern anthropology, cultural history, psychoanalysis and existential philosophy (pp. 101, 118, 143, 164).

The new mimesis is itself no more than a transparent representation of the old. The unified subject (Shakespeare) addresses an ideal reader ('one') about things out there in the world, and its essential or existential truths. The codes, discourses and ideologies that determine this exchange are presented as secondary—as a supplement that falls away to reveal a transcendental *represented* or *signified* which is underwritten by the irreducible categories of the 'self' and its 'experience'. Where the text puts such certainties in doubt, Nuttall recuperates it as offering special instances of *mimesis*. So the impassioned cry of Troilus confronted with evidence of betrayal, "this is, and is not, Cressid" (*Troilus and Cressida*, 3143)[21] approaches the edge of mimesis only to reassert representation's centrality. Here Shakespeare according to Nuttall, "*knows*, experientially, the possible failure of experiential knowing, and that is what he teaches us, his audience" (p. 77). But if this possible failure can be known experientially, it is no failure but a triumph of experiential knowledge, in which the positive and negative both turn out to have been playing for the same side. 'Experience', Nuttall's mantra, is the true touchstone because he experiences it as such, and nothing in modern psychoanalysis or the theory of ideology will convince him otherwise.[22] But his choice of these particular lines to make his point is a revealing one, as an extended reading of the sequence in question would suggest that Troilus is much more of a proto-Lacanian or -Derridean than a friend of empiricism, the subject and unmediated experience. Everything hinges on whether this is *really* Cressida who bestows her favours on Diomedes—which, at the level of mimesis or the play's *locus*, action, it clearly is. But the truths that follow from this truth remove the metaphysical ground from under it, denying it the right to be purely rational, identical with itself, or part of a stable order of significant differences in language:

> If there be rule in unitie it selfe,
> This is not she: O madnesse of discourse!
> The cause sets up, withe, and against the selfe
> By foule authority: where reason can revolt
> Without perdition, and losse assume all reason,
> Without revolt. This is, and is not *Cressid*:
> Within my soule, there doth conduce a fight
> Of this strange nature, that a thing inseparate,
> Divides more wider than the skie and earth:
> And yet the spacious bredth of this division,
> Admits no Orifex for a point as subtle,
> As Ariachnes broken woofe to enter.
>
> (3138–49)

The dividing of the subject, the questioning of identity and significant difference, the undoing of unities and the association of these processes with an abortive construction of sexuality and gender (the 'orifex' and subtle 'point') open up areas that are not accessible to Nuttall's foreclosed discourse, constituting as they do the site of a textual heterogeneity beyond the subject and the mimetic sign. This particular speech could be as seminal to a post-structuralist Shakespeare criticism as Ulysses's disquisition on 'degree' was to the conservative Shakespeare of the 'Elizabethan world picture'. Troilus on the divided subject and sign also indicates the site from which the self-naturalizing hierarchies of the 'degree' speech can be seen as precisely that—ideology, discourse, closure rather than 'insight' or 'how Shakespeare saw the world'. On stage the intricacies of this position are themselves domesticated in an empirical truth. There is a sense in which "this is, and is not, Cressid" is no momentary loss of experiential bearings but a recovery from the trance of mimesis in a

simple statement of fact about acting. This should be the case
not only for Jacobean audiences familiar with plays that called
for a 'double' vision, incorporating a response to the action *and*
a continuing recognition of theatricality, but also for those
later theatre-goers who, under the influence of Brecht or
Artaud, are unable to wholly forget themselves and their part
in a specific social transaction by submitting to the discreet
charm of the bourgeois realism many critics and consumers
would like Shakespeare's work to be. But historically the plays
were more than the "storytelling psychology" Artaud found in
the Shakespeare of his day. And the interruptions to what
Nuttall calls "the natural *coitus* of reader and work" (p. 83), the
mimetic fantasy, come not only from the probings of "mechan-
ical" theorists but from the textual process that can be des-
cibed, in the terms of Troilus's speech, as making "nature"
seem "strange".

Notes

1. For the Renaissance theory that the poet, like God, creates *ex nihilo*,
   see Puttenham, 1589, p. 1. Cf. *A Midsummer Night's Dream*,
   V. 1804–9.

2. *Romeo and Juliet*, 1169; *2 Henry IV*, I.ii.444.

3. Roman Polanski's film version of *Macbeth* (Caliban Productions) ends
   with a meeting between Donalbain and the Witches. "Ambiguity,
   whereby evil and good become inextricable, runs through this play in
   which the hero is at once a 'dead butcher' and the most continually
   sympathetic character, while Macduff can on the other hand believe
   Malcolm capable of whoremongering and avarice, and can yet think
   these not unfit characteristics for Scotland's future hero-king. Confusion reigns and 'nothing is but what is not'" (Somerset, 1975, p. 62).
   On the contradiction between the traditional Vice's homiletic function and his role as provoker of "Dionysian laughter", *see* Spivack,
   1958, pp. 113, 121, 128; Somerset, pp. 62–9; Weimann, 1978,
   pp. 151–60. Weimann emphasizes the plebian associations of the
   Vice and his language, his direct contact with the audience, his
   status, even in defeat, as "a powerful symbol of negation and
   unending rebellion" and his role as "an independent instigator of
   actions and reactions" free, to some extent, of the *locus's* "balanced
   contest of allegorical figures".

4. The Folio text of *Hamlet* has no act or scene divisions after Act 2, Scene 2.
5. Hawkes, 1973, pp. 115–16.
6. Cf. I.iii.508–14.
7. Cf. "ranke Corruption mining all within" (2531).
8. On the questionable status of the Ghost, *see*: Wilson, 1951, pp. 52–86; Prosser, 1971, pp. 118f.
9. First Quarto stage direction. For the point that follows, *see* Lacan, 1977b, pp. 44–5.
10. Mahood, 1957, p. 43. *See also* Forker, 1963, pp. 215–30.
11. *See* Rosenberg, 1978, pp. 95–7; Van Laan, 1978, p. 190; Wilson, 1978, pp. 107–14; Kantak, 1963, pp. 42–56.
12. Lascelles Abercrombie, *cit.* Wells, 1973, p. 193.
13. *See* Breuer, 1976, pp. 256–71.
14. *See* Weimann, 1978, pp. 73–84.
15. *See* lines 1849–93.
16. Holloway, 1961, p. 73. Cf. note 3 above on the Vice.
17. On the links between carnival and utopia, *see* Bakhtin, 1968, pp. 8f.; and on popular utopianism and topsy-turvydom generally, Weimann, pp. 20–4.
18. Cf. Lacan, 1977a, pp. 1–7, 164–5, 299.
19. Dollimore, 1984, pp. 82, 135f., *passim*.
20. Nuttall, 1983, pp. 83, 97, 169.
21. In Folio 1 there are no act and scene divisions for *Troilus and Cressida* after Act 1, Scene 1.
22. Cf. Belsey, 1980, pp. 11–14, 45–6.

6
Truth's True Contents

Thinking is what we already know we have not yet started.
(Jaques Derrida, *Of Grammatology*)

The art of narrative consists in concealing from your audience everything it wants to know until after you expose your favourite opinions on topics foreign to the subject. A good story is like a bitter pill with the sugar coating inside of it.
(O. Henry, *A Tale of Central America*)

Truth's Truth

In the last act of *Measure for Measure*, Isabella exposes Angelo as a murderer, an adulterer, a hypocrite and a virgin-violator, proclaiming that all this, in spite of appearances to the contrary, is "ten times true, for truth is truth/To th' end of reckning" (V. i. 2400–1). The Elizabethan proverb "Truth is truth" is also quoted in *Love's Labour's Lost* (IV. i. 1024) and *King John* (I. i. 115) to affirm an incontestable fact, and it lies behind Hamlet's paradoxical protestation of love for Ophelia:

> Doubt thou, the Starres are fire,
> Doubt, that the Sunne doth move:
> *Doubt Truth to be Lier*,
> But never Doubt, I love.
> (II. ii. 1444–7)

In each case the dramatic situation renders this 'truth of truth' problematic to some degree. The frustration of his attempt to have Claudio executed, the technicalities of the pre-contract, and the fact that he has had intercourse not with Isabella but with the willing Marianna make Angelo innocent of all charges except the one of hypocrisy. Costard's "Truth is truth" is an acknowledgment of the force of a riddling and ambiguous comment from the Princess of France, and Faulconbridge in *King John* uses the phrase as a euphemism for his mother's adultery. Hamlet's line about truth and lies, through its play on 'doubt', says two contradictory things at once—"Suspect truth to be a liar" and "Be unsure that truth is a liar". The latter sense, which assumes, characteristically for *Hamlet*, that the truth is in fact untrue, has made this line the despair of all translators of the play (Gerschenkron and Gerschenkron, 1966, pp. 301–36).

'Truth is truth', a tautology, is its own undoing. Any attempt to affirm something solid and transcendent, ultimately beyond language, by pinning one signifier to another, supposedly identical with itself, is heading for trouble. The proverb ends up by doing little more than arresting itself at the level of words, defeating its own purpose. In Shakespeare's text, however, this and related tautologies extend from the sphere of popular wisdom to the refinements of philosophy and her-

145

meneutics. "Truth is truth" is the domain of Feste's old hermit of Prague, who explained to a niece of King Gorboduc "that that is, is . . . for what is that, but that? and is, but is?" (*Twelfth Night*, IV. ii. 2000–1). It is also familiar ground to Touchstone, who tells the story of a heathen philosopher who, "when he had a desire to eate a Grape, would open his lips when he put it into his mouth, meaning thereby, that Grapes were made to eate, and lippes to open" (*As You Like It*, V. i. 2375–8). In spite of the obvious risks, running from the most vulgar to the most elevated of discourses, Shakespeare returns again to the tautologous dictum at the root of all this in making the marriages and festivity that end *As You Like It* dependent on the stipulation that the truth should contain truth.

In the closing scene of the play, Rosalind and Celia return with Hymen, god of marriage, who announces a reconciliation in his epithalamium:

> Then is there mirth in heaven,
> When earthly things made eaven
>   attone together
>   (V. iv. 2683–5)

Rosalind is returned to Duke Senior who must hand her on to Orlando, a fact which confirms the final frustration of Phebe's hopes in 'Ganymede'. A proliferation of words redefining these positions and alignments threatens the newly achieved 'atonement':

> *Duke S.* If there be truth in sight, you are my daughter.
> *Orl.* If there be truth in sight, you are my *Rosalind*.
> *Phe.* If sight & shape be true, why then my love adieu.
>   (2693–5)

Hymen intervenes in this multiplication of conditionals, appearances and "truths", inviting those assembled on stage to put the matter to rest by acceding to the tautology:

> Peace hoa: I barre confusion,
> 'Tis I must make conclusion
> Of these most strange events:

> Here's eight that must take hands,
> To joyne in *Hymens* bands,
> *If truth holds true contents.*
>
> (2699–704)

This last line, a climactic precondition for the conventional ending of a romantic comedy, has disconcerted a number of editors. Johnson glossed it as "if there be truth in truth, unless truth fails of veracity", and Wright agreed that this appears to be "the only sense of which this poor phrase is capable". Furness sees it as a demand stronger than the occasion requires, but adds in explanation that Hymen "is *always* a little incomprehensible".[1] The *New Cambridge* editors show no such tolerance, regarding the whole Hymen sequence as "not in the least Shakespearean" and this in particular as a "feeble line" there only because "it provides a rhyme for 'events'" (Quiller-Couch and Wilson, 1926, pp. 163, 167).

Hymen's words may, however, be justified in terms of a fairly straightforward, conventional reading of the play. If the society that returns to the court under the restored rule of Duke Senior at the end of *As You Like It* is based on a truth which holds true contents, it will stand in contrast to the corrupt order of Duke Frederick, in which those in power manipulate language to sustain official versions of 'truth' that are patently false. The "gentle" and "noble" Orlando (I. i. 162), for example, has been publicly branded a "villanous contriver" against his elder brother (141–2). Rosalind's innocence too has been misrepresented as treachery, and in this inverted order her "verie silence, and her patience" are seen to "Speake to the people" and promote discontent (I. iii. 539–40). Here 'exile' in the forest becomes 'liberation' as Celia, at the end of Act 1 bids Rosalind, "now goe we in content/To libertie and not to banishment" (I. iii. 602–3).

In contrast to the distortion and flattery at court, Duke Senior's long speech at the beginning of Act 2 sets up a 'truth' true in its contents. This is based on an experiential dialogue with nature's "counsellors/That feelingly perswade me what I am" (II. i. 616–17). Duke Senior's 'nature', which acknowledges the fall and "The seasons difference, as the Icie phange/And churlish chiding of the winter's winde" (612–613), brings with it a knowledge of human limitation and mortality, in stark opposition to the pastoral fantasies that hold sway at the court, where the exiled Duke and his followers are imagined to "fleet the time carelesly as they did in the golden world" (I. i. 118–19). But the truth based on nature and self-knowledge is also opposed to other forms of escapist illusion. While Duke Senior hears the voice of nature, the "tongues in trees" (II. i. 622), Orlando insulates himself against its force with his love poems—"Tongues Ile hang on everie tree" (III. ii. 1325)—which interpose the wilful absolutes of a debased petrarchanism. Thus the first instance of distortion, in the 'truth' of the court, gives way to a second, in the literal adherence of youth to the literary conventions of romantic love. Silvius and Phebe act out their "pageant truely plaid/Betweene the pale complexion of true Love,/And the red glowe of Scorne and prowde disdaine" (III. iv. 1760–2) while Orlando reproduces the same pastoral and petrarchan scenario by languishing in solitude for a distant, deified Rosalind. Confronted with the anguish of true love in Silvius, Touchstone remembers his own idolatrous passion for the personified rustic come-on Jane Smile, and recalls "the wooing of a peascod instead of her" (II. iv. 832–3). As a reference to either fetishism or masturbation ('peascod'—'codpiece'), the Fool's comment punctures the complacent 'truth' of romance. Love in the forest is, at best, a solitary vice deprived of the dialectic and reciprocity Touchstone restores with his obscene commentaries and parodies. Delivered from the limiting identity of the goddess Rosalind, the disguised 'Ganymede' can work in similar ways on Orlando's limited repertoire of platitudes. She/he challenges his stereotype of the divine lady with another, more mortal and carnal Rosalind, who will laugh when he is sad, weep when he is inclined to be merry and sleep with his neighbour. When Orlando protests that he will die for love, Ganymede, acting the role of 'Rosalind', dismantles Troilus, Leander and the other literary models that validate such ridiculous protestations: "men have died from time to time, and wormes have eaten them, but not for love" (IV. i. 2017–19).

Artaud's view that all writing is pigshit would have incorporated his critique of Shakespeare. But here the Shakespearean text itself re-presents writing as a 'dead letter' cut off from the 'spirit' or full presence of speech. Pastoralism, petrarchanism and classical romance are all incorporated into the presentation of love in *As You Like It*, and here these conventions encounter other instances of the already-written. Corin's rustic home-truths on the realities of court and country life, for example, are confronted by the duplicity of Touchstone's language, which proves the shepherd to be, like the lovers, half-baked, an "ill roasted Egge, all on one side" (III. ii. 1235–6). The trite generalizations of Jaques, written in proverbial lore, are also dislodged from their 'single' idiom, in this case by Touchstone's parody:

> it is ten a clocke:
> Thus we may see (quoth he) how the world
>   wagges
> 'Tis but an houre agoe, since it was nine,
> And after one houre more, 'twill be eleven,
> And so from houre to houre, we ripe, and ripe,
> And then from houre to houre, we rot, and rot,
> And thereby hangs a tale.
>
> (II. vii. 995–1001)

The fact that Jaques misses the point and takes such tedious generalizing to be the proper function of the Fool indicates how far gone he is. Through his language the text offers its closest parallels to Artaud's image of writing and the references in Barthes to the self-naturalizing constructions of received wisdom, "the residual condensate of what cannot be re-written", as a staling, a rotting, or as vomit (Barthes, 1974, pp. 21, 98, 206). Touchstone's euphemistic reference to Jaques as "good Mr what ye cal't" (III. iii. 1681) reveals the text's actantial function 'jakes', shithouse of language. Duke Senior's reference to the "imbossed sores, and headed evils" Jaques wishes to "disgorge into the generall world" (II. vii. 1041–3) points to another revealing wordplay, in the melancholic's relentless pursuit of 'matter'—at once 'truth's truth' beyond the play of language and a linguistic pus.

Jaques is beyond redemption. In his conversation with Orlando it becomes clear that both parties speak the already-written—the lover has taken his lines from trite mottoes engraved on love-tokens, while Jaques speaks the "right painted cloath" (III. ii. 1466) of cheap didactic wall-hangings. But Orlando at least shows the humility which, according to a more subtle didacticism,[2] is the basis of self-knowledge. He refuses to join Jaques in railing in general terms against the world and fortune: "I wil chide no breather in the world but my selfe against whom I know most faults" (1471–2). If Duke Senior's achieved self-awareness and Ganymede's advice to Phebe, "know your selfe" (III. v. 1830), resound behind the play's scrutiny of simple-minded adherence to the 'single' code, Orlando's reaction to Jaques anticipates his ultimate inclusion in the new order in which a more personal, experiential wisdom may seem to guarantee that "truth holds true contents" at last. The melancholic, in contrast, will exclude himself from the renewed society headed by Duke Senior and seek out instead the repentant Duke Frederick and the "much *matter* to be heard, and learn'd" from him (V. iv. 2762).[3]

To stay, for the moment, with this interpretative and unifying mode of ventriloquial criticism, Hymen's invitation to the four couples on stage to take hands in wedlock "If truth holds true contents" invokes the freedom of choice accorded to those who wish to become subjects of Duke Senior's society, regenerated by contact with nature. "Much vertue in *if*", says Touchstone immediately before Hymen's entrance, "Your *If*, is the onely peace-maker" (V. iv. 2675–6). The final need for consent marked by Hymen's "If" is reinforced by a play on "contents" made possible by its pronunciation in Elizabethan English, in the primary sense of "that which is contained", with the stress on the second syllable (Kökeritz, 1953, pp. 335, 397); '*contents*' here also signifies 'joys' or 'pleasures' (*OED*), so the lovers must not only subscribe to a 'truth' that is true, but they must also now *contentedly* accept reality as it really is. 'Contents' in this sense picks up a strand of supplementary references in the play. Rosalind and Celia leave the court for the forest "in content" (I. iii. 602), while Orlando and Adam escape to "some setled low content" (II. iii. 772) and Touchstone, footsore in Arden, consoles himself with the gnomic observation that "Travellers must be content" (II. iv. 799–800). Before 'Ganymede' exits for the last time she/he promises the lovers, "I wil content you, if what pleases you contents you, and you shal be married to morrow" (V. ii.

2522–3), and Duke Senior finally announces the marriages and the dance in terms that recapitulate this sense of Hymen's "true contents": "Proceed, proceed: wee'l begin these rights,/As we do trust, they'l end in *true delights*" (V. iv. 2774–5).

The pun on "contents" may seem to accord with the other forms of "atonement" brought by Hymen at the end of the play, bringing reality and desire together as it does. The matter begins to become more complicated, however, when another wordplay is taken into account, this time on "truth" as both 'that which is true' and 'fidelity', specifically the 'troth' plighted in marriage vows (*OED*). Still following a conventional thematic reading, this second sense of 'troth' would give Hymen's "If truth holds true contents" a climactic position in the play's treatment of love. The youthful lovers have been 'educated' out of their stereotyped romantic idealism and brought to self-knowledge, found in nature with its inevitable corollaries of limitation and mortality. This latter state amounts to an achieved adulthood, in which the commitment to wedding vows is the 'atonement' and 'making even' of the conflicting perspectives of the carnal, given rein in the speeches of Touchstone and 'Ganymede', and the spiritual, taken to its debilitating extreme in the pastoral and petrarchan posturing of Silvius and Phebe. Thus Hymen requires that marital fidelity be a realistic proposition, and that marriage should hold true pleasure. But by this point, the horizon of a stable signified is beginning to recede, particularly as the play on "truth" extends to "true", and eight different permutations arise from Hymen's one conditional clause. The puns work with the disconcerting circularity of Hymen's tautologous formulation to prise open the 'natural' unity of the sign, and to do particular damage to the notion of a 'truth' ultimately true and beyond language. Syllepsis, like condensation in the dreamwork, short-circuits 'serious' uses of words. In Freud's description of this process, the wordplay focuses "our psychical attitude upon the *sound* of a word instead of upon its *meaning*", making the "word-presentation itself take the place of its significance as given by its relation to thing-presentations" (Freud, 1960, p. 119). In the circumstances the best explanation of Hymen's "mirth in heaven,/When earthly things made eaven/attone together" is Nietzsche's:

> And if the gods too philosophize, as many an inference has driven me to suppose—I do not doubt that while doing so they also know how to laugh in a new and superhuman way—and at the expense of all serious things! Gods are fond of mockery; it seems they cannot refrain from laughter even when sacraments are in progress.
>
> (1973, p. 199)

Much Virtue in If

Hymen's injunction, described by Quiller-Couch and Dover Wilson as a "feeble line", is four times double:

			true	contents	1
	truth	holds		pleasures	2
			faithful	contents	3
				pleasures	4
If			faithful	pleasures	5
	fidelity	holds		contents	6
			true	pleasures	7
				contents	8

Each permutation applies in some way to the play. (1) is Dr Johnson's explanation of the line, "if there be truth in truth"; (8) "if fidelity is a realistic proposition'; (2) "if the truth can be accepted contentedly"; (7) "if there can be true pleasure in marriage"; (5) "if that pleasure can be sustained by remaining faithful". (1) and (6) are tautologies, and (3) is a semi-nonsensical critique of empiricism—"if the truth is chaste", which approximates to Nietzsche's "dogma of the immaculate perception". These are not out of place in a text that includes Touchstone's heathen philosopher with his grapes.

If Hymen's words still seem to be imposing a 'unity' or 'atonement' by incapsulating so many of the play's central concerns, another sense of "contents" (cognate with 'malcontents') as 'contented people' adds a further four chains of signification to the eight already in place. As a dissemination rather than a recuperation of meaning, "If truths holds true contents" recapitulates the earlier work of the text in a different way.

If Rosalind and Touchstone 'educate' those they meet in the

forest out of various forms of simple-mindedness, they do so not
by imparting any positive, portable wisdom but by undermining the 'single' truth. Wordplay and ambiguity are central in
this process. Just as each 'humour' is complicated by a vision of
changing perspectives, so unequivocal meanings are compounded in the play of words. After seasoning Orlando's bland
romanticism with cynicism, 'Ganymede' confronts Jaques's
banal scepticism with pert common sense, commenting "I had
rather have a foole to make me merrie, then experience to make
me sad, and to travaile for it too" (IV. i. 1941–3). The play on
"travaile" points to the laborious quality of the melancholic's
discourse while also referring back to the spurious claims of this
"Mounsieur Traveller" to a particularly extensive and experiential knowledge of the world and its ways. But Jaques's own
language has already been his undoing. Defining his narcissistic
malaise, he describes it as being not the scholar's, the musi-
cian's, the courtier's, the soldier's, the lawyer's, the lady's or
the lover's, but:

> a melancholy of mine owne, compounded of many simples,
> extracted from many objects, and indeed the sundrie contem-
> lation of my travells, in which by often rumination, wraps me
> in a most humorous sadnesse.   (1931–5)

The uniqueness of this melancholy is already undercut in the
inconvenient excess in "simples", a term which may be neutral
and innocent as 'ingredients', but which discloses the derivative
and over-simplified quality of the elements from which this
"humourous sadnesse" is concocted. Orlando's language too
makes such disclosures. At the end of a lyric which follows
Touchstone's comments on idolatry and masturbation, Orlando
describes the goddess Rosalind in conventional terms as "The
faire, the chaste, and unexpressive shee" (III. ii. 1210). The
standard editorial gloss of "unexpressive" as 'inexpressible' can
be justified as an example of the flexibility of Elizabethan
grammar,[4] and this sense is in keeping with Orlando's petrarchan versifying. But "unexpressive", through *enallage*, is also
present in its more customary senses. The object of idolatry,
robbed of its personality and physical presence, is at once
symbolically 'speechless' and 'dead'.

These minor disseminations of sense anticipate Hymen's climactic wordplay. The puns do not merely correct or distance 'single' utterance, but dismantle it in the pleasure of turning meaning away. The presence of 'whore' in Touchstone's "from houre to houre, we ripe and ripe" and "rot, and rot" indicates the source of melancholy in Jaques, who has been "as sensuall as the brutish sting it selfe", (II. vii. 1040), but here, as in the other ambiguities, specific additional senses relating to character and theme are less important than a cumulative linguistic density. *As You Like It* begins to take on the character of the "galaxy of signifiers" envisaged by Roland Barthes, where senses divide and multiply—in "bills" and "presents" (I. ii. 286–7), "hem" (I. iii. 478), "feete" (III. ii. 1366) and "stairs" (V. ii. 2446) all occurring in the speeches of Rosalind/ 'Ganymede', and in Touchstone's "ranke" (I. ii. 272), "crosse" (II. iv. 796), "manners" (III. ii. 1239), "linde", "pricke" and "mounted" (III. ii. 1288–310), "capricious" and "Gothes" (III. iii. 1620), "honest" (III. iii. 1636) and "Jaques" (III. iii. 1681). When the Duke and his men sing "The horne, the horne, the lusty horne,/Is not a thing to laugh to scorne" (IV. ii. 2145–6), the item they celebrate takes in the quarry hunted by these merry usurpers of the forest's natural lords, the sound that heralds the pursuit, the phallus and the cuckold's crest. "Horne" itself is a minor galaxy whose elements escape the categories of the signified through accidents of sound, throwing into new and gratuitous combinations the disparate concerns of the text, from wedded love to the "brutish sting" and "headed evils" of venereal disease, from Machiavellian intrigue to an innocent nature. Here the differences that establish thematic structure dissolve to be precipitated again at random, and an indeterminacy in the language becomes part of the more general "holy-day humour" (IV. i. 1982) of Arden as a whole, manifest in the hunting song's evocation of the traditional *charivari*.[5] In the forest scenes that take up its greater part *As You Like It* is an intertext in which the 'single' truths of unreflexive discourses, including the pastoral romance, popular and courtly petrarchanism, the rhetoric of corrupt leadership and the proverb collide and re-emerge fragmented.

From this play and delirium the prospect of recovering a stabilizing centre, some uncompromised notion of 'truth's truth', might still be possible by appeal to the empirical presence of 'nature' and to a dynamic 'self-knowledge' which is more complete when wrested from a vision of multiple, and conflicting, perspectives. But this prospect fades in Duke Senior's great set-piece on nature and self-knowledge, the main source of empirical and metaphysical certainty in the play, which affirms its unmediated 'truths' in the most mediated terms:

> *Duk.Sen.* Now my Coe-mates, and brothers in exile:
> Hath not old custome made this life more sweete
> Then that of painted pompe? Are not these woods
> More free from perill then the envious Court?
> Heere feele we not the penaltie of *Adam*,
> The seasons difference, as the Icie phange
> And churlish chiding of the winters winde,
> Which when it bites and blowes upon my body
> Even till I shrinke with cold, I smile, and say
> This is no flattery: these are counsellors
> That feelingly perswade me what I am:
> Sweet are the uses of adversitie
> Which, like the toad, ougly and venemous,
> Weares yet a precious Jewell in his head:
> And this our life exempt from publike haunt,
> Findes tongues in trees, bookes in the running brookes,
> Sermons in stones, and good in every thing.
>
> *Amien.* I would not change it, happy is your Grace
> That can translate the stubbornnesse of fortune
> Into so quiet and so sweet a stile.
>
> (I. ii. 607–26)

What is remarkable about the speech is the way its transcendent givens—the natural world, life and the body—all nominally set apart from the culture and artifice of the court, are themselves suspended in a dense layer of artifice and mediation which incorporates such terms as "chiding", "counsellors", "perswade", "tongues", "bookes", "sermons" and, in Amiens's response, "translate" and "stile". Like the play as a whole, this is a meeting place for a number of other texts and voices. In the use of antithesis, alliteration and recondite scraps of natural history, this interweaving of tongues, sermons and

books—further intensified by the fact that after "I smile, and
say" Duke Senior is quoting himself—is compounded by an
overlay of euphuism more insistent and obtrusive than in any
other play by Shakespeare except perhaps *Love's Labour's Lost*.
The conventions of the pastoral tradition are also still very
much present. If the "old custome" which has "made this life
more sweet" indicates experience gained during the sojourn in
the forest, it also connotes the antiquity of the pastoral *topos* of
the country's superiority. The syntactical ambiguity of "Heere
feele we not the penaltie of *Adam* . . .", usually smoothed over
in modern editions by altering the punctuation and making
this the third in a series of rhetorical questions or explaining
that the line means "we are none the worse for" (Latham, 1979,
pp. 29–30), again straddles the distinction between a 'real'
fallen nature and the Golden Age construction which affirms
"good in everything".

These ambiguities are crucial, as they work with the density
and 'textuality' of the speech as a whole to dislodge the
culture–nature axis conventional interpretations take from it
and use as a reliable thematic opposition for the entire play.
What they disclose about the Duke himself is unimportant.[6]
Even to ask that question is to ignore the ways in which this
'doubleness' interrupts mimesis. The 'character' fades into the
play of the language, which also blocks any simple denotation
of nature. When Amiens reinterprets Duke Senior's natural
communion as a 'translation' of the stubborn into the sweet, the
pun on "your Grace"—title and the specific quality which
'translates'—instigates a play of subject, attribute, title con-
ventionally reflecting status and, in this case, title 'genuinely'
reflecting personal attribute. In this movement the character as
subject, already flattened and made emblematic by the name
'Senior', is subsumed in its actantial function as "the wisdom of
age and authority", set beside the language of the Fool, the
idiom of "Signior Love" (III. ii. 1484) and the waste-matter
consigned to the "jakes". In response to this wisdom Amiens,
ample proof of the flattery that *does* exist in the forest,
actantially signals his 'Amens'.

Duke Senior's speech and Hymen's 'atonement' are the two
main props of a conventional, metaphysical reading of *As You
Like It*. Such readings can, at best, muster only a bewildered

vision of play which struggles to keep 'Shakespeare' in place as the law of culture and value: "One must not say Shakespeare never judges, but one judgement is always being modified by another. Opposite views may contradict one another, but of course they do not cancel out" (Jenkins, 1955, p. 45). In this discourse there must, finally, still be some form of judgment or affirmation, kept in place by the same strategic myopia that recovers from the play a mimetic concept of drama and a naturalized subject and sign. In the text, mined with puns and crossed by the bursts of other texts, such affirmations dissolve in the language and the negative, or multiple, identity of the Fool and the girl who disguises herself as a boy, who acts out the role of the girl, who becomes the boy again, climactically reveals herself to be the woman she really is and then, in the Epilogue, discloses that she/he/she/he/she/he was in fact a boy all along. In the midst of all this there is Touchstone's heathen philosopher concerned with the meaning of lips and grapes, a warning to interpreters who seek 'truth's truth' in the *essence* of the play and its characters.

The problems of such essentialist constructions as 'nature', 'self-knowledge' and 'atonement' become even more acute when Hymen's "If truth holds true contents" resumes its play. "Holds" implies at once 'supports' and 'restrains', or the opposite meanings—'sustains' and 'interrupts'—contained in its synonym 'suspends'. This adds another wordplay to the three already in progress, and a further twelve possible permutations of meaning to the line as a whole, making twenty-four in all. Among the new preconditions for marriage and an ending produced by the division in "holds" are "If an abstract concept of 'truth' interrupts a movement towards the real" and "If marital fidelity *prevents* true pleasure". Since many of the twenty-four stipulations now contradict one another, even the 'peacemaker' *If* is ambiguous. The marriages will proceed whether fidelity sustains or impedes true contentment. The new order of the 'legitimate' patriarch Duke Senior, to be inaugurated with this sacrament, will be installed whether the "truth" it affirms is a valid container of the 'real' or a limit imposed arbitrarily on its play. The "If", then, is both the conditional which implies an invitation to consent, and a fiction belied by the fact that marriages, new dispensation and ending will carry on regardless. This fissured "If" is the mark of the contradictory subject of humanism—"the totality of discourse through which Western man is told: 'Even though you don't exercise power, you can still be a ruler. Better yet, the more you deny yourself the exercise of power, the more you submit to those in power, then the more this increases your sovereignty'" (Foucault, 1977, p. 221). Hymen's "If" indicates at once the *active* subject of grammar and subjection to the father and the sovereign, Duke Senior, whose voice is amplified in that of the god.[7] The choice confronting those about to become his subjects is no choice at all.

This dual "If" brings to forty-eight the number of separate conditional clauses at play in Hymen's tautology. This is a 'truth' beyond editorial footnotes, which generally limit polysemy in the cause of a Shakespearean text that affirms the unity of subject and sign in a serious, communicative use of words. The current Arden edition, for example, limits this line to one narrow contextual reference: "If you are still contented with your marriage partners now that disguises are cast off and you know the truth about them" (Latham, pp. 127–8). The unwitting effect of this denotative straitjacket is to release yet another dimension, in which 'truth' refers to the immediate presence of 'characters' on the stage. When Hymen says of the transformation of Ganymede, "If this is *truly* Rosalind", "truth" means 'what we see before us' in addition to 'troth' and 'truth' in its more general, abstract sense. By this time the possible permutations are too many to describe without recourse to a mathematical model. If the five words of the clause are a, b, c, d and e respectively, and each is accorded the appropriate number of potential significations, the resulting set, $\{a_{1-2}\ b_{1-3}\ c_{1-2}\ d_{1-2}\ e_{1-3}\}$ has seventy-two values, each representing a different "If truth holds true contents". The line which finally puts Rosalind in her place has assumed the character of a dictionary or thesaurus in which signifiers refer perpetually to each other and the self-present truth is barred indefinitely. When Rosalind ceases to be herself and the Epilogue says *"If* I were a woman . . ."* (2791), it affirms a content which is at last unconditionally true—that the truth is as ever other than itself, always already somewhere else.

The Truest Poetry

The final transformation and "If" in the Epilogue points to another aspect of play in *As You Like It*. Here, as later in *Hamlet* and *Macbeth*, the 'doubleness' of language is redoubled in relation to the specific languages of the theatre. The action is itself theatricalized in a way that adds a continuous reflexivity to the illusion. Rosalind resolves to "play the knave" (III. ii. 1448) with Orlando and to be "a busie actor" (III. iv. 1768) in the romantic pageant of Silvius and Phebe. The "circle of this forest" (V. iv. 2611) is the "wooden O" of the theatre, which upholds a "holiday humour" set aside from "this working day world" (I. ii. 471). The relationship between the forest and the court mirrors that of the theatre to the world outside, itself a "wide and universall Theater" which, as Duke Senior says, "Presents more wofull Pageants than the Sceane/Wherein we play in" (II. vii. 1115–7).

Jaques's "All the world's a stage . . . ", like Macbeth's "poor Player" speech, unravels the idea of the stage pointing out the pointless stage, while the theatricality of the Fool and the actor/actress who lead the counterfeiting and revelry in the forest points in other ways to the containing presence of a performance and an exchange with an audience. When Jaques attempts to usurp Touchstone's role, asking Duke Senior for a "motley coat" (II. vii. 1016), his act is directly related to the illusion in progress. Delighted by the Fool's banal meditation on time, and missing the puns on 'houre'/'whore', 'tale'/'tail' and the point of the parody, Jaques wants only a license to persist in his tedious generalization. His desire to "anathomize" folly and administer "medicine" to "Clense the foule bodie of th' infected world" (1034–5), speaking to everyone in general and nobody in particular, is expressed in terms used by Jonson in a very different type of comedy. In *Every Man Out of his Humour*, performed at the Globe in 1598, Asper, the author's spokesman, talks about administering "physic of the mind" to those who are "sick in taste" and showing "the time's deformity/Anatomized in every nerve and sinew" (Jonson, 1925–52, pp. 432–3). Rosalind and Touchstone, in contrast to this didacticism, control the play in which all such absolutisms fall apart. Here a text already occupied with two of the most popular literary fashions of the 1590s, the petrarchan sonnet and pastoral romance, mobilises a third, satirical comedy, and each is subjected to the more general fragmentation of discourses and signs.

A major difference between this ensemble and satirical comedy alone is in the relation of each to its audience. The early Jonson's player is licensed to expose evil and make the moral point. Those who dissent are defined from the outset as foolish, evil or sick, while "Good men and virtuous spirits, that loathe their vices;/Will cherish my free labours, love my lines" (Jonson, III, p. 433). *As You Like It*, as its title implies,[8] has nothing to correct except such constraint and single-mindedness. The sustaining contract of stage and audience is implicit in all the acknowledgments of play and illusion, and the invitation to consent is finally made explicit. The play is altogether very *obvious*. Jolly foresters in green tights sing "Heigh Ho" at the drop of a leaf, while the boy disguised as a woman disguised as a boy pretends to be a woman, and malefactors undergo perfunctory conversions that pick at a threadbare convention. It is no surprise when Hymen, at the last moment, appears from the trees to perform the embarrassing role of *deus ex machina* with nothing to do, no probability left to save in the nick of time, and his stipulation for an ending addresses the audience as well as the figures assembled on stage.

Earlier in the play Audrey has complained "I do not know what Poetical is", and asked "is it honest in deed and word: is it a true thing?" (III. iii. 1628–9). Touchstone's reply, "the truest poetry is the most faining" (1630), puns on 'fain'/'feign' to suggest sincerity and insincerity at once, complicating the basic paradox that poets speak the truth by lying. This introduces another sense of "truth" into Hymen's "If truth holds true contents", in which *As You Like It* will move to its conclusion if this most feigning of confections holds a paradoxical significance and a prospect of contentment for its audience. In this doubling of Hymen's utterance, applicable both to subjects on the stage and in the audience, each of the other seventy-two possible senses of the line takes on an additional dimension. In relation to the audience, and in the larger ritual context which embraces the mimetic action and displays its own presence as an excess, each sense of 'truth's truth' appears again, as if in brackets, as an item on an ideological agenda. So if a 'character' on stage, for example, becomes a subject of Duke Senior's new order by accepting that its truth is really true, the same proposition for the audience would appear as a tautologous condition for the ideological construction of subjects on the 'stage' of the world, the undisclosed closures of which would be mirrored in those of the 'world' realized on stage if the process of its production were not made visible in the 'doubleness' of the linguistic and theatrical signifier. With the dual context of stage (S) and audience (A) and the additional reference to the "faining" truth of the play, which applies only to the audience, Hymen's simple request that the truth be present to itself now presents 168 permutations:

$$S \{a_{1-2}b_{1-3}c_{1-2}d_{1-2}e_{1-3}\} + A \{a_{1-2}b_{1-4}c_{1-2}d_{1-2}e_{1-3}\} = 168.^9$$

Pierre Macherey compares the classic movement of narrative to a detective's logical deductions, proceeding through disparities and enigmas to the moment of "a transparent reading", which requires "delay and opacity" for its production but finally banishes all such constitutive complexities: "Understood, released and discovered, the truth seems so dazzling that it pushes aside all the moments that heralded it. In a sudden flourish, its presence abolishes all previous disguises" (Macherey, 1978, pp. 36–8). If this is the case, Hymen's 'truth' burlesques the climactic moment of conventional plots by increasing the opacity of its constitutive materials and deferring further the presence of this final illumination to itself. The inconclusive 'atonement' is an accelerating dissemination of 'truth' in which the medieval Hymen who presides over the 'marriage' of words and wisdom moves closer to the 'hymen' of Jacques Derrida, which marks the edge of the symbolic and interpretable—"describes a margin where the control over meaning or code is without recourse, poses the limit to the relevance of the hermeneutic or systematic question" (Derrida, 1979, p. 99).[10]

To recover from this a transparent reading which affirms 'legitimacy', 'self-knowledge' or an essential 'nature' is to embrace the folly implied by the text's second sense of 'natural' and to become one of Touchstone's "naturall philosophers" (III. ii. 1230). The option to interpret, thus acceding to 'truth's truth', is of course there, although each 'single' reading is incorporated and dispersed in the play. *As You Like It* proffers a 'nature' at once constructed and unmediated, 'character' and its impossibility, and *carte blanche* for the distribution of ironies, or not, as you like it. Orlando is a callow youth who needs to be educated in love and the true lover whose passion negotiates all obstacles and tests, emerging unchanged to project love at first sight into a 'happily ever after'. He is also subsumed in a play of actants, "Signior Love" to Jaques's "Monsieur Melancholy" to 'patriarchal wisdom' in Senior—wise and legitimate leader, pompous buffoon, usurper and murderer of the forest's natural lords the deer. Jaques is at once 'jakes' and the positive function of the text that resists the hopelessly compromised closures of the Duke's new symbolic order and stays in heroic pursuit of the "matter" of a full unblemished word.

Any single interpretative path may be privileged, but only in the cause of simplifying the play, transforming Hymen's "truth" into the conventional narrative flourish described by Macherey, and proposing an ideal, unitary subject position which, in the text's own terms, is that of a 'character' on a stage who mistakes a production for an undivided reality. Hymen's final invitation to the audience to concur in the pleasure of a divided 'truth' which is also a 'feigning' is much less naive. As in *Hamlet* the mirror is again on display, along with the variety of subjects that may be composed in it and the heterogeneity from which mirrors and their reflections are produced. Here the conventional form that leads to the climactic clarity of a moment of truth is itself unmasked. Romantic comedy, with its marriages and atonements, is as much on display as an aesthetic ideology as the sonnet, satire, and the pastoral romance, working not only as a convention or form which articulates the 'sense' of *As You Like It* but as another item set on its unconcealed agenda.

Goodnight Ladies/If I Were a Woman

"It is the critic's task, and there is hardly a more comical one, to coagulate an island of meaning upon a sea of negativity." Julia Kristeva's remark (1980, p. 109) expresses the predicament of the interpreter of Shakespeare, and particularly of *As You Like It*, who confronts a text which *reads back* the theoretical assumptions of its criticism, the particular closures by which the dominant discourse pins truth to truth and congeals its own articles of faith—in the unified, gendered subject which bears the weight of sacrosanct individual rights and responsibilities; the sign which alludes to an irreducibly 'concrete' experience; the author who vents eternal truth and beauty into the world.

When Dover Wilson calls Rosalind Shakespeare's "ideal woman" (1962, p. 167) for example, this broad assessment of a character's significance, and of the author's feelings towards her, relay assumptions about the text and the world that tell us more about the critic than about Shakespeare. For Dover Wilson, Rosalind is the ideal essence of womanhood but also a person who lives and breathes in the subtlety of Shakespeare's characterization. The Rosalind in *As You Like It* on the other hand, enmeshed in language and theatricality, is part of a process of constructing and undoing images of gender and authority which tends to undermine an essentialist discourse on what is proper and 'natural' to the female and male. Duke Senior, who institutes his own language, true because it is truth, does so as a sort of Absolute Subject—supported by the god Hymen—who has won the Oedipal struggle by a symbolic castration of the Father and murder of grammar. When he speaks of the "churlish chiding of *the winter's winde,*/Which when it bites and blowes upon my body/Even till I shrinke with cold, *I* smile and say . . . ", his modest shrinkage is less striking than the violent displacement from its *subjecting* position in the clause of the biting winter wind, authoritative breath of the father, by the 'I' of Duke Senior as 'little me'—the biter bit. The theatrical actant which is woman acting man acting herself, then man, woman and boy who says "*If* I were a woman" resists the whole sorry business of the signifying phallus and its role in the creation of symbolic orders by summarily slipping from the until-death contract of sexed individuals, sustained by the voice of Seniority in the family and the state, and by reaffirming its own final location in play, in the theatre.[11] It takes a hardy resistance to what Kristeva terms the "negativity" of a text to emerge from this process with prior notions of an 'ideal' womanhood (or manhood) unscathed. [12] In *Macbeth* a recurring concern with what is 'becoming' to men and women, and with different forms of 'unsexing', is similarly inscribed in the hurly-burly of "imperfect speaking" and the shadow who signifies nothing, the clamour which precedes and breaks open the subject's "single state of Man". [13]

With the emergence of a feminist Shakespeare criticism from the mid-1970s on, the text's representations of gender, seen at times as an index of Shakespeare's own attitudes, have become a major topic for investigation. This is also a key area in which the history of the criticism appears as a history of ideological reproduction, marked by the changing shape and configuration of the islands that coalesce on the sea. The nineteenth-century vogue for books on Shakespeare's 'heroines' is an important case in point. These primers in Victorian womanhood, written mainly by women to be read by young women and girls, and bearing such titles as *Shakespeare's Garden of Girls*, *The Girlhood of Shakespeare's Heroines* and *The Sweet Silvery Sayings of Shakespeare on the Softer Sex*, [14] attribute to Shakespeare imaginative judgments that doubly validate essentially 'feminine' and 'masculine' qualities given by nature. Thus Lady Macbeth's ambition, accompanied by her "masculine indifference to blood and death", is gratified at the expense of "every feminine feeling" but redeemed in part by the "touch of womanhood" which determines that "she is ambitious less for herself than for her husband" (Jameson, 1904, pp. 291, 6–7). Rosalind, in contrast, already represents the ideal later celebrated by Dover Wilson and others. An "exquisite creature", she displays a "deep womanly tenderness' coupled with "active intellect disciplined by fine culture" which never exceeds the bounds of the feminine and charms the reader or audience "by her wit, her fancy, by her pretty womanly waywardness playing like summer lightning over her throbbing tenderness of heart, and never in the gayest sallies of her happiest moods losing one grain of our respect" (Faucit, 1891, pp. 236–7).

This waywardness, so alluring when contained, intimates the more dangerous aspects of the 'feminine' [15] and points to the category of the 'indefinable' incorporated into the definition of woman read out of the Shakespearean text by these commentaries. So Mrs Jameson's Cleopatra is "a brilliant antithesis, a compound of contradictions, of all that we most hate with what we most admire", a figure marked by its "*consistent inconsistency*", an enigma which resembles "one of her country's hieroglyphics". Her predominant qualities, vanity and the love of power, mingle with a hundred others, "and shift, and change, and glance away, like the colours in a peacock's train" (Jameson, p. 193). The hint here of another discourse, one which may disturb the 'truth' of the patriarchal order, is, however, recuperated for that order by the firm attributions that trail behind this figure—the "woman's wiles", "female enchantment", "feminine spite and jealousy", "womanly feeling", and regret that "there was no room left in this amazing picture" for the "passionate maternal tenderness which was a strong and redeeming feature of Cleopatra's historical character" (Jameson, pp. 193–204). If the 'wayward', with all its sliding, deflection and transformation, opens up onto a play through which the commentaries themselves might be deconstructed, their discourse is, nevertheless, overtly and unrelentingly homiletic, devoted to teaching women what they are and must be: "Modesty, grace, tenderness. *Without* these a woman is no woman but a thing which, luckily, wants a name yet; *with* these, although every other faculty is wanting or deficient, she might still be herself. These are the inherent qualities with which God sent us into the world" (Jameson, p. 110).

The Victorian cult of Shakespeare's heroines is a particularly tangible instance of criticism or commentary as a *production* which constructs its subjects in specific ways (here calling 'women' into being) and which can either challenge or, as in this case, generally reinforce a dominant ideology. In recent years feminism has done an important service to Shakespeare criticism at large by making it clear that all readings serve particular interests, and especially by emphasizing the relations of power that have already been settled in the universal humanist subject 'man', whose normative preoccupations determine what '*one*' feels' about a text, what it '*means*' or how '*we*' respond. While the Victorian celebration of Shakespeare-as-hero or the concept of a 'religion of culture' remain, behind the modern 'flexible' and 'imaginative' approach, installed in the institutional prestige of English Literature and in the shaping of its syllabus, the student or academic, encouraged to concentrate on 'the words on the page', is not necessarily called upon to confront these issues directly. But the representation of gender in the plays is a difficult topic to avoid, even when the discursive brief is limited to character, theme and plot. So a feminist literary theory, well placed to recognize that reading has always been *reading for*, is more sensitive to the history of criticism as a history of ideological production and, in the particular matter of gender, to the way that positions stated dogmatically in nineteenth-century commentariës survive as unstated assumptions in more informal and 'intuitive' twentieth-century criticism.

L. T. Fitz, drawing on a range of influential modern accounts of *Antony and Cleopatra*, discusses a number of motifs that point to this continuity. These include the habit of comparing characters simply because they are women, when no parallel practice exists in relation to men (Fitz, 1977, p. 298). Thus Angela Pitt in *Shakespeare's Women*, part of a publishing revival in the 'heroines' genre addressed, ironically, to a market created by the concerns of the women's movement (albeit in a diluted, appropriated form), links analyses of Cleopatra and Juliet with the observation that "there is an immediate reduction in scale and tone", and that here is "no sensual goddess, but instead a young, innocent girl" (1981, p. 45). The same critical and ideological assumptions, as Fitz shows, are also manifest in the recourse to equating a particular character with Shakespeare's view of 'woman', and in the use of a double standard to assess the significance of male and female characters' attitudes to love and power. [16] Finally, 'women's wiles' and similar formulations remain in the vocabulary of twentieth-century Shakespeare criticism even when, as Fitz points out, the women in the plays, apart from perhaps Cleopatra and Cressida, fail to live up to the stereotype. The wiles of Prospero, Richard III and a host of other male characters, meanwhile, are never presented in the criticism as specific to men. [17]

Feminist Shakespeare criticism is sufficiently well established in England and the United States to have made it clear, from this theoretical position if from no other, that the critical mainstream has sustained more than an urbane 'disinterested' dialogue. [18] The priorities of feminism in the analysis of

attitudes to gender in the plays also pose questions to any
concept of an absolute literary value divorced from considerations of what is valuable to particular interests in perpetuating
or opposing a hegemonic 'culture'. But a feminism which
operates outside the post-structuralist critique of the subject
and the sign runs the risk of inadvertently reproducing the
more fundamental aspects of the discourse nominally under
attack, while also disregarding modalities of the text that could
be used to reinforce the theoretical challenge. If Marilyn French
is right in claiming that "Truth, as defined by a 'masculine'
culture, is that which stands, which is permanent, which
endures" (1981, p. 37), then *As You Like It*, *Macbeth* and
Hamlet at least, in spite of monumental endurance of 'the Bard',
are in their way profoundly 'unmasculine' texts. Neoclassical
criticism, founded on the permanence of such a 'truth',
discovered in the excesses of the signifier the "*Delilah*'" or "fatal
Cleopatra"[19] that seduced Shakespeare away from the prospect
of a flawless excellence. There are glimpses of a more positive
evaluation of this linguistic seduction in Mrs Jameson's
unguarded excursion into Cleopatra as the hieroglyph of the
peacock's train, where specific 'qualities', as in the language of
Rosalind, Hamlet and the Wayward Sisters, mingle, "shift,
and change, and glance away" (p. 193).[20] French herself
underlines the threat of wordplay to the "masculine principle":
"'Masculine' minds (even in our day) believe that words have
fixed meanings, that there should be a unity of 'heart and
tongue', and thus, implicitly, that feelings as well as words can
be fixed, made permanent, irrevocable. . .Play with language
denies all this. It implies doubleness, even duplicity" (French,
p. 37). If wordplay poses such a threat, then the extension of
play to the level of the theatrical signifier—the text's refusal to
allow dramatic representations, including 'characters', to be
fixed, permanent, irrevocable—doubles it. And so we arrive
back at the text's processes of representation *and* deconstruction—at the "negativity" described by Kristeva.

In Lacan's rereading of Freud and Saussure, the division of
'feminine' and 'masculine' is part of the process in which the
infant—the "*hommelette*" who is at once the 'little man',
'feminized man' and 'broken egg' with fluid, undefined
margins—gains access to a 'world' constituted by language and

symbolization. At the point of access the infant becomes a human subject, a coherent, unified 'self' which, having coalesced in another place, in the imaginary unit of the mirror-image, is also divided from and other than itself. This subject exists for and in what Lacan calls the "Symbolic Order"—reached through the Oedipal phase—an 'objectifying' language which will eventually permit the child to distinguish experience into 'I', 'he', 'she' and 'it', and an order in which the sliding of signifiers across signifieds has been halted by a privileging of certain key signifiers, such as the Phallus and the 'name of the Father', around which 'meaning' is pinned down and organized.[21]

Lacan assigns to the same complex process the production of the subject, the social construction of 'masculine' and 'feminine', and the subject's induction into a language in which signifier and signified are held in the unity of the sign—roughly the sort of 'rational' or 'logical' language Marilyn French associates with the "masculine principle". But French's own analyses of the plays, by taking no account of such theories of the subject and the sign—and the most damaging omission here is the work of Kristeva, Cixous and other French feminists—succeeds, at the moment of interrogating a 'masculine' language in which truth is truth and certain characteristics are distinctly 'male' or 'female', in sustaining an aesthetic which entertains no possibility of locating the text anywhere but firmly within the bounds of the Symbolic. French's account of a Shakespeare who marshals dramatic conflicts, themes and characters[22] to express a particular world view, one which moves progressively towards a probing of his personal sexual attitudes and a partial revision of the polarizing imperative of a cultural "gender principle", sacrifices the deconstructive movement of the text, or what Weimann calls its element of formal "disenchantment", to theoretically naive assumptions about an undivided author, mimesis, reader and work.[23] The critical discourse based on these assumptions leaves the text no option but to reproduce the complex of closures—in language, gender and the subject—which, in the case of French's *Shakespeare's Division of Experience*, is the object only of a selective and contradictory attack.

The "division of experience" posited by French overlooks

another, prior division, as if it were already accomplished, forgotten and out of reach. This is Kristeva's distinction, which echoes others made by Barthes, Derrida and Lacan, between the 'symbolic' and the 'semiotic', or the 'thetic' (equivalent to Lacan's symbolic order) and the *'chora'*. French's discourse, in spite of its marginal recognition of a shifting, indeterminate order of language antagonistic to the "masculine principle", restricts itself to the 'symbolic', or the "thetic predicative operation and its correlatives (signified object and transcendental ego)", which, as Kristeva argues, "though valid for the signifying economy of poetic language, are only one of its *limits*: certainly constitutive, but not all-encompassing" (1980, p. 132). While certain uses of language—for example, scientific discourse—aspire to the status of a knowledge by reducing as far as possible the presence of the *semiotic*, 'literature', in contrast, is distinguished by the fact that "the semiotic is not only a constraint as is the symbolic, but it tends to get the upper hand at the expense of the thetic and predicative constraints" (p. 134). The semiotic, associated with the "sea of negativity" in which Kristeva sees criticism comically coagulating its thetic islands, implies, particularly in poetic language but to a lesser extent in any language, a *"heterogeneousness* to meaning and signification" which is always in sight of meaning "or in either a negative or surplus relationship to it" (p. 134).

This central distinction has an obvious affinity with other now familiar post-structuralist double-acts: *écrivance* and *écriture, lisible* and *scriptible*, difference and *différance*, sign and *trace*, etc. But the particular emphasis in the 'symbolic'/'semiotic' pairing on the construction and undermining of gendered subjects in language suggests Kristeva's model as one of the most useful for an Anglo-American feminist Shakespeare criticism which lacks a sufficiently developed problematic of the subject and the sign. Poetic language, resembling in some ways that of the psychotic,[24] reactivates a heterogeneity which can be detected "in the first echolalias of infants as rhythms and intonations anterior to the first phonemes, morphemes, lexemes and sentences" (Kristeva, p. 133), compelling the intact, self-identical subject who confronts it to become a "questionable *subject-in-process*" (p. 135) and dislodging the masculine-feminine distinction of a symbolic order dominated by the phallus while intimating another 'feminine' this order cannot contain—a pre-symbolic, imaginary area of first intonations and identification with the mother's body. This site of the semiotic is already expressed as the *'chora'* in Plato's *Timaeus*—"receptacle ... unnamable, improbable, hybrid, anterior to naming, to the One, to the father, and consequently, maternally connoted to such an extent that it merits 'not even the rank of a syllable'" (Kristeva, p. 133).[25]

In poetic language the semiotic appears where the jurisdiction of the symbolic is weakest, in disrupted syntax, rhythmic and musical effects, elision, excesses of meaning, and attempts "to wipe out sense through nonsense and laughter" (Kristeva, pp. 133–5, 142). In Shakespeare's plays, written to be published only in performance, this modality of signification was reinforced in vocal timbres, physical movement and the very presence on stage of bodies reassembled in the text[26] both as representations of the unified subjects of the symbolic order and as processes anterior to, and always in excess of, these subjects—the shadowy motions of writing, speaking and acting that signify nothing except signification's own surplus in relation to the symbolic or mimetic. In concrete terms the semiotic, with its implicit undermining of symbolic gender distinctions, is in evidence from the minutiae of language to some of the basic conditions of production: from the "double, double" nursery-rhyme doggerel of the sexually indeterminate witches for example, echoed in the language of the 'unsexed' Lady Macbeth[27] and the "sound and fury" of her partner, to the opposition of the female character and the boy actor who played her—and its reverberations in a text as intent on exploiting such technical 'problems' as concealing them or letting them pass. Such considerations tend to be lost on a criticism devoted to mimesis or interpretation, even if that criticism concerns itself with such issues as Shakespeare's 'feminist' vision,[28] his endorsement of patriarchal values or, as in Marilyn French's analysis, his only partially successful struggle to free himself from these values.

Character, as everyone who studies Shakespeare criticism is supposed to know, is what the twentieth century left behind in discovering dramatic poetry and then poetic drama. But it is difficult to find many pieces of modern Shakespeare criticism, however much in flight from what Juliet's nurse's husband ate for breakfast, that do not accord to character the status of at least a token personage, a version of the "*whole* subject . . . conscious, knowable" sustained by a symbolic aesthetic in which "the enunciatory 'I' *expresses himself* in the text, just as the world is *represented*. . ." (Cixous, 1974, p. 385). Character, in this sense, has remained a focus for commentaries concerned with 'truth's truth' in matters relating to the text's representation of gender. (What are we meant to *think* when personage *a* or *b* says this or that, and how are we placed in relation to values implicitly challenged/reinforced/'probed', etc.?) This emphasis is apparent (1) in the nineteenth-century texts that dogmatically affirm a particular construction of 'woman', (2) in a more 'open-minded' modern academic criticism, nominally less attached to character, but in which some of the earlier assumptions remain embedded, and (3) in the first stirrings of a contemporary Anglo-American feminist criticism. It follows that an intervention in this tradition from (4) the ground of a post-structuralist critique of the subject and the sign will function where character *falls apart* as a support of the enunciatory 'I' and represented 'world' projected onto the text, at the point where it *never was* except as an unstable function of language, a provisional hieroglyph or inscription that bears the trace and negation of all others. As this process of 'charactering' and 'de-characterization' is inseparable from the text's particular production of authority and 'legitimacy' in ideologies of the family and the state, a matter already considered above in relation to *Hamlet*,[29] the case of Ophelia, a favourite of 'heroines' criticism, is as good a place as any to begin a systematic illustration of these four historical stages of reading.

Anna Jameson's claim that modesty, grace and tenderness are woman's God-given attributes, without which she is a thing that "wants a name yet", appears in the chapter of *Shakespeare's Heroines* devoted to Ophelia, an exemplary model of feminity and one which attests to the fact that, as long as these three special ingredients are present, woman is herself "though every other faculty is wanting or deficient" (Jameson, p. 110). Ophelia is no less exquisite, and more a woman, for her passivity and weakness. As befits her age and sex, love is her first concern.[30] She loves Hamlet, "not for what he is in himself, but for that which appears to her" (p. 115)—"The'expectancie and Rose of the faire State,/. . . Th' observ'd of all observers" (1809–10). Her self-delusion in this requires no further investigation, for "what can be more natural?" (p. 116). It is also natural that she should be less intelligent than Hamlet, and that he should love her for this. A woman's intellect, Mrs Jameson argues, is subject to her feelings and "bears the same relation to that of a man as her physical organization—it is inferior in power, and different in kind" (p. 11). Hamlet, made "unspeakably interesting" by his powerful male intellect, lights on "the tender virgin innocence of Ophelia" and, without demeaning himself or detracting from his own grandeur, loves in the delight "with which a superior nature contemplates the goodness which is at once perfect in itself, and of itself unconscious" (pp. 115, 119). When the time comes, it is Ophelia's bad luck that her innocence, perfect goodness and fetching lack of intelligence have to be thrust aside for more weighty matters of state. But at least she has the comfort of retaining her femininity to the last and dying "a spotless victim offered up to the mysterious and inexorable fates" (p. 122).

The one potential blemish on this ideal of martyred innocence is intimated in the warnings by Polonius and Laertes to Ophelia about opening her "chast Treasure" to her wooer's "unmastred importunity" (I. iii. 494–5), in Hamlet's rhetorical question "Are you honest?" (1759) and in her own songs, in which her madness is associated not only with grief for a dead father but also with the prospective husband who *"dupt the chamber dore,/Let in the Maid, that out a Maid, never departed more"* (2792–3). This opens up the prospect of a division between, on the one hand, an image of feminine grace and pliability, of a fluid presence awaiting control or definition by men and, on the other, the threat to patriarchal structures of authority, legitimacy and exchange posed by female sexuality—the "indistinguish'd space of Woman's will" as negatively connoted in *King Lear* (IV. v. 2724).[31] Mrs Jameson anticipates the interpretation that the advice of Ophelia's father and brother may already be too late, a view which amounts to a slur on the 'character' (in a dual sense, moral and dramatic) she describes as a seraph who has wandered out of bounds, a snowflake that dissolves in air "before it has caught a stain of earth" (p. 112). No impropriety, she argues, is indicated by what Ophelia says and sings in madness. On the contrary, the fact that she then utters precisely what she would not have said when sane "is an additional stroke of nature". This, according to the most respected physicians, is a classic symptom of insanity, and Mrs Jameson herself has been acquainted with "a young Quaker girl", as innocent as Ophelia, who behaved in the same way and "whose malady arose from a similar cause" (p. 112).

This division on the question of Ophelia's 'honesty' is a telling instance of the process which prolongs the shadow of Mrs Jameson's type of discourse into the modern period. Some of the most influential Shakespeare scholars of the twentieth century, including Bradley, Dover Wilson, Kenneth Muir and Harold Jenkins,[32] have felt compelled to address the question of Ophelia's chastity and to insist, against her detractors, on something not far removed from the Victorian image and the assumptions that accompany it. Words like 'victim', 'innocence', 'poignancy' and 'pathetic beauty' recur in the criticism with a dismaying frequency. At the beginning of this line Bradley cites Mrs Jameson as an authority on Ophelia's madness,[33] and in her translation for the 1980s of Shakespeare's 'heroines' into his 'women' Angela Pitt sums it up in familiar terms by referring to the "pathos" attached to the death of a character who is "a poor innocent, oblivious of danger to the last" (1981, p. 53). Never in the history of Shakespeare criticism has so much special pleading been provoked from so many by so few. It is as if there would be nothing to say about Ophelia were it not for this minor irritant on the margin, a point to be forcefully rejected as something that should not have been added to the debate in the first place. A handful of interpreters, mainly foreigners (Tieck, Boerne, Kott, Madariaga),[34] have claimed Ophelia is no innocent maiden, and a host of others—mainly male and Anglo-Saxon—spring to her defence like outraged uncles.

The evidence on both sides is rather thin. First there is the belief that Ophelia is simply 'not that kind of girl' and that suggestions to the contrary are based on literal-minded misreadings of Hamlet's attack on her in the 'nunnery' scene, with

all its misdirected anger and brutality, and on the hint of
sexual betrayal and the phallic imagery that crop up in Ophelia's madness. On the other hand, Jan Kott, making Ophelia a
'contemporary' for readers and audiences in the 1960s, takes it
for granted that she has slept with her boyfriend and leaves it at
that (1964, pp. 58–9). On the side of the detractors, Salvador
de Madariaga has pursued the investigation further and made
at least a *prima facie* case for the prosecution. His Ophelia is a
"fast girl", a typical Tudor courtesan who, like Anne Boleyn,
aims to ascend to the throne via the royal bed-chamber but
under the cover of impeccable virtue.[35] In the sources—both
the *Historiae Danicae* of Saxo Grammaticus and Belleforest's
Histoires Tragiques—the decoy left for Hamlet in the equivalent
of the 'nunnery' scene is a specifically sexual lure to test his
show of madness, and their encounter almost certainly ends in
intercourse.[36] From this, and from Ophelia's songs and her
comportment before 'The Murder of Gonzago', Madariaga
extrapolates an intimacy with Hamlet which has existed from
before the beginning of the action and which has clear implications for the actor's interpretation of the character on stage. If
the actor is to understand that the text unfolds evidence for this
physical intimacy then the 'Ophelia' of Mrs Jameson and the
majority of subsequent commentaries is in fact only the character's performance of herself, a fiction analogous to the role of
Claudius as "vice of kings" or to Hamlet's own "antic disposition".

The debate, such as it is, has been set up more often in
interpretations that argue there should be *no debate* than in
those that question whether poor Ophelia is *really* a virgin.
More striking than the disagreements is the fact that the
discussion has remained for so long at this level, of a confront-
ation between one discourse which resembles the prurient
'probes' of tabloid journalism and another which reproduces
the sexual assumptions and emotional range of Victorian melodrama or of parlour disquisitions on the life and death of Little
Nell. And the meeting of the 'pathos', 'innocence' and 'poignancy' image with that of the 'fast girl' reproduces, beneath the
apparent conflict, an ideological agreement on the dual essence
of 'woman'. These two Ophelias represent the "inlaw" and
"outlaw" feminine, which according to Marilyn French consti-

tute a division that Shakespeare was never able to go beyond or reconcile.

Although French conjures up these categories in a historical vacuum, aiming in general terms to enhance "our understanding of Shakespeare" and "our understanding of our own lives and our thinking" (p. 18), this dualism *within* the 'masculine'–'feminine' opposition does, of course, have a historical basis. It was at the beginning of the third century that Tertullian described woman as "a temple built over a sewer" and the medieval idealization of the Lady, in courtly love and the emergence of mariolatry for example, is shadowed by the idea that women need no respite after orgasm, and by Avicenna's warning to men that one ejaculation is more debilitating than forty bloodlettings. A belief in the stronger sexual desire and capacity of women, which can be traced back at least as far as Aristophanes's *Lysistrata*, was certainly not unknown in the age of Shakespeare. The persecution of witches often had an acknowledged link with this view: "All witchcraft comes from carnal lust, which in women is insatiable".[37] In the Homily on Marriage, read out in English churches from 1562 onwards, woman is described as "a weak creature not endowed with like strength and constancy of mind", one "more various in fantasies and opinions", and "more prone to all weak affections and dispositions of mind" (Stone, 1977, p. 198)—a construction which underlines the need to *contain* female sexuality, given its obvious bearing on the legitimacy of the male line in the inheritance of property and on the exchange of women in marriage, an arrangement in which sexual attraction and romantic love played a relatively minor role until the second half of the seventeenth century.[38] The very weakness and variability through which women were considered suited by nature to be shaped to the structures of the patriarchal family also constituted the greatest potential threat to their smooth functioning.[39]

So there is no reason why Shakespeare should *not* have subscribed to the dual view of the 'feminine', which is not only reproduced in nineteenth-century commentaries on Ophelia and in the continuing modern debate, but is also specific to Elizabethan and Jacobean discourses on women. The belief that he did is implicit in the criticism which insists that the play has an answer to Hamlet's question about Ophelia's chastity, an answer which embodies one or other of the types of womanhood. There is, however, another sense to "Are you honest?", which shifts the focus in the text from the closed circuits of the 'feminine' to a problematic which incorporates the production of that category in ideology. Within the constraints and freedoms of 'character' Ophelia is clearly *not* honest in the sense of 'truthful'. Hamlet asks "Where's your Father?" and, knowing very well that Polonius is "seeing unseene", she replies "At home, my lord" (1785–6). During the whole 'nunnery' scene Hamlet's invective, often regarded as an attack on Gertrude and women in general cruelly directed towards Ophelia, is exactly this *but also* a specific comment, strategically generalized and 'antic' for the hidden audiences that characterize Elsinore,[40] on one who has made her "Wantonnesse' her "Ignorance" (1801). The force of this remark is that here true abnegation and promiscuity exist not in a breaking of sexual codes but in a willing acceptance of the compliant, intellectually inferior 'feminine' role—the status of "green girl" or "baby", the sexuality to be cajoled, curbed and exploited to the point where it is complicit with the forces massed against Hamlet.

The painted puppet who lisps, jigs and ambles, the manipulable object who accepts definition from brother, father and king, is too much 'woman', and Hamlet's particular attack echoes through associated images of sugar and paint. The "sweet maid" on whose body Gertrude will scatter flowers as "Sweets to the sweet" (3435) is also an instance of the "Candied tongue" that licks "absurd pompe" (1911), and is more directly implicated than Polonius realises in his comment before the 'nunnery' scene: "with Devotion's visage,/And pious Action, we do *sugre* o're/The divell himself' (1698–1700). Hamlet's attack on the 'painting' of visage and action refers back to Claudius's prologue to the scene, concerning the "Harlot's Cheeke beautied with plaist'ring Art" (1703) and the prince's earlier "vilde Phrase' about "the most *beautified* Ophelia" (II. ii. 1138–9).[41] The fate of the one who accepts the 'feminine' attribution so completely is a gradual fading out of will and reason to the point where, between accident and suicide, "incapable of her own distresse" (3170) the subject who has become invisible behind the adjustments of an outer show is pulled down to "muddy death" only by the weight of her sodden garments (3175–4).

"Poor Ophelia. Far too soft, too good, too fair, to be cast among the briers of this working-day world and fall and bleed upon the thorns of life" writes Mrs Jameson (p. 111), a sentiment echoed by Judith Cook, but with an edge of recognition that such a fate is not entirely decreed by a natural law of gender: "Poor Ophelia . . . unlike most of the rest of Shakespeare's girls she seems to have little or no will of her own—docile, frail, used by her father and the Court, she fragments into madness when confronted with a frightening series of events" (1980, p. 92). The play's emphasis on costume,[42] painting and confectionery edges the issue of gender towards this question of *construction*. Having dispensed altogether with the handkerchiefs and the *sal volatile*, Juliet Dusinberre locates the problem squarely in an ethic of integrity and responsibility which is beyond gender and in the *cultural* reproduction of 'masculine' and 'feminine' subjects:

> Her whole education is geared to relying on other people's judgements, and to placing chastity and the reputation for chastity above even the virtue of truthfulness. Ophelia has no chance to develop an independent conscience of her own, so stifled is she by the authority of the male world. The consequence is, that being false to herself, allowing herself to acquiesce in the deception by which her father and the king overhear her conversation with Hamlet, she is inevitably false to Hamlet.
>
> (Dusinberre, 1975, p. 94)[43]

Thus the text's repeated question about Ophelia's chastity is not so much one that invites an answer as a teasing irrelevance which, however much it lures directors and commentators to reveal their own presuppositions, functions more to *display* than to reaffirm familiar ideologies of the feminine. The open question concerning chastity is pointed by Hamlet's play on 'nunnery'. This term's secondary connotation of 'brothel' is equally applicable to an Ophelia whose "wantonness" and "ignorance" are one and the same. It is not only in its primary sense that "Get thee to a *Nunnerie*" (1776) ridicules "a morality which thinks chastity compatible with hypocrisy" (Dusinberre, p. 94). It addresses at once a virgin prostituted by her father and king and a woman who may have been Hamlet's lover but whose assumption of a manipulable 'innocence' still fits her only for a cloister. The victim of patriarchy is also, to a degree, complicit in her own downfall[44]—a figure of melodrama who remains, nevertheless, tenuously within the domain of tragedy.

For Mrs Jameson, Ophelia is the antithesis of Gertrude, the "wicked queen" who merits no separate consideration as one of Shakespeare's 'heroines', but whose affection for this "gentle and innocent creature" is "one of those penetrating glances into the secret springs of natural and feminine feeling that we find only in Shakespeare" (p. 112). From a position critical of such constructions of the 'natural and feminine', it is possible to see much more in common between the two figures. In Gertrude too the pressures of patriarchal attribution are coupled with what has often been interpreted as a lassitude and abnegation, summed up in Bradley's view of her as one who "was not a bad-hearted woman" but "very dull and shallow", who "loved to be happy, like a sheep in the sun" and was pleased "to see others happy, like more sheep in the sun" (1904, p. 167). The paradigm here, signalled by Bradley's use of the past tense, is that of the novel or biography, which supply the appropriate analogies to both Gertrude and Ophelia in Augusta Leigh, who "suffered from a kind of moral idiocy since birth" (Mahood, 1957, p. 125),[45] Conrad's Winnie Verlock who thinks that things do not bear much looking into, and in Fanny Assingham's gloss on 'wantonness' and 'ignorance' in *The Golden Bowl*: "But stupidity pushed to a certain point *is*, you know, immorality". Bradley's account of Gertrude has provoked its own critical debate, to which contemporary feminist critics have contributed accounts of what the queen is 'really like'— interpretations which in turn secure the hold of 'character' criticism on this area of concern.[46] To Mrs Jameson, Ophelia was marked by "an exclusive sense of her real existence without reference to the wondrous power that called her into life" (p. 111), and although Bradley inadvertently anticipates his own demise in the observation that "the analysis of her character" seems "almost a desecration" (p. 160), his approach to the plays survives nowhere more strongly than in the

Anglo-American feminist criticism which insists on sustaining an unproblematized notion of the 'representation' of women and which can even state that a "microscopic examination of individual personalities may still profitably be undertaken" (Berggren, 1980, p. 18).

"Like other revisionist enterprises", write Lenz, Greene and Neely in their introduction to *The Woman's Part*, "feminist criticism struggles to free itself from the assumptions, the dichotomies, the styles of traditional criticism and thought; and this effort itself, if it cannot entirely succeed, can generate new illuminations" (1980a, p. 10). While a feminist reassessment of Ophelia, or any other Shakespearean 'character', may attack the traditional dichotomy of the 'feminine' and move polemically towards a concern with the construction of gender, its arrest at the level of a mimetic 'personality' will nevertheless perpetuate what Hélène Cixous calls the "treadmill of reproduction" and its phallogocentric separation of the author (subject) from the world (object) of which he/she speaks, however heroically divided or interrogative his/her vision may seem.[47] The meanings that coalesce in this mode of criticism still undermine the more fundamental challenge of the text and remain precisely a *revision* rather than a decisive theoretical break, which comes only at the point where 'character' and 'meaning' are themselves in doubt.

When Horatio first reports Ophelia's madness to Gertrude, he does so in an opaque and tentative idiom, which compounds rather than clarifies the 'nothing' and the hermeneutic problem he addresses:

> [she] speaks things in doubt,
> That carry but halfe sense: Her speech is nothing;
> Yet the unshaped use of it doth move
> The hearers to Collection; they ayme at it,
> And botch the words up to fit their owne thoughts,
> Which as her winkes, and nods, and gestures yeeld them,
> Indeed would make one thinke there would be thought,
> Though nothing sure, yet much unhappily.
>
> (2751–8)

The circumlocution, untypical of Horatio's language generally,[48] complements the contributions labelled 'Polonius' or

'Osric' to the rhetorical surplus in speech at Elsinore. Its discreet ambiguity and hesitance at this point—not exactly thinking but thinking what might be thought—leads not only to the question of Ophelia's chastity but to any way of construing her madness that thinks "nothing sure, yet *much unhappily*", in other words to any interpretation that does not view it with indifference or positive delight. Behind this expression of a range of interpretations, itself in its way 'botched', lies a plenitude of Ophelias conjured in an unspecified lexicon of nothings, winks, nods and gestures, a process not yet called to the closures of one particular inscription or 'character'.

The figure who actually appears on stage after this preamble is no longer the unified subject of an anchored, symbolic language, the 'Ophelia' interpellated by father, brother and king. The processes intimated earlier in the play by the distance between, on the one hand, narrative and rhetoric and, on the other, the position of "green girl" and "baby"[49] now break through the unities of subject and character in:

> Poore Ophelia
> Divided from her selfe, and her faire Judgment,
> Without the which we are Pictures, or mere Beasts.
>   (2821–3)

But a picture is what has been on view all along, one which is never moved aside to reveal a coherent subject that is being manipulated or a novelistic individual-society dichotomy. Behind the constructed image there is only heterogeneity, which becomes itself in the course of Ophelia's insanity. This corrosion and pluralization of the subject, signalled in the Folio stage-direction "*Exeunt Ophelia*" (2950), is simultaneously at work on the level of dramatic form, where extraneous blocks of text slide into the space of this 'character' to further impair its mimetic and ideological standing as personage. The comments of Polonius and Claudius immediately before the 'nunnery' scene, on "sugred" piety and the harlot's painted cheek, are instances of this movement, which occurs again when Gertrude's comment on her own state, delivered just prior to the entrance of the mad Ophelia, shifts to the latter

figure as prologue to the compromising St Valentine's Day
song:

> To my sicke soule (as sinnes true Nature is)
> Each toy seemes Prologue to some great
>   amisse,
> So full of Artlesse jealousie is guilt
> It spills itselfe, in fearing to be spilt.
>   (2762–5)

In the last couplet the question about Ophelia's chastity is
triggered again, but in a way which advances a series of textual
effects that formally cut the ground from under its feet.

   Where Ophelia ends, the recuperations of interpretative
criticism begin, unaware of their own contortionism and
paradox in securing the unique, unified 'individual' of humanism—Ophelia as a victim who "gains her independence
through madness", etc.[50] The 'fast girl'/'innocent maid' aged
into the 'aunt-mother' constitutes a negativity in which patriarchal, symbolic discourse, in both text and criticism,
coagulates its islands of meaning. In the language of Laertes,
Polonius, Claudius and the Ghost, the interpellation of 'feminine' subjects is relatively straightforward, operating within a
narrow range of conventional ideological structures later reproduced in nineteenth-century commentaries and the modern
debate about Ophelia's chastity. Hamlet's language, it almost
goes without saying, is more problematic.[51] While castigating
the betrayal of a "symbolic" feminine virtue, it remains, in its
persistent erosion of the subjects and meanings pieced together
around murder and incest, a deconstructive venture into the
"semiotic" domain which, in Kristeva's terms, is always
threatening to break through self-naturalizing centred structures, including those elaborated around gender. The subject
who holds up a mirror to fix Gertrude as transgressor in the
closet scene is itself unmanned, feminized, divided by the
processes of the unconscious and of the "antic" in its dual sense
of madness and acting.[52] The prince, like the mad Ophelia, is
multiple, already "tane away" from a Hamlet who is radically
"not himselfe" (3686)—an effect of language and theatricality
never conclusively extricated from speaking "things in doubt",
"nothing", "wild and hurling words". Even as it calls women

to account, the text of *Hamlet*, and pre-eminently of the speaker who bears its name, translates attempts to reconstitute order from the rot of its negation at Elsinore into the more fundamental negations of the 'chora', a space which does not yet know, but always signifies more than, the binary oppositions of phallocentrism.

The analysis of Ophelia's 'character' leads eventually into a textual process which suspends forms of interpretation that insist, contrary to Sidney's dictum, that the poet should be *affirming* something, in this case making thetic or symbolic predications about 'woman' or already gendered subjects. *Hamlet* acts out its own transformations of the 'truth's truth'/ girl-boy-girl-boy-girl-boy coupling in *As You Like It* and the association of the androgynous Sisters, 'imperfect speaking', and the perplexing of the protagonist's "single state of man" in *Macbeth*. And here too the level of the theatrical signifier, the raw material of performance, comes into play. Just as a divided 'Hamlet' divides further into the actor and the prince whose acting exceeds and postpones action, so the 'feminine' which is interrogated, shaped and cajoled in the *locus* is wholly dismantled on the *platea*, into its components of paint, costume, interpellated subject, the veiled, un/reachable body of 'woman', and the hidden sex of the actor. In relation to 'Gertrude' and 'Ophelia', this sexual intertext is prevented from decorously vanishing into mimesis not only by the play's persistent theatrical reference but also by the particular presence of the boy actor who acts the boy actor who is the Player Queen—a hieroglyph of language, the hymen, homoeroticism and the patriarchal exchange of women whom Hamlet addresses as "your ladyship" and ambiguously abstracts in the fervent, mildly indecent wish that "your voice *like a peece of uncurrant Golde* be not *cracked within the ring*" (II. ii. 1472–3).[53] This figure is on stage when Hamlet tells Ophelia, by allusion to puppetry, that he would like to be a voyeur/ participant—the classic 'interpreter'—in her intercourse with a lover:

Ham. This is one *Lucianus* nephew to the King.
Ophe. You are a good Chorus, my Lord.
Ham. I could interpret betweene you and your love: if I could see the Puppets dallying.

Ophe. You are keene my Lord, you are keene.
Ham. It would cost you a groaning, to take off my edge.
Ophe. Still better and worse.

(2113-19)

The 'groaning' implies defloration and/or the ungoverned female orgasm, the question the play persistently unanswers.[54] Ophelia's language has been appropriated as evidence of, variously, a prior, secret intimacy with Hamlet and a maidenly modesty coupled with compassion: "Still better and worse" as a decorous expression of tender solicitude for the prince's state of mind *or* something approaching the English dame-comedian's lusty "You are awful, but I like it".[55] This seeming choice in the business of 'interpreting' is, however, qualified by the image of the genitals as mere 'puppets', wooden items for staging a whole production of gender.[56] Ophelia, by association with the Player Queen and with the puppet she was in the 'nunnery' scene, is already what she will become in the poor jest of the grave-digger, neither man nor woman (3323). The strongest link in this pattern of associations, which cuts across the gendered subject of mimesis, has occurred immediately before the entrance of the Player Queen and his colleagues. Joining the audience who await the beginning of the play, Hamlet asks Ophelia "shall I lye in your *Lap*?", a term which, in Jacobean English, connotes both the female genitalia and, more specifically, the clitoris:[57]

Ophe. No my Lord.
Ham. I meane my Head upon your Lap.
Ophe. I my Lord.
Ham. Do you thinke I meant Country matters?
Ophe. I thinke nothing, my Lord.
Ham. That's a faire thought to ly between Maids legs.
Ophe. What is my Lord.
Ham. Nothing.

(1966-74)

The first rule of an illusionist drama (we should attribute this, perhaps, to Castelvetro) must be:

If you are compelled by law to employ male actors in female roles do not, under any circumstances, draw the audience's attention to the question of what lies between the heroine's legs.

The second:

> If a breach of the first rule is unavoidable, ensure at all costs that it is not followed by a scene in which a character already established as male acts the part of a woman.

It is recognized that in Shakespearean comedy at least the technical 'limitation' of the boy-actor is exploited to promote a confusion of sexual identity. Lisa Jardine has extended this principle to *Cymbeline* in a persuasive analysis of the ambiguities in what Posthumus Leonatus calls "the woman's part"— *pudenda*, constructed 'feminine' and dramatization (1983, pp. 12–14). Less than thirty lines before Cleopatra becomes "Marble constant", announcing "I of *nothing*/Of woman in me" (3488–90)[58] she pictures some "squeaking Cleopatra" who will "Boy my greatnesse/I'th' posture of a whore" (3462–3). In the case of Ophelia, the "nothing" in his/her lap connotes the pre-symbolic surplus so often associated with the term in Shakespeare—here a palimpsest of genitalia in which attributions of presence and lack patter indiscriminately across the phallic and vaginal signifiers. From this primordial play there emerges a rudimentary phallocentric binarism which is by turns elaborated and undercut in the text at large. Hamlet's "head" (*glans penis*) is, by the pun, identified with and divided from the "head" as seat of reason. The symbolic feminine placed between Ophelia's legs, 'nothing' in the sense of mere lack, is also what women *think* under a male hegemony—"thinke your selfe a Baby", "I thinke nothing, my Lord"—a bind which brings, with compliance, the attribution of unreason.[59]

In a mimetically sealed reading of the play this taunting of Ophelia is one of the subtler instances of male violence to women. But the subject positions such a reading imposes are suspended, distanced, rendered critical by the linguistic and theatrical processes of the text. "We see her once again, playing a sort of automaton part in the play-scene", wrote Helena Faucit (Lady Martin)—almost as touched by Ophelia as was Anna Jameson—"sitting patiently, watchfully, with eyes only

for the poor stricken one who asks to lay his head upon her lap",
one who has, "in all their former intercourse" [*sic*] been a model
of courtesy, but whose "rude, meaningless words" in the
'nunnery' scene have convinced her that he is indeed mad
(Faucit, 1891, pp. 14–16). This chapter on Ophelia depicts
Shakespeare, condemned to write at a time "when boys and
beardless youths were the only representatives of his women on
the stage", anticipating the triumphs of Faucit herself in the
nineteenth-century theatre:

> Yes, he must have looked beyond 'the ignorant present' and
> known that a time would come when women, true and worthy,
> should find it a glory to throw the best part of their natures into
> these ideal types which he has left to testify to his faith in
> womanhood, and to make them living realities for thousands of
> whom they would else have been unknown ... Women's
> words, women's thoughts, coming from a man's lips, a man's
> heart—*it is monstrous to think of*! One quite pities Shakespeare,
> who had to put up with seeing his brightest creations thus
> marred, misrepresented, spoiled.
>
> (Faucit, p. 4)[60]

In her own performances of Rosalind, Helena Faucit found the
Epilogue, the last resting place of 'truth's truth' and such 'ideal
types', the "one drawback to my pleasure". On stage this
moment, "fit enough for the boy-actor" but "out of tone with
the Princess Rosalind" became the occasion of a "painful
shyness", "a kind of shrinking distaste" and "a kind of nervous
fear, too, lest I should forget what I had to say" (p. 285).
Estrangement, monstrosity, the unconscious—the Victorian
Lady-in-process as she writes from Byntysilio, Llangollen to a
yet unknowing world in a piece dated September 1884. A
century later, with the 'heroines' on ice, there is scope for a
reappraisal of representation and gender in this monstrous
regiment. But to even ask about Shakespeare's 'women' is to
have answered too many questions in advance. Closing the
cipher at "*If* I were a woman", and following Hamlet's rule that
"the Lady shall say her minde freely; or the blanke verse shall
halt for it" (II. ii. 1371–2), the last word goes to Ophelia, the
one/many who think(s) only the "nothing" between the legs,
the item which is neither itself, hawk nor handsaw: "Good-

night Ladies: Goodnight Sweet Ladies: Goodnight, goodnight"
(2809–10).

Notes

1. Furness, 1896, p. 280.
2. "The trodden worm curls up. This testifies to its caution. It thus reduces its chances of being trodden on again. In the language of morality: Humility" (Nietzsche, 1911, pp. 5–6).
3. Dr Johnson: "The character of Jaques is natural and well preserved . . . By hastening to the end of his work, Shakespeare suppressed the dialogue between the usurper and the hermit and lost an opportunity of exhibiting a moral lesson in which he might have found matter worthy of his highest powers" (1969, p. 107).
4. On the equivalence of many '-ive' and '-ble' adjectives in Shakespeare, *see* Abbott, 1870, p. 19.
5. *See* Montrose, 1981, p. 49.
6. *See*: Pierce, 1971, pp. 73–4; Latham, 1975, p. lxix.
7. "Humanism invented a whole series of subjected sovereignties: the soul (ruling the body, but subjected to God), consciousness (sovereign in a context of judgment, but subjected to the necessities of truth), the individual (a titular control of personal rights subjected by the laws of nature and society), basic freedom (sovereign within, but accepting the demands of an outside world and 'aligned with destiny'). In short, humanism is everything in Western civilization that restricts the *desire for power*: it . . . excludes the possibility of power being seized. The theory of the subject (in the double sense of the word) is at the heart of humanism and this is why our culture has tenaciously rejected anything that could weaken its hold upon us" (Foucault, 1977, pp. 221–2).
8. Cf. *"Twelfe Night, or, What you will"* (Folio title).
9. Not all of these 172 permutations yield combinatory senses. There is repetition, back-tracking, tautology, nonsense and *reductio ad absurdum*. But there are also *significant* changes rung on truth/fidelity, sustains/impedes, true/faithful and pleasures/contents. And preceding all of these is the conditional (also merely hypothetical) 'If' which requests closure and confirmation always from elsewhere. The reader or hearer must decide for her/himself the true significance, or *significance*, of Hymen's injunction. How many permutations will you allow? Where and by what authority do you draw the line beyond which the interpretation of these words itself ceases to hold true

contents? Edward Harrison says *"As You Like It*—Take It or Leave It" (p. 74).

10. See Curtius, 1953, p. 38; cf. Derrida, 1979, pp. 92, 138, and 1972, pp. 240–5, 293–4.

11. Cf. Althusser, 1971, pp. 178–81; Lacan, 1977a, pp. 5–6, 20–25.

12. Vanessa Redgrave's 1961–62 RSC Rosalind seems to have been a significant factor in cultivating just such a resistance. Dover Wilson admits to having been enchanted by this particular performance and Bernard Levin, in his review of the production, recaptures all the throbbing tenderness of Mrs Jameson (see below): "virtually faultless, a creature of fire and light, her voice a golden gate on lapis lazuli hinges, her body a slender reed rippling in the breeze of love . . . this is not acting at all but living, being loved" (*cit.* Cook, 1980, p. 19).

13. There is an extensive literature on what constitutes 'man' and 'woman' in *Macbeth. See*, for example: Veszy-Wagner, 1968, pp. 242–57; Hawkes, 1973, pp. 142–57; Biggins, 1975, pp. 255–77; Horwich, 1978; Klein, 1980. *See* Jameson, 1904 (first published 1832 and reprinted throughout the Victorian period); Faucit, 1891; Eliott Leigh-Noel, 1885; Clarke, 1850–52. See also *The Sweet Silvery Sayings . . .* (1877) and Dowden 1885. Charles and Mary Lamb assumed that their *Tales from Shakespeare* would be read mainly by girls because boys were more capable of dealing with the original texts ('Willingly to Shakespeare', *TLS*,. 15 November 1957, pp. xii to xiii).

15. Victorian productions of the plays in which women disguise themselves as men took particular care to redeem any hints of impropriety by stressing the feminine qualities of the speech and behaviour of these figures (*see* Jackson, 1979, pp. 15–26).

16. Fitz, 1977, pp. 304–5.

17. *Ibid.*, p. 300.

18. *See* the extensive bibliography of feminist Shakespeare criticism compiled by Lenz, Greene and Neely (1980b) and supplemented by Ziegler (1982).

19. *See* Vickers, 1974–81, II, p. 477 and V, p. 68. Johnson's "fatal Cleopatra" is, as M. M. Mahood points out, itself an inadvertent pun connoting both *destiny* and *death* (1957, p. 9).

20. Cf. Mrs Jameson's Rosalind: "To what . . . shall we compare her, all-enchanting as she is?—to the silvery summer clouds, which, even while we gaze on them, shift their hues and forms, dissolving into air, and light, and rainbow showers" (p. 52).

21. *See* Lacan 1977a, pp. 5–6, 20–5, 67, 99, 310; Althusser, pp. 195–219.

22. French, like other contemporary Shakespeare critics, renounces character criticism while continuing to practice it (*see* Erickson, 1982, pp. 192–3).

23. According to Marilyn French, Shakespeare probes dramatically questions of power and legitimacy and also his own sexual attitudes and feelings about women. He is prepared to "plumb the consequences of his own sexual disgust" and, throughout these investigations, he struggles for "a vision of a proper ordering of society" (pp. 18, 144). His work progresses towards a partial disengagement from the "gender principle" and a recognition that extremes must be reconciled and "the masculine principle must be feminized" (p. 322)—a kind of synthesis, albeit one towards which only male figures in the plays are allowed to strive, and which is accompanied by a continued endorsement of more limited and conventional concepts of the feminine.

24. The "semiotic" appears in the intonations, rhythms and glossolalias of psychotic language, working as the "ultimate support of a speaking subject threatened by the collapse of the signifying function" (Kristeva, 1980, p. 133).

25. For an account of contemporary *écriture feminine*, women's writing which explores the "semiotic" and emerges from "'without', from the heath where witches are kept alive; from below, from beyond 'culture'" (Cixous, 1981, p. 247), *see* Cixous's article "The Laugh of the Medusa" (1981) and Jones, 1977.

26. That is, written text in performance but *not* the sort of modern production that would take "this is not acting at all but living" to be a compliment (*see* above, note 12).

27. "The Thane of Fife, had a wife: Where is she now?" (V. i. 2135–6). *See* Charney and Charney (1977) on the language of mad women in the work of Shakespeare and his contemporaries, and Briggs (1972, p. 173f.) for a "semiotic" element common to nursery rhymes and sixteenth-century witchcraft. Thomas (1971, pp. 180–2) argues that the efficacy of such charms resided partly in their loss of meaning: "the very impenetrability of the formula helped to give it its power". The priorities of neoclassical criticism represent a revenge of the symbolic on the semiotic. In 1767 Richard Farmer remarked: "How would the old Bard have been astonished to have found that he had very skilfully given the *trochaic dimeter brachycatalectic*, commonly called the *ithyphallic* measure, to the Witches in *Macbeth*!" (Vickers, V, p. 265).

28. Dusinberre, 1975, pp. 5–6.

29. *See above*, Chapter 5, section on 'Wild and Hurling Words'.

30. "All Shakespeare's women, being essentially women, either love or have loved or are capable of loving" (Jameson, p. 60).

31. I have adopted the Q1 reading here. Folios 1, 2 and 3 have the "*indinguish'd* space of woman's will", a semiotic intervention at the point of a scapegoating which confirms the closures of the symbolic. It is not clear whether this intervention comes from Edgar, Shakespeare, the scribe or the compositor.

32. Bradley, 1904, pp. 160–5; Muir, 1963, pp. 24–8; Jenkins, 1982,

pp. 151–2; Wilson, 1951, pp. 328–9.

33. Bradley, p. 165.

34. *See*: Kott, 1964, pp. 58–9; Madariaga, 1948, pp. 40f.; Furness, 1963, I, p. 179n., and II, pp. 284–90.

35. Madariaga, pp. 42–3.

36. *See* Bullough, 1973, pp. 12–13, 64.

37. Stone, 1977, pp. 494–5, 501–2. Flaubert's *Dictionary of Received Ideas*, which is the best source for this division of the 'feminine' in the nineteenth century, defines "YOUNG LADY" as "pale, frail and always pure", one to be kept away from the monkey-house at the zoo (1954, p. 84) and taught that a "STALLION" is "a larger type of horse" (p. 77). It also includes the following entries:

> BLONDES. Hotter than brunettes (see BRUNETTES).
>
> BRUNETTES. Hotter than blondes (see BLONDES).
>
> HAMMOCK. Characteristic of Creole women.
>
> HYSTERIA. Confuse with nymphomania.
>
> NEGRESSES. Hotter than white women (see BLONDES & BRUNETTES).
>
> PROSTITUTES. A protection for our daughters and sisters, as long as we have bachelors. Should be harried without mercy.
>
> REDHEADS. See BLONDES, BRUNETTES and NEGRESSES.
>
> (Flaubert, 1954, pp. 20, 21, 45, 49, 67, 70, 71)

38. Stone, 1977, pp. 102, 104, 180f.

39. The stigmatization of female sexuality in the persecution of witches served an evident ideological function in relation to the social and economic place of the family. But the persecutions were themselves determined by economic considerations, being often directed at one of the most vulnerable, and least 'useful', groups in society—older women without family support or, in the wake of enclosures and engrossments, the means to support themselves. Keith Thomas also points out that, almost without exception, accusations of witchcraft were directed from a higher to a lower social position. *See* Thomas, 1971, pp. 510, 560–1; Salgādo, 1977, pp. 86–7; and Stallybrass, 1982, pp. 190–2.

40. For an account of the 'nunnery' scene on stage, and traditional strategies for making Hamlet *directly* aware of his hidden audience, *see* Carlisle, 1967, pp. 129–40.

41. Unknown to Polonius, the "vile" or "ill" phrase "beautified" speaks the sickness of the harlot in the conventional deification of the maid.

42. Cf. Act 1, Scene 2, where the emphasis in Ophelia's account of Hamlet's approach is on disordered costume.

43. Cf. French, 1981, pp. 149–50.

44. Her earlier speeches employ narrative, rhetoric and archaism in ways that exceed the part of "green girl" or "baby" while never allowing a

definite 'character' to coalesce *behind* the interpellated 'Ophelia'. *See above*, Chapter 5, section on 'Wild and Hurling Words'.

45. Molly Mahood directs this comment towards Gertrude alone.

46. *See*: Heilbrun, 1957, pp. 201–6; Smith, 1980, pp. 194–210; Pitt, 1981, p. 58.

47. *See*, for example, Marilyn French's conclusions on *Hamlet*: "In this play, Shakespeare challenges, examines, probes his own ideals—male legitimacy and female chaste constancy—which, like all ideals, are based on faith rather than knowledge, and finds them shaky and untrue to actual human life, which is based on sex and killing. To do such a thing requires enormous moral courage—a willingness to cut away the foundation from under one's feet. Shakespeare's probing led him into pain so severe as to appear in the play as despair" (1981, p. 158).

48. Most modern editions follow the Second Quarto in assigning these lines to an unnamed Gentleman.

49. *See above*, Chapter 5, section on 'Wild and Hurling Words'.

50. Suzanne Bertish, quoted by Cook, 1980, p. 94. Cf. Faucit, 1891, p. 3.

51. *See above*, Chapter 5, section on 'Wild and Hurling Words'.

52. *See* particularly Gertrude's response "Speake no more . . . " (2464–8). On the 'feminine' in Hamlet (theoretically un-deconstructed or -reconstructed version), *see*: French, 1980, pp. 57–8; Leverenz, 1978, pp. 291–308.

53. The currency/trade image recalls Polonius's advice to Ophelia: "thinke your selfe a Baby,/That you have tane his tenders for true pay/Which are not sterling. Tender your selfe more dearly;/Or not to cracke the winde of the poor Phrase,/Running it thus, you'l tender me a foole" (I. iii. 571–5). For the bawdy "ring" image, cf. *The Merchant of Venice*, Act 5, Scene 1.

54. The Arden editor, committed to defending Ophelia's chastity, overlooks the possibility that "groaning" might imply orgasm as well as the loss of virginity (Jenkins, 1982, p. 303n.).

55. *See*: Pitt, 1981, p. 55; Madariaga, pp. 43–4; Wilson, 1951, p. 186.

56. Cf. *Bartholomew Fair*, V. v. 96–117.

57. H. M. Hulme, 1962, p. 119. This throws new light on Guildenstern's claim in the First Folio text that "on Fortune's lap, we are not the very Button" (II. ii. 1273–4). *See also* Wilbern, 1980, p. 245.

58. The First Folio text of *Antony and Cleopatra* has no act or scene divisions.

59. Cf. Gertrude compared to the "beast that wants discourse of Reason" (I. ii. 334); and Ophelia, "Divided from her selfe, and her faire judgment,/Without the which we are Pictures, or meere Beasts" (2822–3).

60. My italics.

7
Star Wars

He wove a net of such a scope
    That Charles himself might chase
    To Carisbrooke's narrow case;
That thence the *Royal Actor* borne
The *tragic scaffold* might adorn,
    While round the armed bands
    Did clap their bloody hands.
He nothing common did or mean
Upon that memorable scene;
    But with his keener eye
    The ax's edge did try
(Marvell, 'An Horation Ode Upon
Cromwell's Return from Ireland')

Whereat with blade, with bloody blameful blade,
He bravely broacht his boiling bloudy breast.
  (*A Midsummer Night's Dream*, Act 5, Scene 1)

Jacques Derrida Meets the Sledded Pollax

Cockaygne is an imaginary land of plenty to the far west and to reach it you have to wade through pig-shit for seven years (Weimann, 1978, pp. 20, 34). Up a creek off the main route a minor altercation is in progress concerning what the "sledded Pollax" in Hamlet (I. i. 79) really is or are. The school of James Joyce holds that Old Hamlet is striking the ice with a frightening implement of war, a pole-axe which is either studded ('sleaded') or fitted with a sledge-hammer.[1] The tradition upheld by Harold Jenkins (1982, pp. 425–6) maintains in contrast that "He smot the sledded Pollax on the Ice" speaks of many Polish persons on sleds, whizzing towards this thundering "front of Jove" (2440) to be picked off like space invaders. Who knows? Shakespeare, who could certainly have expressed himself more clearly, has left only a very large sledge to crack some very small Pollax. The image as a whole, doubly exposed, does roughly show in visual terms how the elements of the sign and the subject work, while suggesting an additional homonymic pun on 'Pollax' and some computer programmes for teaching Shakespeare in schools. In the first game, the programme of traditional Shakespearean exegesis outlined by Morris Weitz in *Hamlet and the Philosophy of Literary Criticism*, the reader is assaulted by signifiers and takes out as many as possible to recover from play the 'truth' of the text.[2] In the second, 'Hommelette, Prince of Process', the enemies are the text's centres, metaphysical affirmations and transcendental signifieds, to be shot down for the materiality of the signifier (2500 points) and the abolition of 'man' (5000 and repeat).

Quoting another critic, Hilda M. Hulme in *Explorations in Shakespeare's Language* concurs that the characteristic bad jokes and off-colour puns in the plays are strictly " 'on the surface' " and that, more fundamentally, " 'there are in his major characters, no stopping places between the white of purity and the black of sin' " (1962, p. 95). This naive presentation of normally unstated principles of moralizing criticism is common in texts like Hulme's that approach the abyss of subjects and signs inhabited by the likes of Hymen and the sledded Pollax. In retreat from the implications of their own linguistic analyses both Hulme and M. M. Mahood contribute to a primer of their discourse's basic assumptions. However complex the language, "an intuitive comprehension of the whole Shakespearean design" is "the final purpose of Shakespeare scholarship" (H. M. Hulme, p. 60). Shakespeare appears in person as the immortal Bard, literally rising above his material conditions to give his own words proverbial force: "His delights, like Antony's, were dolphin-like; they showed their back above the element they lived in" (Mahood, 1957, p. 19). His 'mature' language is what Coleridge called the "I thinking", his style, after a youthful phase of intoxication with words, comparable to that which strives for a *"peinture de la pensée"*. Mahood, who makes these claims for an unproblematized subject and sign in the thick of the mediations of wordplay and the letter, can even endorse as still "substantially valid" Dryden's pronouncement that Shakespeare " 'needed not the spectacle [*sic.*] of books to read nature' " (Mahood, pp. 19–20).

Such 'limit-texts' of Shakespeare criticism offer a primer of their discourse in marking the edge of its ground. Nature, unity, intuition, *la pensée*, black and white, the major characters and an amphibiously sportive author erect a barrier against the unspeakable. These items are all specific instances of the more general terms on Derrida's list of "transcendental signifieds", marked by an "invariable presence", which have centred the structures of Western metaphysics: "essence, existence, substance, subject, transcendentality, consciousness, God, man and so forth" (Derrida, 1978, pp. 279–80). Other limit-texts add to this primer of Shakespeare studies. The interpretations of *As You Like It* that come closest to Hymen's delirium recover from carnival festivity, the multiple dimensions of play or the insistence of 'if' Shakespeare's unequivocal assertion of the presence of truth's truth in love, nature or political 'legitimacy'.[3] In the 1960s and 1970s vogue for Shakespearean 'metadrama' too, the dominant tradition exacted its dues from the materiality and doubleness of the theatrical signifier, arresting its play to produce a number of recuperative readings, including a *bildungsroman* on the poet who becomes progressively embittered and disillusioned with illusion (Righter, 1962), a view of Shakespeare as a social thinker who expresses opinions on roles and play that anticipate Weber and modern American positivist sociology (Lyman and Scott, 1975), and an uplifting belief that the "created world" of the text is revealed in order that we might actively seek in the real world "the inherent goodness and moral order we have encountered in Shakespeare's art" (Egan, 1975, pp. 88–9).

Confronted with heterogeneity and play, texts at the limit of metaphysical criticism conjure away the abyss by acts of faith in their own first principles, recovered from an informal empirical approach as fragments of a lost originary creed. These fragments keep in place the 'Shakespeare' of Jonson, Arnold, Carlyle and Newbolt, who speaks across time and space to all those who have in them still a touch of nature and Touchstone's 'natural philosophy'. Here the eternal verities, felicities and powers of discrimination remain intact in the work of the one who, pre-eminently, knew the proverbial hawk from the handsaw—a distinction which, in context, dismantles such distinctions. Simultaneously a corruption of 'heronshaw' and a 'sore', or a young falcon still in the hands of its keeper, Hamlet's "Handsaw", in its opposition to the "Hawke", collapses distinctions of youth and age, predator and prey (II. ii. 1426). The 'hawk' is also a plasterer's mortar-board or a 'hack', a crude cutting implement set against the precision of the handsaw. But since proverbs, as Harold Jenkins points out, "often delight to join incongruities", the "Hawke" and "Handsaw" are also simply a hawk and a handsaw. Truth holds true contents, grapes were meant to eat and lips to open, and "alliteration is quite as important as likeness, or unlikeness" (Jenkins, 1982, pl. 474). The 'saw' also implies a fruitless discussion, caught up in which are mangled fragments of some of the scores of 'saws' or proverbs deployed in the text—"Many kiss the hand they wish to cut off", "Empty hands no hawks allure", "He doesn't know a buzzard from a hawk" and "hand the saw", meaning to alternate or take turns. (H. M. Hulme, pp. 56–60). This is not only a Saussurean play of differences without positive terms but a cumulative undermining of difference itself, which is displaced by a *différance* that indefinitely divides and defers the presence and plenitude of a signified. In proving his sanity through the hawk and the handsaw, Hamlet makes it identical with the delirium of his "antic disposition", while the double sense of 'antic' also brings

into play the prince of the *platea*, the actor who conducts the
rites of semiotic maiming and disruption in collusion with his
audience. The crisis of the differentiated sign is also that of the
subject and in most of his multiplicity Hamlet at this point,
outside the narrowest of mimetic frames, does not in truth
know a hawk from a hole in the ground.

Hamlet's burlesque proverb does for significant differences
what Hymen's "truth" does for its true contents. Midway
through her analysis of "Hawke" and "Handsaw", which
incorporates most of the detail outlined above, Hilda Hulme
suggests that "at this point of my exposition the present-day
reader may feel that enough is enough" (p. 59). This is clearly
the problem of the present-day reader, whose anxieties are
nevertheless shared by Hulme. Here, as in other commentaries
at the limit of traditional criticism, there is an uneasy cohabi-
tation of two modes of invading the space of the text, the
dominant discourse laying down its law in a louder voice than
would normally be necessary, the other more diffuse and
transgressive.

The contradictions most visible in these marginal works are
also in evidence in the more central gestures that constitute the
'great tradition' of twentieth-century Shakespeare criticism.
L. C. Knights's famous attack on Bradleyan character analysis is
now re-presented as a landmark, a releasing of the 'poetic' and
'dramatic' in the text—albeit in senses that fall far short of
Puttenham's "doublenesse" or Sidney's "nothing". But
Knights's specific condemnation of the habit "of regarding
Shakespeare's persons as 'friends for life' or, maybe, 'deceased
acquaintances'", which accounts for "most of the vagaries that
serve as Shakespeare criticism" (Knights, 1946, p. 27), failed
to interrogate directly the *category* of character, lacking a theory
of the subject and the sign to displace the critical practice which
simply took their unity as given. Meanwhile the work of
recuperation continues in what has become a routine acknowledgment that Shakespeare's characters are not like those in
novels, preceding discussions that inevitably ascribe to characters the qualities of the humanist subject. In the 1980s, with
Bradley supposedly eclipsed, the true nature of the madness
that afflicts the unfortunate Macbeths and the sort of therapy
that might have helped them are still considered topics worthy

of discussion in print: "In the event there could be no psychotherapeutic intervention to slow or arrest the progress to disaster, and each died a lonely death without reconciliation" (Davis, 1982, p. 227).

The other main advance in twentieth-century Shakespeare criticism, like the attack on 'character', suffers from arrested development within the idealist problematic but proposes a line of inquiry that may be taken to its logical conclusion through contemporary theories of the subject and the sign. The invention of the 'problem play' has set aside a generic space in the Shakespearean canon for texts that contain contradictions without necessarily resolving them, allowing for divided reactions in the mind of the individual auditor and the possibility, scandalous to traditional exegesis, that people in the same audience might take away different meanings from a play.[4] This moves some way from the interpretation which seeks a metaphysical centre towards that which rejoices in the play of signs, and if all Shakespeare's plays were not problem plays in this sense, a special generic ghetto for polysemy might serve some purpose other than that of confirming an unproblematic, unequivocal and no longer tenable norm.

One of the most extreme limit-texts of the older, canonized criticism, the one which articulates most clearly the conflict between a dominant and an emergent discourse, is *Seven Types of Ambiguity* (Empson, 1953), where numerous displays of the Shakespearean signifier are finally pulled back towards unity. Here, in order to establish an "adequate skeleton of metaphysics", Empson eventually states his assumptions about the relationship of meaning to its dispersal in play. Citing Pavlov's experiments on the brains of dogs, he maintains that the poet and the commentator must at all costs avoid "giving something heterogeneous" and present instead "something which is at every point compound", which forces the reader to grasp a "total meaning" and bear "all the elements in mind at the moment of conviction" (Empson, 1953, pp. 238–9). In "conviction", the ambiguity of Empson's own language points at once to the 'natural' requirements of the Pavlovian subject and the operations of an ideological law, reproducing the classic contradiction of identity/subjection and the play in Hymen's "holds".[5] At this point the text stands in the middle of the main route to contemporary theory, looking back with nostalgia towards *total* meaning and the unitary "mind" of the reader, both almost bursting but heroically intact. By naming the site of discursive exclusion as the "heterogeneous", Empson prepares the ground for a theory of heterogeneity which will see unity and identity as the imposition of a metaphysical limit that can never finally hold.

The apparent pluralism of traditional humanist criticism is based on a solid and reductive orthodoxy on the unified subject and sign. Its negation arises from within, visible in the first steps towards the undoing of 'character', the inauguration of the 'problem play' and the various studies of the signifier in wordplay and metadrama. The unspeakable heterogeneity mobilized in such concepts as *écriture*, *jouissance*, *différance* and the subject-in-process is already at work in the older discourse, compelling its more adventurous texts to don metaphysical life-jackets and recite the portions of the creed they can recall in the face of what Derrida has called "the as yet unnamable which is proclaiming itself and which can do so, as is necessary whenever a birth is in the offing, only under the species of a nonspecies, in the formless, mute, infant, and terrifying form of monstrosity" (Derrida, 1978, p. 293). The theoretical break, when it comes, bears the culturally and academically 'alien' mark of French post-structuralism, Russian formalism, psychoanalysis and the theory of ideology, but it is already foreshadowed in the internal strain and the impasse of humanist Shakespeare criticism.

Owing perhaps to the special conservatism of Shakespeare criticism, attached as it is to the monumental figure of the Bard, the 'terrifying monstrosity' of contemporary literary theory, at the time of writing this chapter, has yet to produce much in the way of new readings of the texts, although it is safe to assume that there are already numerous dissertations in progress in this area and articles being rejected by the more prestigious journals.[6] The threat, such as it is, may be more immediately discerned in the pre-emptive strikes of the more traditional way of doing things against "structuralist fundamentalists" allegedly opposed not only to "literature" but to "life" (Barry, 1981), and in attempts to close ranks by curbing the symptomatic prodigality of conventional interpretations and imposing more 'sensible' consensus readings on the plays.[7] The work of producing intellectual arguments against contemporary theory is left to a small number of metaphysical hit-men whose hostile summaries of the state of play can be cited, if necessary, by those critics who choose to remain theoretically monoglot.

Among those who do directly address the innovations in literary theory are M. H. Abrams, who defends humanist criticism with some illuminating illustrations from Shakespeare while branding deconstruction with the usefully dismissive catchphrase "how to do things with texts", as if the texts in conventional readings, like Touchstone's "wooing of a peascod", do whatever is being done to themselves. Addressing a claim attributed to J. Hillis Miller, "that no textual passage has a determinable meaning, but simply sets off a freeplay, or *suspens vibratoire*, of innumerable significations", Abrams shows with reference to *King Lear* that the question of meaning is relatively straightforward providing the reader and the author share the same "implicit rules" which "make it possible for us to say what we mean and to understand what someone else says" (1977, p. 183). Thus literature may, after all, be extricated from the entanglements of *écriture* for the phonocentrism of what Wordsworth called "a man speaking to men" (Abrams, 1979, p. 566) and if the "overall structure, or 'meaning'" of *King Lear* permits a limited plurality of interpretations, the sense is unequivocal in matters of detail:

> When Lear says, "Pray you, undo this button," or again, "As flies to wanton boys are we to the gods;/They kill us for their sport," there is no ground in the constitutive rules of English for a difference between a Marxist, Freudian or archetypal interpretation of his utterance. All readers of Elizabethan English know what Lear meant—to put it more specifically we know what Shakespeare meant Lear to mean—however variously we may relate this meaning, according to our critical stance, to the evolving characterization of Lear, or to the play of imagery in the rest of the text, or to what we posit as the organizing principle of the drama as a whole.
>
> (Abrams, 1977, p. 183)

While it is true that the "button" and the "flies" are less problematic than the sledded Pollax, Abrams puts these to use in ways that suggest less a man speaking to men than a specific discourse doing things with texts. On the agenda again, behind an apparent pluralism of possible readings, are the embracing assumptions based on unity, character and a taming of the dispersive 'doubleness' of poetic language into the order of what Caroline Spurgeon called "iterative imagery" (Spurgeon, 1933), a concept which, reiterated in 1977, is quite different from the one it attempts to repeat. In this context it becomes a metaphysical stance against Derrida's view of repetition, in which the impossible act of 'reiterating' what is not a self-present identity in the first place serves only to emphasize a prior *différance*. The comfortable atmosphere generated by the critic, his author, character and reader all talking man to man is also disturbed by the fact that when Lear, as Abrams claims, utters the words "As flies to wanton boys . . . " he is for some reason speaking Gloucester's lines, thus also usurping Macbeth's function of the poor player who struts and frets his hour on the stage and crossing this converse of urbane subjects who all speak Elizabethan English with Freud's *Psychopathology of Everyday Life*. 'M. H. Abrams' at least, if not his Shakespeare and Lear, is a process happening in places not dreamt of by his discourse of unified meaning.

By assuming the metaphysical priority of intention over accident, the slate can always wipe itself clean and confront the real issues again fresh. Two years later, in "How to Do Things with Texts", Abrams meets Derrida head on and pole-axes his freeplay with an empirical proverb of the signified from the Reverend A. E. Sims. Setting all this nonsense aside, Derrida or anyone else could still, in an emergency, presumably succeed in "identifying and warning a companion against an onrushing autobus". And even in a "sign-world of absolute indeterminacy", as Abrams claims while changing his bus-driver's hat for that of a single-minded Hamlet, it should still be possible "to achieve the 'effect' of telling a hawk from a handsaw" (Abrams, 1979, p. 575).

Nature's Bastards

In the long pastoral scene in Act 4 of *The Winter's Tale* the action is briefly interrupted by a debate on horticulture. Perdita insists that she will keep in her garden none of "Nature's bastards" (IV. iv. 1891), 'unnatural' flowers created by the gardener's grafting. Polixenes replies:

> Yet Nature is made better by no meane,
> But Nature makes that Meane: so over that
>   Art,
> (Which you say addes to Nature) is an Art
> That Nature makes
>   (IV. iv. 1900–4)

He goes on to argue that attempts at cross-breeding are perfectly acceptable because the gardener's art is a natural accomplishment, given by the divine artist who has created nature and in whose image humanity creates to improve upon it: "This is an Art/Which do's mend Nature: change it rather, but/The Art it selfe, is Nature" (1906–08). Later in the play this question posed to simple distinctions between art and nature recurs when Leontes, before the statue of his 'dead' wife Hermione, observes that "There is an ayre comes from her" and asks in amazement "What fine Chizzell/Could ever yet cut breath?" (V. iii. 3279–80). The text gives no answer, but editors and commentators have taken it to be the art of God, the one creator who can work in the 'breath' of *life*.

According to this interpretation, the 'art' of the play finally acknowledges at this point its own limitations, and its strictly supplementary status in relation to 'nature'. There is, however, another answer to Leontes's question. That the statue should come to life again is the work of the artist who made Hermione in the first place and then killed her off. This artist, who chisels not stone but the "breath" of speech, flaunts the improbable and 'unnatural' artifice through which his text constitutes "Nature". This is the case no less in the statue scene than in the guest appearance of Father Time, the shipwreck off the non-existent sea-coast of Bohemia[8] and "Exit, pursued by a bear". The very title of the play connotes the far-fetched and during its protracted happy ending this quality is re-emphasized. A sequence of events "so like an old tale, that the veritie of it is in strong suspicion" (V. ii. 3038–9) is later "Like an old Tale still" (3070) and finally, after Hermione's resurrection, Paulina's comment dispenses altogether with the hand of the divine chiseller: "That she is living,/Were it but told you, should be hooted at/Like an old Tale" (V. iii. 3326–8).

Leontes's comment on the sculpture harnesses the breath-taking embarrassment always imminent in mimetic drama, exploiting the space between subjects and signs that pretend to be what they are not and the Elizabethan and Jacobean audience's willing suspension of belief. "What child", asks Sidney, "is there that, coming to a play, and seeing *Thebes* written in great letters upon an old door, doth believe that it is Thebes?" (1966, p. 195). The comments on the "old Tale" too tap this residual scepticism and transform the duplicity of mimesis into the doubleness of the sort of theatrical rite that concedes "If this were plaid upon a stage now, I could condemne it as an improbable fiction" (*Twelfth Night*, III. iv. 1649–50). This is an art which refuses to make itself merely supplementary to or parasitic on the 'natural' or the 'real' and which makes the transcendent patterns of renewal and redemption figured in the seasonal and Christian imagery of *The Winter's Tale*[9] contingent on the operation of codes and discourses displayed as being in their own way fictive. Monolithic identities of metaphysics revolve in a semiotic turnstile in which affirmation and negation alternate. This process is condensed in the syntactical play of subject and object in "an Art,/That nature makes", where priority moves from one term to the other, and in the backhanded compliment to the Almighty, also the poet, as the only one who can "cut breath". Art is nature, nature art, resolving both into the category of *production*.

"Shakespeare's Art", Carlyle wrote, "is not Artifice: the noblest worth of it is not there by plan or precontrivance. It grows up from the deeps of Nature, through this noble sincere soul, who is the voice of Nature" (Carlyle, 1841, p. 174). This extreme statement of the essential priority of nature, so central to the historical construction of the Bard, contains an assumption about the secondary, intrusive role of artifice which remains, albeit in more subtle and temperate forms, in the incrusted Shakepeare of both modern criticism and so-called popular or mass culture. This assumption is repeated in the work of theorists from Castelvetro in the sixteenth century to Mahood in the twentieth, who value drama because of the presence on stage of persons and properties which ensure that it "comes nearest to life of all forms of *mimesis*". [10] It is this 'natural' imperative that turns conventional studies of metadrama away from the full doubleness of the constitutive theatrical dimension towards acting 'imagery' which unifies a structure of representation or gives biographical details about the artist's concept of his art, with its sycophantic acknowledgment of limits in relation to the unmediated 'real' it seeks to capture. From this derives the critic's duty of discovering *within* the artifice Shakespeare's "insights into the human condition" (David, 1978, p. 46), an activity not unlike that of the Reverend Sims whose work goes on. The most recent *Birthday Book*, compiled by the Vice-Chairman of the ISA, Dr Levi Fox, and on sale in Stratford-upon-Avon, carries its own wry health-warning in the entry for 1 November, "The devil can cite Scripture for his purpose" (*The Merchant of Venice*, Act 1, Scene 3).

In *Mythologies*, the *locus classicus* for the analysis of such self-naturalizing contrivance, Roland Barthes describes another layer of incrustation added to Shakespeare in the modern cinema. In Mankiewicz's *Julius Caesar*, the hairdresser becomes according to Barthes, "the king-pin of the film" by scraping together, even from the most sparsely covered scalps, the forelock or fringe that is "quite simply the label of Romanness". Thus all historical determinants in the production of signs—in Rome, the Shakespearean text and in Hollywood—merge into one sign which seems perfectly natural:

> The frontal lock overwhelms one with evidence, no one can doubt that he is in ancient Rome. And this certainty is permanent: the actors speak, act, torment themselves, debate 'questions of universal import', without losing, thanks to this little flag displayed on their foreheads, any of their historical plausibility. Their general representativeness can even expand in complete safety, cross the ocean and centuries, and merge into the Yankee mugs of Hollywood extras: no matter, everyone is reassured, installed in the quiet certainty of a universe without duplicity, where Romans are Romans thanks to the most legible of signs: hair on the forehead.
>
> (Barthes, 1973, p. 26)

If the hair leaves anything in doubt the sweat clinches it, conveying through buckets of vaseline the inner struggles of the conspirators and the essence of tragedy "in the locus of a horribly tormented virtue". Again the natural and universal take priority in a sign which deletes its own artifice: "To sweat is to think—which evidently rests on the postulate, appropriate to a nation of businessmen, that thought is a violent, cataclysmic operation, of which sweat is only the most benign symptom" (Barthes, 1973, pp. 27–8). Across the obvious divide between the traditional practices of Shakespeare criticism and this instance of 'culture' administered to the 'masses' by those in control of its means of production, there remains here the ideological orthodoxy of a unified, self-naturalizing sign and subject. Be it 'Shakespeare' speaking man to man on nature and the unchanging truths of the human condition or the sweat pouring from beneath Marlon Brando's fringe, the triumph is that of a "duplicity which is peculiar to bourgeois art", of a sign "at once elliptical and pretentious, which is pompously christened '*nature*'", of "Nature and History confused at every turn" and the "ideological abuse" hidden in "*what-goes-without-saying*" (Barthes, 1973, pp. 11, 28).

In the tradition of Saussure and the Russian formalists, Barthes in *Mythologies* emphasizes the *production* of meaning in linguistic and semiotic systems. The later, post-structuralist interrogations of metaphysics deal specifically with the 'essences' and transcendental signifieds that assume priority over the material production of signs. At the impossible 'centre' of Derrida's project is a definition of metaphysics which comes closer to the mutually disintegrative movement of "an Art/That Nature makes" than anything in the vast commentary on *The Winter's Tale*. The metaphysician's enterprise, for Derrida, is that of "returning strategically, ideally, to an origin held to be simple, intact, normal, pure, standard, self-identical, in order to think in terms of derivation, complication, deterioration, accident etc." (Derrida, 1977, p. 247). Thus Western philosophy and ideology are constituted around differences *with* positive terms, the 'original' term, in each case, set against its 'weaker' companion which denotes a falling away from the unity and perfection of the source. So nature precedes art in a movement repeated in the relationship between reality and fiction, speech and writing, man and woman and in the procedures of "all metaphysicians from Plato to Rousseau,

Descartes to Husserl" who conceive "good to be before evil, the positive before the negative, the pure before the impure, the simple before the complex, the essential before the accidental, the imitated before imitation" (Derrida, 1977, p. 247). The dominant term, which subsists only by and in the other, claims its absolute status as presence, essence or interiority by reproducing the other as species of exteriority and adulteration—as "a supplement, something inessential and yet detrimental to that essence, an excess that should not have been added to the unadulterated plenitude of the within" (Derrida, 1977, p. 247). The "old Tale" which maintains, from what it takes to be the ground of its own production, that "The arte it selfe, is Nature" confronts the transcendental gangsterism of metaphysics with the true art, and nature, of the supplement.

Human Interest

British press coverage of the Cambridge 'structuralist' show-trial of 1981 still awaits the sort of analysis produced by Barthes in *Mythologies*. In the absence of a satisfactory definition of the theoretical issues at stake, the 'human interest' angle became predominant, with the strident voice of tradition in this "Battle of the Dons" calling for a clampdown on dehumanizing jargon and algorithms and affirming "It is our job to teach and uphold the canon of English Literature".[11] On the other side the subversive proponents of foreign ideas dismissed the pedagogical practice of a decadent humanist criticism as the exquisite group-congress of "students loving their tutors and tutors loving their students, and both together expressing their great love of English literature by a sensitive examination of the eternal moral truths contained in George Eliot".[12] Against contemporary theory, persistently lumped under 'structuralism', stood the standard empiricist argument that the proof of the pudding is in the eating, and overworked journalists were unable to procure any convincing 'structuralist' readings of standard texts. Meanwhile, even a representative of the progressive faction could acknowledge the supplementary status of philosophy and theory in matters of taste and judgement, recognizing that literary criticism is, after all, "rather like

riding a bicycle", the more you think about it the greater the
danger of falling off. [13] If the most direct parallel to all this in
Mythologies, essays first published in the 1950s, is the analysis of
all-in-wrestling as moral melodrama, a more fitting analogy in
a post-Falklands Britain full of unemployed school-leavers is
the patriotic computer game. In "Gotcha!", the model which
swamped the arcades in the summer of 1983, advance reviewers
of the Special Boot Squadron roar down from Cambridge on
their bicycles, studded gowns proclaiming "Nature's Bastards", to lay deadly pudding-fields and defend the beaches
against invading forces from Paris and Yale.

This mythic battle was, in many respects, an elaborate metaphysical sideshow, another proof of the 'pluralism' entertained,
at least in its higher echelons, by the British educational apparatus as a whole if not by Cambridge University. Metaphysics goes
beyond 'the white of purity and the black of sin' and other eternal
verities. The metaphysical, as Fredric Jameson argues, is based
not only on "so-called humanism, which is always grounded on a
certain conception of 'human nature' ", but also on "the possibility of questions about the 'meaning' of life (even where these
questions are answered in the negative, by the various exist-
entialisms)" (Jameson, 1983, p. 59). Having accommodated
French intellectual fashions of the 1940s and 1950s, metaphysics can also appropriate those of the 1960s and early 1970s.
David Lodge and Jonathan Culler, for example, have recovered
from these theoretical innovations safe, depoliticized forms of
textual analysis that merely add to traditional Anglo-American
critical and pedagogical practice the allure of scientificity. [14]
Lodge distinguishes between the branch of 'structuralism' he
employs in his own work, which "aspires to the status of a
science", and another, more accurately termed post-structuralism, which encompasses Foucault, Lacan and Derrida, is "ideological in orientation", and is probably not "susceptible of being
assimilated and domesticated in a critical vernacular" (Lodge,
1981, p. ix). The fact that all criticism is ideological, however
carefully it covers its traces, and that the informality of a "critical vernacular" is one of ideology's most secure hiding-places,
should certainly have emerged from even a perfunctory reading
of the post-structuralists Lodge names and cut off his retreat to
the comforts of a nominally ideology-free position.

What is most striking about the stance of the conservative forces in the Cambridge controversies is that it did not even reach this level of ideological sophistication, when the work of Lodge and Culler is itself now lagging behind in the business of defusing contemporary theory. "To open a book or article by, for instance, Derrida or one of his disciples", Lodge claims, "is to feel that the mystification and intimidation of the reader is the ultimate aim of the enterprise" (Lodge, p. ix). But in the case of the disciples at least, such intimidation and mystification is more likely than not to be located in the vanguard of the metaphysical discourse or, more directly, critical ideology to which Lodge himself subscribes and which is led from the rear by the generals who uphold the canon. By the mid 1970s Michel Pêcheux recognized that "the 'battle-field' of Writing, the Text, etc.", with its " 'excesses', 'overflowings' and 'transgressions' " offers "a supplementary pretext for humanism . . . to cling to the settled stability of its evident truths" and, in the words of Etienne Balibar and Pierre Macherey, that such inversions represent " 'a privileged figure of ideological conservation' " (Pêcheux, 1982, p. 180). The same point is made more graphically in Terry Eagleton's description of the "critical sceptic sensually thrilling to the unfounded play of signs" as "the son of a metaphysical father rapt before the ritual of ultimate meaning" (1976, p. 168) or as the prodigal who "testifies to the impossibility of language's ever doing more than talk about its own failure, like some bar-room bore", and whose revolutionary gestures, committed to "affirming nothing", are "as injurious as blank ammunition" (Eagleton, 1983, pp. 145–6). The game that purports to detach the 'metaphysical' from the ideological is always in danger of transforming it into a cumbersome scapegoat which is easy prey for the text's frenetic 'materiality', itself no more than a metaphysical concept, a transference of an essential nature which is "elusive, evanescent, richly ambiguous" from the world to the word (Eagleton, 1983, p. 146).

Derrida, a declared communist, recognizes in American appropriations of deconstruction an "institutional closure" which not only defuses its more challenging political implications but directly serves the contrary political and economic interests traditionally sustained by the educational apparatus,[15] interests which, if pressed, will drop more than metaphysics on their antagonists. His conservative following, in the wake of the Yale school of Bloom, Hartman, de Man and Hillis Miller, remain, while denying its very possibility, in something not unlike the "pure intellectual sphere' designated by Arnold as proper to criticism. This poses no real threat to the canon or to the continuing institutional role of 'literature'. The same set texts may present themselves to an ideal reader, still concealed but now 'deconstructing' rather than 'interpreting':

> All hid, all hid, an old infant play,
> Like a demie God, here sit I in the skie,
> And wretched fooles secrets heedfully ore-eye,
> More sacks to the myll.
>
> (*Love's Labour's Lost*, IVa. 1412–15)

In conservative deconstruction there is no reason why the text should not remain the commodity it was for interpretative criticism, its historical production and reproduction deleted, if not by its spontaneous presence then by a signifier which has taken on the mantle of all productive labour, leaving the reader or writer to encounter its relentless motions either in metaphysical embarrassment or in polymorphous delight. At play in 'freeplay' itself, and returning to undermine any celebrations of this as an end in itself, is Marx's use of the term to denote free trade in the commodities assumed in classical political economy to be 'things' called into being when nature decreed the capitalist mode of production.[16] In depoliticized deconstruction the Shakespeare of Newbolt and Carlyle is not only kept intact but given a new lease of life, reinstated as the one in whose work "the latest generations of men will find new meanings . . . new elucidations of their own human being" (Carlyle, p. 174).

M. H. Abrams echoes Carlyle in conceding the attraction of this form of deconstruction, which "can persistently discover new meaning even in a classic text". This activity provides "a freshness of sensation . . . at least until we learn to anticipate the limited number of meanings it is capable of generating" (Abrams, 1979, p. 588). The latter insight is confirmed in one of the few such readings of Shakespeare produced so far, which ends in summary: "the *'jeu de signification'* (Derrida's term) exceeds what is signified", and [*x*] "as a whole, is itself a play of signification" (Dawson, 1982, p. 221). That *x* in this case is *Much Ado About Nothing* is incidental. It could equally, and undoubtedly will in time, be any other play by Shakespeare or anyone else for that matter.[17] Lacking a visible purpose of *ideological* intervention, such work can only propagate a state of affairs already in existence at Yale where, as Michael Ryan observes:

> 'textuality' does indeed boost 'the literary' to a status it has not enjoyed in years, and it helps resuscitate a profession that is witnessing a secular decline in the value of its treasured fetishes, in the face both of the politicization of the canon by women's and black studies and the inevitable coming to the fore of media and popular culture studies.
>
> (Ryan, 1982, p. 103)

The ideological teeth have been drawn from this version of Derrida, pending his long-deferred encounter with Marx, first promised in *Positions* in 1972. Also forgotten in this critical practice is Barthes's warning in *Mythologies* that the task of dealing with "the essential enemy (the bourgeois norm)" calls for "the necessary conjunction of these two enterprises: no denunciation without an appropriate method of detailed analysis, no semiology which cannot, in the last analysis, be acknowledged as *semioclasm*" (Barthes, 1973, p. 9). A deconstruction which sacrifices ideology to 'metaphysics' and unfounded 'play' fails on the second count and is ultimately less disruptive than the work of skinheads who set fire to Anne Hathaway's cottage, which may fail on the first but which at least has the virtue of a *lumpen*-semioclasm.

The shortcomings of depoliticized deconstruction do not, of course, imply a necessary return to the even more conservative position of "a man speaking to men" or the 'disinterested' study of the "inexhaustible variety of literature as determinably meaningful texts by, for and about human beings" (Abrams, 1979, p. 588). In its undoing of unified subjects, signs and texts deconstruction contributes to the "appropriate method of detailed analysis", which, according to Barthes, must accompany the semioclasm guided by ideological purposes. It begins to articulate some of the concerns towards which Edward

Harrison, in one of the passages quoted earlier, was reaching in 1929—a "self", a "book" and a "Bard" all immersed and produced "in the relations that make object, subject, commodity what they are" (Harrison, pp. 7–8). Some of its concerns are foreshadowed in Brecht's view of "the continuity of the ego" as a myth and in the *Verfremdungseffeckt* which distances the mimesis of bourgeois realism, foregrounding the semiotic processes and social transactions in which meaning is produced.[18] Althusser's account of the ISAs, still the firmest ground from which to mount a critique of conservative deconstruction, itself draws on the theoretical baggage of post-structuralism, taking from Lacan a subject produced in signifying practice— the "involuntary, conscripted candidate to humanity" who is "interpellated" as a subject by ideology, which exists "only by subjects and for subjects" (Althusser, 1971, pp. 170, 216). Deconstruction is at least closer to, and more compatible with, a contemporary ideological criticism than is the work of critics still intent on riding their bicycles and proving their puddings. And because of its potential for conservative appropriation, it now represents a relatively safe middle ground for a preliminary dismantling of the 'naturalized' text of traditional criticism and an articulation of some key concepts prior to the more overtly ideological intervention which, in the present academic climate in Britain at least, increasingly runs the risk of being seen as directly sponsored by the KGB and calls for the presence in the classroom of an archbishop, a Nazi and a Conservative Member of Parliament to ensure that the proper 'balance' is seen to be maintained.[19]

Carnival

While English readers were acquiring the first copies of *Practical Criticism*, Mikhail Bakhtin, in the Soviet Union, was producing a critique of Saussurean linguistics (published in 1930 under the name of V. N. Vološinov) in which the central precept, "The sign may not be divorced from concrete forms of social intercourse" (Vološinov, 1973, p. 21), still has a bearing on post-structuralism. But Bakhtin's later work shows how deconstruction, when applied to Shakespeare and other Renaissance texts that draw on the popular tradition of inversion, might hit on important aspects of a more concrete historical analysis. The account of carnival in *Rabelais and his World* encompasses in their historical and social setting a number of practices analogous to those of deconstruction which, like carnival itself, has conservative and potentially subversive dimensions. [20] This conjunction can make even conservative deconstruction, almost in spite of itself, less the routine operation of "More sacks to the myll" than a form of reading which, in ways not available to the vocabulary of traditional humanist criticism, begins to disclose the text's own ideological raw materials and its ways of working them.

The medieval carnival and similar celebrations, perpetuating an unbroken tradition which descended from the Roman Saturnalia, evolved in parallel with the official feast. The latter—feudal, ecclesiastical or arranged by the state—was "monolithically serious", sanctioned and reinforced the existing social hierarchy, and remained "a consecration of inequality" (Bakhtin, 1968, pp. 8–10). Carnival, in contrast, was "organized on the basis of laughter" and gave access to a "utopian realm of community, freedom, equality and abundance" (Bakhtin, pp. 8–9). Tolerated and even legalized, this tradition of inversion and levelling was turned over to the market-place where it expressed itself in the ritual spectacle of carnival pageants and popular shows. Linked, as Bakhtin maintains, only "externally" to the feasts of the Church, carnival festivity invaded the solemn forms of religious ritual and subjected them to "grotesque degradation", replacing liturgical responses with laughter or animal noises and allowing "gluttony and drunken orgies on the altar table, indecent gestures, disrobing" (Bakhtin, pp. 74–5). Central to this tradition were disorderly language—curses, oaths, nonsense, ritual abuse—and parodies, not only of gospel readings, the Lord's Prayer and church ritual but also of secular proclamations and blazons giving official information on prices, the progress of wars and so on. These blazons, early forms of constructing and managing the news, were transformed in carnival into catalogues of nonsense, syntactically and semantically deranged, or topsy-turvy lists in which hay, straw and oats, for example, might appear as luxury items while sugar-coated strawberries were advertised at the price of last week's herring.[21]

Historically, such festivity is the home of the popular forms of ritual inversion and parody described by Robert Weimann as they reappear in medieval drama and survive on the Elizabethan stage. Its status is that of the *supplement* as defined by Derrida. In terms of the dominant ideologies of feudalism the festive is attached to primary social experience as a falling away from good sense, a deterioration which proposes the serious norm as original, pure, intact and not dependent on the supplement for its being. The Feast of Fools was described in an apologia prepared by the Paris School of Theology in 1444 as existing so that "foolishness, which is our *second* nature and seems to be inherent in man, might freely spend itself at least once a year"; Bakhtin describes carnival as "the people's *second* life" (pp. 8, 65). But such festivities undermine the apparently singular norm and install the supplement in its place, discovering in the secondary world a plenitude of liberty, familiarity and indulgence. From this viewpoint the ideological norm that constitutes the primary becomes a deterioration, a suppression, a supplement. The divinely and naturally ordained system which 'permits' carnival and the other days of popular festivity is, from the position of this supplementary privilege, the parasite grown monstrous on the blood of the host, which it now relegates to the parasitic status.

The supplement, excess, *jouissance*, the signifier are all concepts that bear the mark of the carnivalesque and its unhinging of normative metaphysical and ideological discourses. A deconstruction of the 'Shakespeare' produced in traditional criticism can work on the text in ways that echo the text's own recapitulation of festive materials and motifs. From the late sixteenth century on, carnival and festivity were increasingly suppressed or transformed into what became the modern 'holiday' then 'leisure', brought progressively under the control of the family and the state.[22] But older festive materials and practices, absorbed into the popular dramatic tradition, survive in Elizabethan and Jacobean drama, re-presented in the context of other forms of supplementarity. Puritan attacks on the theatre itself associated it with traditional 'pastime' and celebration, usually occurring at key points in the agricultural calendar—with maypoles, jigs, bull- and bear-baiting, even football.[23] 'Play', as the supplement of 'work', was stigmatized as 'idleness', the primary scapegoat of the puritan contribution to an ethic in which the surplus-value extracted from labour was more than repaid by labour's inherent virtue of staving off moral bankruptcy and damnation. This supplementarity was reinforced by the geographical location of all the great Elizabethan public theatres, forced outside the city of London by the civic authorities to areas like Bankside and, to the north of Bedlam, Shoreditch. It was also implicit in the legal and economic standing of actors. Shakespeare's organization and others of its kind occupied a unique position in this respect, caught between the past and the future. As companies jointly financed and managed they were in the vanguard of capitalist enterprise, but as groups of players they assumed the status of feudal retainers by seeking the support of an aristocratic patron, compelled to do so by the Tudor legislation against vagabonds, 'sturdy beggars' and 'masterless men'. This legislation was designed, with a maximum of punitive violence, to control a mass of people ousted from their traditional livelihoods by changes in feudal patterns of land-holding, and to shape this mass to the needs of emergent capitalist industries. Although the history of the successful actor during this period is one of accumulating wealth, court patronage and gentrification,[24] the legal and theological stamp of the supplement, "an excess that should not have been added to the unadulterated plenitude", remains.

In the classic mode of carnival festivity, recapitulated in deconstruction, Shakespeare's text recovers the supplement from its secondary status, an act which confounds plenitude with heterogeneity. It associates the theatre with its own second worlds of transformation and illusion—the heath, the wood, the island—further complicating an already problematic relationship, in which the 'art' of the city or court may be either dominant (Prospero, 'cultivation') or excrescent (Duke Frederick, 'artifice'), by locating its own 'art' in the marginal world associated with 'nature'. In the self-consciously theatrical dimension of the plays the second world assumes another form of primacy, at odds with that of the 'nature' connoted by woods, heaths and islands. As the text's representation of its own source of utterance it precedes, in the absent plenitude of 'nothing', any actual production of 'nature' or a 'world', undoing the metaphysical priority of the represented over representation.

Madness, dreams, the 'thickening' of narratives and the invasion of sense by sound in wordplay bring other instances of the transvaluated supplement to bear on the self-naturalizing ideological forms reworked in the mimetic illusion of the *locus*, an action stalked from downstage by the direct heirs of the carnival tradition—the fools, parodists, lords of misrule and corrupters of words. As in carnival the text's upending of loaded binary oppositions disturbs the strategies of exclusion and prioritization by which metaphysics represses the supplement and constitutes its founding unequivocal values— presence, ideality, the signified. In the course of this inversion a sort of priority is ascribed to the supplement, but one which can never make it intact, innocent, purely original in the manner of the dominant it has displaced. Difference is now prior to identity while exteriority and adulteration are conditions of metaphysical self-presence and purity. The priority of the supplement is the abolition of the *merely* supplementary. From its site the art itself is nature and the truest poetry the most feigning. The world is a stage only in the sense that the stage, like the text, has no outside, no 'represented', the process of differentiation being ultimately denied the validating certainty of a 'within' which in truth contains truth.[25]

As You Like It, *Hamlet* and *Macbeth* all deploy elements of the popular festive tradition, reproducing the carnivalesque trope, the supplement which assumes a barred priority, in relation to specifically theatrical materials—the stage, illusion, action, language. In the terms of the rhetorical handbooks of the period this figure is variously paradox, *chiasmus*, *aporia* or "making doubt of things when by plaine manner of speech we might affirme or deny", *procatalepsis*, which Puttenham describes as snatching a bouncing ball, besting a domineering antagonist by anticipating his or her line of argument and speaking it in mockery, and *antimetabole* or "the counterchange"—'balling a bouncing snatch' (Puttenham, 1589, pp. 174, 189, 294). This trope is present not only in *As You Like It* but in many other comedies and romances, most notably Peele's *The Old Wives'*

Tale, *A Midsummer Night's Dream* and *The Winter's Tale*. The importance of the festive tradition in English Renaissance comedy was recognized before the appearance in English of the work of Weimann and Bakhtin.[26] But the Elizabethan platform stage's provision of a position near the audience comparable to the medieval *platea* also sustained the presence, even in a tragic action, of festive practices constituting a "second dramatic process or dimension" which varies in its function: "supplementing, enriching, modifying, criticizing or generally distancing the main action" (Weimann, 1978, p. 238).

This supplementation, superimposing the *process* of theatrical presentation, upstages mimesis while drawing the audience from the plenary site of the 'real', itself presented as only a stage, into the production. Present in *Hamlet*, *Macbeth* and also in *King Lear*, this elaboration of a marked dramatic difference within a single text perpetuates the generic "hodge-podge" with its "mingling of kings and clowns" scandalous to classicizing criticism in the 1580s and 1590s.[27] But the insistence of the supplement in tragedy is not unique to Shakespeare or entirely dependent on comic materials. In *The Spanish Tragedy* for example, Hieronimo's madness inflects already highly wrought forms of rhetorical address further towards the signifier, while the downstage *platea*-like space is occupied throughout by an audience, Revenge and the Ghost of Don Andrea, who watch from the stage as the action unfolds and comment between acts. Early in the play the theatre audience watches this audience of two watching another audience further upstage who view a pageant put on by Hieronimo. In the closing scene three levels of audience again look out over the shoulders of those before them and the receding horizons of the real as they play within the play, a linguistic *pot-pourri* in which each actor speaks a different foreign language, moves relentlessly to its bloody climax when the actors who play the characters who seem to be killed turn out to have been killed 'in fact' by Hieronimo, no mere actor but the revenger who really was, although of course not *really*.

G. K. Hunter has argued that the framing action of Don Andrea and Revenge introduces an ironic distance between divine justice and the efforts of Hieronimo and others to secure satisfaction within the limitations of an imperfect earthly justice (Hunter, 1978, pp. 214–19). Unknown to the actor whose frustrated struggle for justice turns into a quest for revenge, his choice, even if it entails his own damnation, is part of Revenge's larger play in which a higher order of retribution is acted out. Catherine Belsey develops this point in identifying *two* dramatic modes in the text, "the medieval, allegorical, divine comedy of the Andrea-Revenge dialogue" and "the quasi-realist tragedy of Hieronimo's revenge", which places the protagonist "at the intersection of the feudal scheme of justice and a newly glimpsed, but not yet authoritative, bourgeois order in which the individual acts on behalf of society" (Belsey, 1981, p. 177). But however much the levels of illusion in *The Spanish Tragedy* contribute to a mobilizing of discourses on justice, resolved into a unity in Hunter's analysis and sustaining a contradiction in Belsey's, there remains a residue which addresses specifically the space of the theatre and binds conflicting concepts of the 'nature' of the subject and of justice in the relations that determine the moment of their production on the stage. The play at once speaks and refuses to speak. Like Hieronimo after the play within the play it holds its tongue in its hand, deploying a constitutive hall of mirrors never "to reveale/The thing which I have vowed inviolate" (IV. 1879–80), which in fact amounts to no more than what has already been said.

English tragedy of the late sixteenth and early seventeenth centuries is, as Catherine Belsey maintains, the product of a "discontinuity between one social order and another" (Belsey, 1981, p. 183) and its marshalling of contradictory discourses breaks through the bounds of structural 'unities' proposed by thematic or reflectionist criticism. But superimposed on discourses that affirm particular constructions of justice, nature, the family or the state there is often a discourse on the theatre itself. This is in no way *truer* or *less ideological* than other discourses in the text, but it does counter their metaphysical and affirmative mode with the historical trope (literally 'turning') of the supplement, evolving from carnival and other festive and ritual forms to be adapted and extended in the theatre, and addressing the production of subjects and discourses rather than reiterating their 'natural' character. While Kyd's play is a seminal instance of the 'doubleness' which reappears in *Macbeth* and is intensified in *Hamlet* to the point of producing "a world where words and gestures have become largely meaningless" (Danson, 1974, p. 48), the 'deconstructive' mode of Shakespearean comedy, particularly evident in *As You Like It*, is anticipated in Peele's *The Old Wives' Tale*, a text intent on abolishing altogether any mimetic 'content' of plots, characters and themes.

The pages Antic, Frolic and Fantastic, lost among the trees in the opening scene of Peele's play, meet a "wooden" ('mad') dog described in a pun which brings together the location, madness and the signifier. As the play proceeds this series is extended to include dream and theatre in a chain of supplements which eventually assume their own form of priority. Rescued by Clunch the blacksmith, two of the pages are entertained by the "old tale" of his wife, Madge, while the other sleeps. The narrative, immediately materialized as a play for which Madge, Frolic and Fantastic are the audience on stage, subjects materials drawn from folk tale and festivity, romance, burlesque romance and classical comedy to a process of dislocation and overdetermination which confuses not only the sparse modern commentary on the text but also the protagonist of the play within the play, Eumenides, who speaks for an imaginary audience in his response to the particularly enigmatic advice of the hermit Erestus: "This man hath left me in a *Laborinth*" (449).[28] The tale's various plots, with their sudden fissures and disjunctions, allude to conventional forms in such a way that they offer an interpretative lure, but each path is brought to a dead end and the whole coheres only by analogy with dream. The framing action of the old wife's narrative, offered by Madge to Frolic and Fantastic while Antic takes his "unnatural rest" with Clunch in the only bed available, provides a rationale for this heterogeneous material. "A tale of an howre long", says Fantastic before Madge begins, "were as good as an howres sleep" (84–5), and the dramatic dream-labyrinth that springs from the tale stands in the same relation to the 'real' world of the old wife and the pages as dream to rational waking experience. Their level, in turn, mediates this analogy for the theatre audience's experience of the play and its relation to the world outside. At the end of the bewildering journey there is an affirmation only of the comic destructuring itself and of the basic value of generosity, the virtue which permits the containing transaction in the theatre to be completed successfully. Generosity is shown to the old man Erestus by all who emerge from the inner action unscathed. And it is embodied again in the hospitality of Madge's narrative and the simple breakfast of bread and cheese prepared for the lost travellers before they leave the wood. The whole play resounds with Erestus's repeated warning, "Things that seem are not the same" (160, 169) which foregrounds and breaks the illusion while underlining a contrast between an enchantment that enslaves the senses—worked by the "vile conjuror, Sacrapant", the antitype of the narrator Madge—and the enchantment of the theatrical fiction, freely entered, acknowledged in the course of the action and as indispensable (as a punctual presence, and absence, in the 'real') as dream to waking 'reason'.

In its own terms *The Old Wives' Tale* must differ from such a reading of it in one crucial respect. If the distinction between reason and dream, or the real world and the fictive world of play, issues from the play itself then it is the dream or the fiction that is speaking and the 'real' state of affairs must be different. When the supplementary term assumes its barred priority in this way, the valorised metaphysical distinction which defines it as only a supplement in the first place can no longer hold true. If Erestus's "Things that seem are not the same" is a warning against false appearances, it is also, in a supplementary sense, a recognition that illusion is not illusion in any way that would distinguish it from, and thereby distinguish, a self-present real. The text's combination of pluses and minuses always yields, at its various levels, another minus and makes peering too far into its regress with positive intentions a schizophrenic project. The play really only dreams that it is really only a play really only dreaming that it is really only a play and so on. At each juncture, echoing the device of a distorting echo that appears in the play within the play, the positive affirmation is a distortion of the supplement, and the supplement (dream, theatre, signifier) a place for reproducing the metaphysical affirmation as no longer innocent and complete, but wearing on its sleeve a bracketed absence, an echo of a plus constructed as a barred minus. The 'outside' of the play is

where this distorting echo ceases to be heard, the point where
reality and illusion seem to be distinct again and real acting
begins in earnest:

> First Brother: And may we safely come where·Delia is?
> Echo: Yes.

(407–8)

Albion's Confusion

Discourses, as constituted in Foucault's discourse on the topic,
are not just "groups of signs (signifying elements referring to
contents or representations)" but "practices that systematically
form the objects of which they speak" (Foucault, 1972, p. 49).
The 'text' produced in contemporary deconstruction resembles
in many ways that which emerges in the Elizabethan dramatic
discourse on the theatre, of which *The Spanish Tragedy* and *The
Old Wives' Tale* are early, and seminal, instances. But this does
not, of course, go to prove the essential and irreducible
'materiality' of writing, a contemporary transformation of the
older representation of writing as that which remains itself
across time—"*Vox audita perit littera scripta manet*" (Caxton,
1928, p. 51).[29] The 'textuality' of these plays, rather than
constituting a neutral dimension in which discourses simply
collide and fall apart, is itself tied to a discourse, apparent in
other sixteenth- and seventeenth-century texts, which is
directed towards a representation of the text's own space and
the relations and exclusions that operate within it. And this
discourse on the text is a particular production of historical
crisis in the social formation, addressed to manifestations of
that crisis in the 'representations' produced in the text at a time
when various discursive 'essences' of the subject, nature and the
real are in conflict.

The tortuous self-scrutiny evident in the work of Kyd, Peele
and Shakespeare is by no means unique to them or to the stage.
Foucault's analysis of Velazquez's *Las Meninas*, for example,
shows how a constitutive 'doubleness' could also cut across the
visual codes of mimesis in painting to make a portrait of the
Infanta Margarita of Spain, her attendants and the artist "the

representation, as it were, of Classical representation, and the definition of the space it opens up to us". Here, as in *Hamlet*, it is all done with mirrors, in this case one which *should* reflect the spectator who views *Las Meninas* but in fact displays, among the paintings that hang on a wall in the background, the blurred image of Philip IV and his wife Mariana—at once the true objects of the gaze of Velazquez and others in the group whose eyes seem to meet those of the spectator, and the subjects of a canvas, of which only the reverse is visible, on which the painter is working. In the alternating absences of the mirror, which holds "the palest, the most unreal, the most compromised of all the painting's images", mimesis marks the presence of its necessarily excluded *subject*, in the triple sense of the painter, the one who is represented and the spectator who occupies the position from which it may be viewed as a representation. At the centre of the painting's grouping and dispersal of figures in space there is this "essential void" produced to permit representation, freed from its multiple subject, to present itself as "representation in its pure form" (Foucault, 1970, pp. 3–16).

Foucault also discovers this pursuit of 'pure representation', which can only be a misnomer once the 'represented' disappears, in *Don Quixote* where "resemblances and signs have dissolved their former alliances", so that "words wander off on their own, without content, without resemblance to fill their emptiness" and "lie sleeping between the pages of books". Quixote himself is literally the 'character' that constitutes him, a "long, thin graphism, a letter that has just escaped from the open pages of a book" whose being is "nothing but language, text, printed pages, stories that have already been written down", a fabrication of "interwoven words . . . writing itself, wandering through the world among the resemblances of things" (Foucault, 1970, pp. 46–8). This degree of conscious 'textuality' is characteristic of a particular historical conjuncture. If the predominantly realist text—*Sarrasine*, for example in Barthes's *S/Z*—requires something of a smash-and-grab operation before it will yield its codes, the text's discourse on itself during the decades on either side of 1600 frequently leaves doors and windows open, also the strongroom which, more often than not, contains a picture of an open safe.

The abyss into which things are put in deconstruction's *mise en abîme*, also the "essential void" in *Las Meninas*, is familiar in the topography of Elizabethan and Jacobean drama. It is the 'nothing' in the depths of *The Old Wives' Tale* which reappears, along with the bad pun on 'wood', the iconography of the man in the moon, and the equation of wood, dream, madness and theatre, in *A Midsummer Night's Dream*. The ballad of Bottom's dream, to be entitled "Bottom's Dream", is so called "because it hath no bottome" (IV. 1742). In its infinite unfathomability it contains a plenitude which is an emptiness. The dream bares many traces of carnival—orgiastic gratification in a utopian congress of queen, weaver and ass; a parody of St Paul on divine illumination; a praise of folly.[30] It is at once a description of a mystical plenitude beyond words,[31] and a series of mundane truisms about life in the real world of subjects and property— "Me-thought I was, and me-thought I had" (1735)—in which each sense is capable only of the offices proper to it, and anyone who tries to explain what it is all about is "but an Asse" or "a patch'd foole" (1734–6).

This world, in its way quite normal, is the play's dream of a place where its various "translations"[32]—a recurring term which signifies *metaphor* as well as changes in appearance or identity—will be arrested, where "mans hand is not able to taste, his tongue to conceive, nor his heart to report" (1739–40), and things will no longer "seeme small & undistinguishable,/Like farre off mountaines turned into Clouds" seen "with parted eye,/When every things seemes double" (IV. 1712–15). Theseus's language attempts to institute this closure by installing "coole reason" in a position of dominance at the expense of "The Lunaticke, the Lover and the Poet" (V. 1798–9). But Hippolyta's language embraces 'translation' and dream, maintaining that dreams shared communally, "told over" by "minds transfigur'd so together", grow to "something of great constancie" (V. 1815–17), a proposition which applies equally to the experiences of lovers in the wood, the fictive 'truth' consolidated and dispersed in the theatre, and cool reason's production of the world. The last word on Theseus, which joins his magisterial gaze with Hippolyta's parted eye, is that he is the creature of the poet purged and rendered supplementary by his 'reason'. Puck's valediction, "If we shadows have offended . . . " (V. 2207), recalls the Duke's own comment on the "lamentable Comedie" and "tragic mirth" of *Pyramus and Thisbe*—"The best in this kind are but shadowes" (2004)—and funnels the proceedings in general into something "No more yeelding but a dreame" (2112). In the text's representation of itself this is all the work of the poet who, in a more positive sense than that implied by his puppet, Theseus, "gives to aire nothing, a locall habitation and a name" (V. 1808–9). But this discourse too works through exclusions in claiming for its creator the divine prerogative of a fresh start, and even the most "self-molesting discourse" can, as Terry Eagleton argues, be referred back to a "more fundamental realm, that of historical contradictions themselves" (Eagleton, 1981, p. 109). It is this realm that holds the true materiality of the 'nothings' of *A Midsummer Night's Dream*.

As Theseus condemns Hermia to death, perpetual virginity or marriage to the man of her father's choice, this is done in the name of the law of Athens which, as the Duke claims, "by no meanes we may extenuate" (I. 129). When the lovers are woken in the wood after their night of confusion, Theseus lifts this nightmare prohibition as quickly and as arbitrarily as it descended while Egeus still pleads "the Law, the Law" (IV. 1680). The conflict between the letter and the "material of conduct" which, according to Aristotle, is "essentially irregular"[33] is here magically dissolved and with it the contradiction between the absolute sovereignty of law and that of the legitimate leader whose word is law—a conflict of discourses on justice and power which engaged the attention of Queen Elizabeth and was to become central to the struggle between Charles I and Parliament.[34] The law of Athens, like Theseus himself, is and is not absolute. Although banished by the advance of the plot, this contradiction finally remains suspended in the peremptory passage of the lovers through experience to maturity and its ensuing atonement of individual contentment and the social order, which itself remains under partial erasure through the possibility that Demetrius at least is still a prisoner of Puck's love-juice.[35] While *Love's Labour's Lost* declines to "end like an old Play" in that "Iacke hath not Gill" (IVb. 2835–6), *A Midsummer Night's Dream* promises that "*Iacke* shall have *Iill*, nought shall goe ill" (III. 1504) with an enthusiasm belied only by the fact that the spectator may, to the end, find these emblematic Jacks and Jills as difficult to tell apart as they find each other. In the process the play also suspends the contradiction between the patriarchal trade in young women carried out under the auspices of the family[36] and the spontaneous integrity of a unique and individual 'love', which Swift in 1723 could still describe as "a ridiculous passion which hath no being but in plays and romances".[37]

As ever the text is affirming nothing—yielding no more than a dream—and if its shadows offend, it can still hold up the disclaimer of being only a "Fairy toye", albeit one of considerable sophistication. Through its riot of dreams, translation, madness and play, all interrogating the metaphysical supplementarity of 'representation', the text's discourse on itself may distance and problematize more 'single' self-naturalizing discourses. But it is also in a curious way disabled, not so much transcendent as ideologically *hors de combat*. Carnival inversion was, as Bakhtin argues, rooted in a "spiritual and ideological dimension", its true festivity ultimately sanctioned by equality and solidarity—"by the highest aims of human existence, that is, by the world of ideals" (Bakhtin, 1968, p. 9). Its deconstructions go beyond delirium and indeterminacy to a vision of a better world, already in prospect at its own moment of levelling and familiarity. The encounter of a popular festive tradition with elements of the court masque in *A Midsummer Night's Dream*[38] produces an idealism of a more attenuated and prevaricating kind. The utopian moment now binds stage and audience in the production of dreams which, when told over, may grow to something of great constancy, however powerless to intervene in the less subtle, less self-conscious dreaming of discourses that intensify the contradictions in the social formation rather than suspending them in the tremors of the 'double' sign. Within the opulence of this sign, which projects a constitutive communion of stage and audience, the "base mechanicals" are ultimately kept in the place they will occupy in the subsequent history of English Literature, as a broken fragment of the language, or that class of people who, however eager to please, still talk and act funny—"a sound but not in government" (V. 1921). And the emergent puritan bourgeoisie, in the process of excluding itself by choice from the 'unity'

both of the little world of the theatre and of 'Merrie England' at
large, confronted this discursive opulence and excess not as the
forceful utterance of an ideological adversary with which it
shared at least a common language but as a space for unproductive idleness and the indulgence of trivial appetites, a way of
letting the time pass by.[39]

In *King Lear* the abyss of subjects and signs, complete with
its ideological disclosures and abnegations, appears as an *almost*
physical presence, conjured up near the cliffs of Dover during
the scene in which Lear and Gloucester finally meet again on the
"great stage of Fooles" (V. 2014). When Edgar, in one of the
five parts he assumes, describes the view from an imaginary
edge his language is in no way essentially different from that in
which the play's 'real' landscape is produced on the bare
Jacobean stage, and the gap between aspiration and accomplishment in Gloucester's leap, an actor's pratfall with a degree
of forward momentum, displays the gulf that exists between a
mimetic 'referent' and the linguistic materials required for its
production. Like the absence in the mirror of *Las Meninas*, the
vertiginous drop into which Edgar's disguised voice can finally
"look no more,/Least my braine turne, and the deficient
sight/Topple downe headlong" (Iv. v. 2457–9) doubles as a
topography of 'representation' itself. At the foot of the cliff the
"murmuring Surge,/That on th' unnumbred idle Pebble chafes/
Cannot be heard so high" (2555–7), its unmotivated noise
produced as the sound surplus to sense in the words that call it
into being.[40] As this pure signifier moves up from its silence
towards solid ground, a signified is progressively distinguishable albeit deformed by simile and metonymy into a vision of
choughs and crows "scarce so grosse as Beetles", fishermen the
size of mice, a samphire gatherer "no bigger than his head" and
the "tall Anchoring Barke,/Diminish'd to her Cocke: her
Cocke, a Buoy/Almost too small for sight" (2448–56). At the
edge of the cliff the speaking subject is himself again, or at least
the 'self' Edgar is pretending to be, but still faced with a
prospect of his own invention in which he is already swallowed
up and scattered.

Edgar's pretended fear, above the unnumbered pebbles and
the surge, that his brain will turn and "the deficient sight"
topple headlong unites the blindess of Gloucester with the

madness of Lear as their meeting approaches, and the vertical line of Edgar's cliff reconstitutes the axis of representation in the text as a whole. 'Madness' is produced in the play's language as a signifier cut free of its signified and as voices that disperse the unified subject—"Pilicock sat on Pilicock hill", "suum, mun, nonny, Dolphin my Boy, Boy *Sesey*: let him trot by", "Sa, sa, sa, sa". In "Reason in Madnesse", with its obvious parallels in what Gloucester can *see* once he is blinded, meaning begins to emerge as "matter, and impertinency mixt" (IV. v. 2615–16). In 'reason' the sign and the subject have each coalesced but remain beset by an ineradicable heterogeneity anticipated in Lear's majestic, already top-heavy rhetoric in the ceremonial division of the kingdom and recalled when he wakes in Cordelia's tent:

> Pray do not mocke me:
> I am a very foolish fond old man.
> Fourscore and upward,
> Not an howre more, nor lesse:
> And to deal plainely,
> I feare I am not in my perfect mind.
> Me thinks I should know you, and know this man,
> Yet I am doubtfull: For I am mainely ignorant
> What place is this
>
> (IV. vii. 2813–21)

Here the language, like that of the lovers woken in the wood in *A Midsummer Night's Dream*,[41] seeks out the place, the subject who speaks and the relations that shape the utterance. A hesitant shuffling of clauses suggests someone who knows language but is speaking for the first time. In both plays the awakening leaves behind a world of dream and madness which is also the text's representation of the theatre. The heath and the cliffs are, like the wood outside Athens, places of transformation that reverse the supplementary mark of the linguistic and theatrical signifier. While Puck is a quick-change artist who supervises the lovers' "fond Pageant" (III. 1138) for Oberon, the "King of shadowes" (1388), the king driven out into the storm is already "*Lear's* shadow" (I. iv. 744), the poor player whose accomplices will be the professional Fool and Edgar in the part of Bedlam beggar. The performances within

King Lear range from the mock-trial of the daughters, in which
an extra increment of imagination is required from the audience
to amend the joint-stool that represents Goneril, to the "great
stage of Fooles" scene—the densest extended moment of
theatrical doubleness when the two principal players meet over
Edgar's imaginary abyss.

The view from the cliff-edge, inscribed in the theatrical
trope of the supplement, is the absent centre of the play, a
regress into the "nothing" spoken by the Fool (I. iv. 658),
given by Cordelia and promised by her father in return—
"Nothing will come of nothing" (I. i. 96). Lear also tells the
Fool that "Nothing can be made out of nothing" (I. iv. 663),
but ultimately this is the source of any affirmations the play has
to make and the point to which they return. In the main action,
as J. F. Danby's classic study of the play shows, the Tudor
discourse on the state and family as structures given by a
'nature' which will revenge itself on 'unnatural' subjects
confronts an emergent 'nature' in which the fittest survive and
individual enterprise stands against traditional duties—"the
plague of custome", as Edmund calls them, and "the curiosity
of Nations" (I. ii. 337–8).[42] In this struggle neither the
'nature' of Hooker and the Chain of Being nor that of Hobbes is
victorious. Self-interest finally consumes itself, but the 'nature'
Lear and Gloucester invoke to punish their 'unnatural' children
is equally indiscriminate in selecting its targets. Both of these
essentialist views of what nature decrees are suspended in the
text's discourse on the linguistic and theatrical signifier,
produced as the 'nothing' or the excess that precedes the
essences engaged in the discursive closures of conflicting
ideologies. Lear and Gloucester's respective abrogations, of
kingship and paternal duty, bring them to a recognition that
these are parts to be vigorously *enacted*, not positions written by
nature to be taken as read. The 'natural' discourse on power and
the subjects it constitutes are suspended over the blindness,
madness and fragmentation of Edgar's imaginary abyss, which
doubles as the heterogeneity from which 'Lear', 'Gloucester'
and the rest are produced as elements in a mimetic action. In
parallel with this gesture of casting metaphysics down to the
blind spot where its own constitutive blindness becomes
visible, any metaphysical value that endures in the play

emanates from the Fool who multiplies words, the eloquent silence of the "poore fool" Cordelia (V. iii. 3277) and the several roles of the antic released when Poor Tom declares "*Edgar* I nothing am" (II. ii. 1272).

"Men are so necessarily mad, that not to be mad would be another form of madness': Foucault, following Pascal's aphorism, postulates a historical "zero point in the course of madness at which madness itself is an undifferentiated experience, a not yet divided experience of division itself" (Foucault, 1967, p. ix). Out of this zero of undifferentiated experience the rational discourse on madness eventually produces, from the late eighteenth century on, 'mental illness' as a device for separating madness from reason in such a way that the separation can be taken as always having been there. And so psychiatry's "monologue of reason *about* madness" comes to replace a past dialogue which incorporated "all those stammered, imperfect words without fixed syntax in which the exchange between madness and reason was made" (Foucault, 1967, p. x). The Renaissance texts and paintings located closer to the "zero point" are, according to Foucault, characterized by a "proliferation of meaning, from a self-multiplication of significance", an imagery "burdened with supplementary meanings, and forced to express them" and an "excess of meaning" into which "dreams, madness, the unreasonable can also slip" (Foucault, 1967, pp. 18–19).

Pascal's dictum, adapted to the theatre and carrying the echo of a text still in dialogue with madness, sums up the trope of the supplement from *The Old Wives' Tale* to *The Winter's Tale*, through Shakespeare's Comedies, *Hamlet* and *Macbeth*: "Men are so necessarily acting, that not to be acting would be another form of acting". When Edgar assumes madness in the first of his roles, the syntactical arrangement of his words sets up a dialogue in which madness and acting together reply to reason and the self-present real. "*Edgar* I nothing am" speaks rationally of the assumed madness and madly of identity divided to the point where it can no longer recognize significant difference or the logic of self-identity. It also points to the submerging of the actor's identity in the role and the unreality of the one who does the submerging, an 'Edgar' who is essentially no more and no less substantial than Poor Tom. In the Jacobean theatre, as

in carnival, such madness, masking and folly were the occasion
for a social and semiotic license. In making 'nothing' of Edgar,
Poor Tom relates this license to the production of the theatrical
illusion in a way that mediates his transformation on the level of
mimesis to his audience. This layer of mediation, implicit in
the 'nothing' that surrounds and permeates the text, brings
madness, the theatre and traditional forms of festive upheaval
into a particularly sharp conjunction, through which the *locus*
conflict between a feudal 'nature' reformulated by the ideolo-
gues of the absolutist Tudor state, and the discourses of
competitive individualism is played out *behind* allusions to the
festive ideal of equality and plenty.

During the "great stage of Fooles" scene, Lear—dressed in
wild flowers and weeds, at once a May King and a Lord of
Misrule—turns his "Reason in Madnesse" to traditional forms
of topsy-turvydom and abuse of authority.[43] The blind
Gloucester must look with his ears to see that "a Dogg's obey'd
in Office" and that justice and thief are indistinguishable:
"Change places, and handy-dandy, which is the justice, which
is the theefe" (IV. v. 2597–603). The inversion is also a
levelling, handy-dandy a figure not only of 'nothing' but also of
the utopian plenitude associated with carnival and the Land of
Cockaygne. Earlier, in the "Poore naked wretches speech", Lear
has already recognized that the real misrule was before he
became his shadow, and he has urged a personified morality-
play "Pompe" to "Take Physicke" and "Expose thy selfe to feele
what wretches feele,/That thou maist shake the superflux to
them,/And shew the Heavens more just" (III. iv. 1809–17).
This redistribution would not so much *fulfil* as *produce* something akin to divine justice by 'showing' it in the dramatic
sense. Through the breaks he has caused in an order he takes to
be transcendent and divine, Gloucester too is drawn some way
towards inversion and utopia when he "sees feelingly" the
injustice of wealth:

> Let the superfluous, and Lust-dieted man,
> That slaves your ordinance, that will not see
> Because he doo's not feele, feele your powre quickly:
> So distribution should undoo excesse,
> And each man have enough.
>
>   (IV. i. 2252–5)

The festive ideal of equality and plenty that flickers behind these preliminary gestures of shaking off a 'superflux' and 'undoing excess' is expressed more directly in some parts of the Fool's utopian prophecy, which even levels the stage-audience distinction in making the speaker, alive in pre-Christian Britain, momentarily contemporary with his hearers:

> Ile speke a Prophecie ere I go:
> When Priests are more in word, then matter;
> When Brewers marre their Malt with water;
> When Nobles are their Taylors Tutors,
> No Heretiques burn'd but wenches Sutors;
> When every Case in Law, is right;
> No Squire in debt, nor no poore Knight;
> When Slanders do not live in Tongues;
> Nor Cut-purses come not to throngs;
> When Usurers tell their Gold i'th'Field,
> And Baudes, and whores, do Churches build,
> Then shal the Realme of *Albion*, come to great confusion:
> Then comes the time, who lives to see't,
> That going shalbe us'd with feet.
> This prophecie *Merlin* shall make, for I live before his
>   time.
>   (III. ii. 1734–49)

Here the basic festive trope which sets hierarchy on its head is compounded by other internal burlesques and inversions. The whole sequence parodies pseudo-Chaucerian verses in Putten-ham's *Arte of English Poesie* (1589, pp. 187–8), and its ideal community is itself adulterated, inverted in the first four lines of the prophecy—which are at once anti-utopian and directly critical of Jacobean society. The bathetic climax of this apoca-lypse which brings the realm to "great confusion" is that then people will walk on their feet—a tautologous regress, compar-able to the meaning of eating grapes according to Touchstone's philosopher, and a mundane truism like those embedded in Bottom's dream ("the eare of man hath not seene, mans hand is not able to taste")—which inverts inversion by setting every-thing right way up. The parting claim that "This prophecie *Merlin* shall make" sets the whole speech in quotation marks as a burlesque and scrambles the 'present' of the performance and the 'past' of the action with the intervening 'future' of Merlin in a continuous supplementary time shared by the actor as Fool, and the Fool as actor, with his audience.

Robert Weimann argues that here "the theme of Utopia is not merely associated with the inversion motif, it is *expressed* structurally in terms of inversion" and that the "inversion of inversion is highly experimental and itself amounts almost to a method of reason in madness" (Weimann, pp. 42–3). But this double inversion, multiple when compounded with other supplementary tropes, occurs in any number of late sixteenth- and early seventeenth-century plays, from *The Spanish Tragedy* and *The Old Wives' Tale* on, which combine a self-conscious theatricality with one or more of such terms as madness, dream and festivity. The mangled prophecy is a special case only in that it adds another twist or two to a supplement that occupies the front of the stage and continually punctuates the 'fable' of *King Lear*, from the interventions of the mad king, the actor-madman and the professional Fool on the heath to the meeting on the great stage of fools.

Although elements of social criticism are thrown out by its centripetal motion, this play of presence and absence is, like the vision of Albion's confusion, tightly wound into itself. The text's intensification of festive inversion overtakes any shadow it might retain of the plebeian feast's egalitarian idealism. "There is little hope", as Danby rightly points out, "of enlisting the Fool as a social reformer" (Danby, 1949, p. 107), and if traces of a popular utopianism are reproduced in the pleas of Lear and Gloucester for "distribution", they are heavily policed by an Elizabethan discourse on Christian charity, which has less to do with turning the social order on its head than with confirming its inequalities by alleviating the symptoms that pose the greatest internal threat to the dominant religious ideology.[44] Shaking off superfluities has very little to do with shaking the world to its foundations, and Gloucester's attribution of social injustices to the fact that the lust-dieted man "will not see,/Because he doo's not *feele*" contains enough political quietism to fuel a thousand practical criticism seminars. The "powre" that Gloucester calls down to awaken these dormant feelings, "So distribution should undoo excesse", is not of course that of the class of carnival levellers but the power of the "Heavens" (IV. i. 2251), where they may all eventually reap the true rewards of deprivation. There is always a temptation for Marxist humanism to pounce on these lines with great alacrity.[45] But if they do go some way towards undermining an adamantly conservative Bard, seen as a souped-up Hooker or the Tillyard tradition's lickspittle apologist for the Tudor Myth and the Chain of Being, they are scant evidence for regarding Shakespeare as a prototype of the fellow-traveller.

The discourse on representation in *King Lear*, which incorporates timeless prophecy, the imaginary abyss of language, and actors acting (actors acting) madness that contains reason, is a particularly convoluted production of the aesthetic ideology of 'nothing', which is also expressed in the airy nothing of *A Midsummer Night's Dream*, the "baseless fabricke" of *The Tempest*, and the 'nothing' Sidney's poet affirms and from which Puttenham's creates. While the internal distances and inversions of the text it proposes may disclose the contrivance of ideological discourses that present themselves as natural, the 'textuality' that gets in the way of the conflicting doctrines of nature in *King Lear* also traps in its regresses the egalitarian festive ideal. The apparently rational Lear of the play's opening scene is, as Kent claims, in a way already '"mad" (I. i. 155), and when he says "Nothing will come of nothing" there is reason in this madness too. The historical transformations of festive inversion and abuse evident in the play are powerless in the face of the sort of essentialist discourse they debunk, the coercive language of law, proclamation and political doctrine, which determines the material conditions of the theatre—the legal status of actors, the location of buildings, even the gradual squeezing of an anarchic festive solidarity into this safer, less volatile, heavily censored space. In the Shakespearean text's self-reflexive dimension these material conditions of production reappear in the guise of the theatrical contract—a utopian 'converse' of stage and audience in the process of creation *ex nihilo*. But here the festive and its potential for hatching revolutionary ideologies are, for all the text's prioritizing of supplements, firmly in an *institutionally* supplementary place, a 'nothing' where anything can happen but acting is always in excess of action. Behind this unending handy-dandy the play proceeds to the point where Lear cries "Howle, howle, howle" (V. iii. 3217) and moves into either madness, reason or

Foucault's zero-point where somehow an undifferentiated experience of reason and madness can still be called 'madness'. The concluding, inconclusive prediction of Poor Tom, now the 'nothing' of Edgar again, seems a safe bet in comparison with the projections of the Fool: "we that are yong,/Shall never see so much, nor live so long" (V. iii. 3301).

If the indeterminate time of the Fool's prophecy could be pushed forward another hundred years, it would reach an attack on the London stage which recalls those of the Puritans at the turn of the seventeenth century but applies to a theatre, no longer broadly popular, that attracted audiences drawn almost exclusively from the gentry and aristocracy. Thirty-eight years after the restoration of Charles II, Jeremy Collier complained about abuse of the clergy and the higher social orders:

> And has our Stage a particular Privilege? Is their *Charter* inlarg'd, and are they on the same Foot of Freedom with the *Slaves* in the *Saturnalia*? Must all Men be handled alike? . . . I hope the *Poets* do not intend to revive the old Project of Levelling, and *vote* down the House Of Peers.
>
> (Collier, 1698, pp. 175–6)

Collier's correlation of drama, saturnalian inversion and political struggle for the ideal of a greater equality and democracy is clearly alarmist. Held in the asylum of the theatre pursuing nothing, a modified festive topsy-turvydom was relatively harmless. The historical force of the festive ideal was much more in evidence in the aims of peasant revolts in England and Europe in the late Middle Ages and, in the 1640s, of groups like the Levellers, the Diggers and the Ranters, the suppression of whose egalitarian programmes and practices during the English Revolution formed part of the compromise between the merchant classes and the aristocracy which led to the constitutional monarchy.[46] If the utopian ideal went through one form of transformation and redoubling in the Elizabethan and Jacobean theatre, its main political thrust involved a rejection of the theatre along with other types of traditional festivity and play. In the more radical Puritan programmes distribution would "undoo excesse" not only in the sense of personal wealth but in terms of removing the need for a delirious 'second life' of imaginary plenitude.

In the articulation of these aspirations the festive tradition was itself overtaken by a specifically Judaeo-Christian millenarianism in which the press and the pulpit had much more to contribute than the theatre, the vernacular Bibles providing the appropriate authority from within the dominant religious ideology in the promise that the first shall be last and the Pauline proclamation of a kingdom of heaven on earth, attainable through the struggle of true believers who have "turned the world upside down" (Acts 17:6).[47] The polemicists who attacked the theatre and other forms of 'pastime' did so within a much broader vision than that permitted to the kill-joy hypocrites obsessed with the letter paraded in the stage's travesty of Puritanism. In *The Anatomy of Abuses*, for example, Stubbes mentions the theatre as only one target among many, including a lack of provision for the poor, "the fraudulent dealing of Marchant men" and the enclosures of common land that "bee the causes why rich men eate upp poore men, as beastes do eate grasse".[48]

The Tudor enclosures of the commons and engrossment of estates, whose owners also profited from the expropriation of Church property and the legal chicanery through which large numbers of feudal copyholders were ousted from their lands, produced, on the heaths and in the woodland areas that remained open, communities of 'masterless' men and women who, according to Aubrey, lived "lawless, nobody to govern them . . .having no dependence on anybody".[49] Out of this dispossessed class sprang the more radical ideologies of the English Revolution and the political will to transform them into action, from the peasant revolts of the early seventeenth century to the mobilizing of the New Model Army, "a body of masterless men on the move", which was to become the main political power-base of the Levellers.[50] In its preoccupation with heaths and forests the Shakespearean text occasionally produces fragments of their material reality—in the plight of Lear's "naked wretches", in Corin's predicament when he first meets Rosalind and Celia, or the position of women with no means of subsistence who could be dealt with more economically by the persecution of witches than by a redistribution of wealth. But for the most part its dream displaces these social contradictions, reproducing them on the level of language and representation. While the text's woods and heaths resist self-naturalizing discourses, its material equivalents, threatened by a more pressing form of 'closure', were a site for the production of ideologies intent on making history by means other than "faire is foule" and "handy-dandy". Those who were young in 1606 when Edgar spoke his concluding words in praise of *King Lear* might well have lived to see much more than that play could ever encompass—a year later the Digger insurrection against enclosures in the county in which Shakespeare himself was a property-owner;[51] in 1642 the closing of the theatres, inaugurating the greatest age of English drama; and in 1649, in place of the carnival effigy of a mock-tryant, the official feast of a royal beheading.

Notes

1. *See*: the Scylla and Charybdis episode in Joyce, *Ulysses*, II; Haley, 1978, pp. 407–13.

2. "The critics of *Hamlet* assume that their utterance and argument are true (or false) in relation to an objectively existing set of facts in *Hamlet* or the world. They agree that there is the real *Hamlet* . . . and that tragedy, drama, aesthetic comprehension or response, and dramatic and artistic greatness or merit are also facts in the world which are (ideally) definable in terms of their essences. The aim of the critic, thus, is presumed to be the making of true statements about the nature of *Hamlet* . . . and its relation to life and the world" (Weitz, 1972, pp. 212–13).

3. *See*: Barber, 1959, p. 238; Kuhn, 1977, p. 46; Palmer, 1970, pp. 30–40.

4. Lawrence, 1960, p. 4; Schanzer, 1963, p. 6.

5. "*P*. I love a man without any convictions. How many convictions have you got? *D*. It depends what you mean by 'convictions'." (Peter Cook and Dudley Moore, 'Winkie Wanky Woo', *Derek and Clive*, Island Records, 1976.) The contradiction in Hymen's "holds" is also present in the "*Aufhebung*" ("suspension" or "sublation") of Marx and Hegel (*see* Marx, 1973, p. 32 and Slater, 1977, p. 9).

6. Since this chapter was completed, contemporary theory has begun to find its way to Shakespeare. *See* Introduction, *supra*.

7. *See*: Levin, 1979; Rabkin, 1981; Powell, 1980.

8. Cf. Baldick, 1983, pp. 185–6 on the non-existent colonial education

system in British Honduras; also the Harrison material above. *Caveat lector*.

9. For interpretations concerned with myth and fertility ritual, *see* Tinkler, 1937, and Frye, 1962. On Christian symbolism in the play, *see* Bethell, 1947.

10. Mahood, 1957, p. 186. *See also* Catelvetro, 1570, p. 16, and Hibbard, 1969, p. 146.

11. Attributed to Christopher Ricks (*The Guardian*, 17 January 1981, p. 26). *See also* Richard Webster, "Structuralism and Dry Rot", *The Observer*, 1 February 1981, p. 27.

12. Unattributed quotation (Ian Jack, "On the Trail of the Lonesome Don", *The Sunday Times*, 25 January 1981, p. 13).

13. Frank Kermode in conversation "over a pizza in the Sweeney Todd Pizza Parlour on the banks of the Granta" (Jack, *ibid.*).

14. Culler, 1975; Lodge, 1981. For an account of the ideology of Culler's *Structuralist Poetics*, see Lentricchia, 1980, pp. 101f. Lentricchia and Ryan provide detailed analyses of contemporary theory in North American universities and academic publishing, which space prohibits here.

15. *See*: Ryan, 1982, p. xiv; Eagleton, 1982, p. 148.

16. Marx refers to Henry Charles Carey, who declared that capitalist relations of production were eternal laws of nature and reason, whose free and harmonious working [*frie harmonishces Spiel*] was only disturbed by the intervention of the state" (Marx, 1976–81, I, p. 705). The Everyman translation of *Capital* (London: Dent, 1930) uses the phrase 'harmonious free play" (II, p. 616).

17. Cf. McDonald, 1978, who breathes new life into the Bard by arguing at length that "the *presence* of *absence*" in the structure of *Hamlet* is "the source of its vitality" (pp. 36, 53).

18. *See* Brecht, 1964, pp. 15.

19. In the thick of the Cambridge controversies London's only evening newspaper printed a separate story about Marxist teachers "infiltrating Britain's state schools" under the headline "Red teachers 'moving in' " (*The Standard*, 22 January 1981). Journalists covering the Cambridge affair discovered that "structuralism and Marxism seem sometimes to march hand in hand" (*The Observer*, 18 January 1981, p. 3), an issue its protagonist, Colin MacCabe, was called upon to clarify: "As for Marxism, MacCabe says that he is a Labour Party member and 'Marxist only in some senses'. His approach to literature would definitely not appeal to the orthodox Marxist, he says" (*The Sunday Times*, 25 January 1981, p. 13). For a detailed account of the points of contact between Marxism and post-structuralism, *see* Ryan, 1982.

20. On carnival and deconstruction, *see* Eagleton, 1981, pp. 145–6, 150. Eagleton emphasizes the "plebeian solidarity" of carnival. On some

historical aspects of carnival politics, *see* Ladurie, 1980 and Naipaul, 1972, pp. 267–75.

21. Items appearing on a list published at Romans, near Grenoble, during Carnival in 1580 after the town had been declared a Land of Cockaygne (Ladurie, 1980, p. 182). *See also* Bakhtin, 1968, pp. 5, 14–17.

22. Bakhtin, 1968, pp. 33–4.

23. *See* Barber, pp. 16–23, 51–7.

24. *See* Bradbrook, 1962.

25. Cf. Derrida, 1976, p. 158.

26. Most notably in Barber.

27. *See* Weimann, 1978, pp. 237f.

28. All references to Peele, 1970. On the labyrinth image in Peele and Shakespeare, *see* Evans and Vaughan-Lee, 1980, pp. 165–73.

29. Derrida has strategically overlooked this version of the speech-writing duality, emphasizing its phonophile converse.

30. *See*: 1 Corinthians 3:9; Greenfield, 1968, pp. 236–44; Bakhtin, p. 14.

31. "Mystical explanations are regarded as profound; the truth is that they do not even go the length of being superficial" (Nietzsche, 1960, p. 169).

32. *See*: I. 203; III. 936; III. 1054. On metaphor as "translation", *see* Wilson, 1909, pp. 172–3.

33. *Nichomachean Ethics*, 1137b (Aristotle, 1926, p. 315).

34. Caspari, 1968, p. 270; Hill, 1980, pp. 166f.; Belsey, 1981, pp. 169, 179–81.

35. *See* Brooks, 1979, p. 85n.

36. On the overwhelming predominance in the late sixteenth century of arranged marriages, *see* Stone, 1977, pp. 180–95. Puck's "Country Proverb" on Jack and Jill continues: "The man shall have his Mare againe, and all shall bee well."

37. Stone, 1977, p. 283.

38. *See*: Welsford, 1927, pp. 324f.; Olson, 1957, pp. 95–119.

39. *See*: Northbrooke, 1843, pp. 43–56; Stubbes, 1595, pp. 102f.; Gosson, 1869, pp. 33–44.

40. J. P. Collier discovered in these lines "an assonant grandeur and solemnity almost worthy of our own Alfred Lord Tennyson" (Collier, 1842, p. 135).

41. IV. 1671–8.

42. *See* Danby, 1949, *passim*.

43. I am much indebted in what follows to Weimann's account of *King Lear* (1978, pp. 40–3).

44. *See* Joseph, 1971, pp. 61–3; and Mehl, 1975, pp. 154–62.

45. *See* for example, Kettle, 1964a, pp. 166–9.

46. For the recent debate on the extent of Leveller democracy, *see*: Macpherson, 1962, p. 122; Morton, 1970, pp. 197–219; Arblaster, 1981, pp. 220–37.
47. *See* Hill, 1972, *passim*. "Freedom is the man that will turn the world upside downe" (Winstanley, 1946, p. 316).
48. Stubbes, 1595, pp. 33, 81–3.
49. Hill, 1972, pp. 32f.
50. *Ibid.*, p. 68.
51. Both Hill (1980, p. 21) and Kamen (1976, p. 383) use the term 'Digger' to characterize the 1607–08 uprisings in Warwickshire.

8
End of Carnival

Ban
Ban
Cal
-iban
like to play
pan
at the Car-
nival
(Edward Brathwaite, *The Arrivants*)

"Ile be reveng'd on the whole packe of you"
(*Twelfth Night*, Act 5, Scene 1)

Arrested in Dubiety

George Orwell complained that Shakespeare was "noticeably cautious, not to say cowardly" in expressing opinions that might trouble the rich and powerful and that social criticism in his plays is limited to the outpourings of fools and madmen (Orwell, 1962, p. 116). Here, in an essay on Tolstoy's moralizing and its failure to come to terms with *King Lear*, Orwell dons a similar straitjacket, one which has impeded critics from Dr Johnson to Knights, Traversi and Wilson Knight.[1] It is axiomatic in both the 'literature' of humanism and in deconstruction's 'textuality' that the utterance of opinion is not the point at all. On the contrary, both constructions of the text posit discourses which transcend mundane commitment to particular statements or ideological positions. Kenneth Muir counters Orwell's naivety in another way, pointing to the severity of censorship at a time when no play could be performed without first being licensed by the state (Muir, 1964, pp. 66–74). If Shakespeare's plays had done what Orwell required of them there would be no Shakespeare's plays. The history of literature, like that of criticism, has little to do with the mythic Free World of the imagination where subjects utter their personal visions regardless of the discourses in which they are constructed and positioned—who says what to whom and with what authority, and whose fingers are on the institutional controls.

Because we see in it an "endless sport of signs and similitudes" *Don Quixote* is, for Foucault, "the first modern work of literature" (Foucault, 1970, pp. 48–9). For the same reason, Shakespeare's plays become the first 'great works' of modern English literature where language, in Foucault's terms, "breaks off its old kinship with things and enters into a lonely sovereignty from which it will reappear, in its separated state, *only* as literature" (Foucault, 1970, p. 49).[2] The *merely* literary in this sense cannot be explained by the tautologous idealism with decrees that literary works transcend ideology because to do so is the essential nature of literature. It also escapes Orwell's diagnosis of a failure of nerve in Shakespeare and the mechanically materialist explanation that such an ideological abdication would have been due to censorship. The 'literary' text of

Shakespeare is, rather, produced by its ideological overdetermination and its modes of addressing acting and mimesis at a time when crisis in and conflict between self-naturalizing discourses rendered the very category of representation problematic, along with the 'nature' of language itself.

This crisis, for Foucault, precedes the "Classical age" of European discourse,[3] the conclusion of which precipitates again, in the nineteenth century, this "knowledge closed in upon itself", the "pure language" considered "in nature and function, enigmatic—something that has been called, since that time, *Literature*" (Foucault, 1970, p. 89). In academic curricula this subject, at first considered to be more suitable for women and inferior male students,[4] gradually replaced the classical languages as the primary 'humanizing' force and, after the introduction of compulsory education, worked increasingly to reproduce within the specious 'unity' of a national language and culture distinctions between the classes most fully in command of its riches and those who were restricted to a basic fraction, condemned at the lower echelons of the system to have the plenitude administered as the tantalizing inaccessibility of a law of culture, power and creativity. But this institutional process did not simply call its object into being. The 'literary' discourses described by Foucault at the point of their emergence in the sixteenth century, although later valorized and put to work in education, have a historical specificity. "Dialectically, literature", as Macherey and Balibar point out, "is simultaneously product and material condition of the linguistic division in education" (1978, p. 7). The scapegoat Malvolio's promise of retribution was fulfilled in ways other than the closing of the theatres alone. What made the Shakespearean text, for the emergent Puritan middle-class, something akin to 'only literature' ('pastime', 'idleness', 'play') is a material condition of the bourgeosie's deployment in education, at the height of its power, of 'literature' with a vengeance.

Shakespeare, according to a recent survey of the criticism, is a difficult subject for a Marxist reading, first because "his plays have little of a dogmatic spirit about them" (Powell, 1980, p. 14). Being itself dogmatic, Marxism—according to this standard caricature which overlooks not only Althusser and his successors but also Marx himself—can only be crudely reductive when confronted with subtlety or complexity. The greatest strength of critical pluralism, in contrast, is that it proves nothing—"it produces no developing body of knowledge" and therefore "promotes no orthodoxy", and the very "contradictoriness" of Shakespearean critics only goes to confirm "the inexhaustibility of his plays" (Powell, 1980, pp. 1–2). In this schema the essentially literary, here specifically Shakespearean, text claims as an inherent characteristic the place ascribed to it in Macherey and Balibar's account of its institutional *production* as "something outside (and above) the process of education, which is merely able to disseminate literature, and to comment on it exhaustively, though with no possibility of finally capturing it" (Macherey and Balibar, 1978, p. 7). In this process the *constitutive* ideological operations of teaching and criticism modestly renounce their place in production for that of a subservient, parasitic discourse which celebrates but can never contain a central essence, the aesthetic tremor of "literary style" in which the text works its imaginary reconciliations and moves towards a transcendent unity and harmony "by displacing the ensemble of ideological contradictions on to a single one, or a single aspect, the linguistic conflict itself' (Macherey and Balibar, 1978, p. 9).

The criticism which, in this construction, is strictly secondary perpetuates the concealed work of 'literature' in reproducing the relations of production within the divided unity of a common language, while also raiding this inexhaustible fund of representations for specific moral and metaphysical closures that may then be referred back to the unending handy-dandy of a "Yes, but" pluralist debate. In concrete terms this combination of statement and modest renunciation ranges from the interpretation of what the text is 'really saying' to the gilt-edged moralizing which discovers Shakespeare not so much stating as courageously probing or profoundly interrogating. On the author's behalf this latter approach translates " 'last night I was writing a play' " into " 'last night I was engaged in obstinately questioning some of the things that are most deeply disturbing in human life' " (Holloway, 1961, p. 5), and its finest hour is probably D. G. James's discovery in *Hamlet* of Shakespeare's "momentous and profound intention" of exploring "a mind arrested in dubiety before the awful problem of life" (James, 1951, p. 77). Here in all its splendour is the sedentary heroism of the bourgeois critic himself, subtitled "What I did in the long vacation" and held in the stifling orthodoxy of the Great Issues that have supposedly incapacitated all men and women everywhere since time immemorial—Birth, Death, Time, Defecation, the sensitive individual's innate need to obstinately question etc.[5]

In Raymond Powell's equation 'literature' and this type of criticism cohabit successfully while dogma has the status of a scapegoat or supplement. Be it Marxist, a non-Marxist theory of discourse such as Foucault's, feminist or of any complexion that renounces the political paralysis of a mind arrested in dubiety and the pointlessness of a pluralist 'debate' which depends on there being no resolution, dogma is for humanism the excrescence, the thing that should not have been added. Deconstruction, which has a way with such supplements, can disclose the dogmas erected on unified subjects and signs that precede the very limited plurality in traditional forms of reading favoured by the discourse Powell endorses. The poststructuralist text may also serve as a horizon for a history of the more obvious dogmatic productions of a criticism that presents itself as merely explanatory—the "modesty, grace and tenderness" of Victorian womanhood, for example, Kermode's imperial *Tempest*, or Dover Wilson's counter-revolutionary *Hamlet*.[6] At first glance deconstruction has all the appeal of an industrial accident which has blown open the organization's secret files and maimed only the representatives of an invisible management. Its usefulness is limited, however, to that of a theoretical interregnum or a catalyst. As a form of inversion stripped of carnival's class solidarity,[7] it can remain arrested in the position of a delirious 'second life' of bourgeois criticism which reinforces the more fundamental ideological work of an indeterminate literary language. Its unimaginable dominance in literary studies could only underline the existing mark of triviality and supplementarity placed on the 'humanities' in the educational apparatus as a whole.[8] At the end of carnival there are only material conditions of a less dizzy kind than those ascribed to the playfully material text, and a number of discourses—deconstruction included—which produce their objects in ways that either articulate or attempt to displace and gloss over the more fundamental historical contradictions. In the aftermath there is no stigmatized 'dogma' to call an urbane impartiality into being, no approach that is inherently more 'natural' or 'human' than others.

Critical Awareness

A recognition that criticism, in its guise of endlessly circling an immutable object, is complicit in producing 'literature' creates unique opportunities for the favoured Anglo-American doctrines of pluralism and balance to be put into effect in literature teaching for the first time. Rather than a token acknowledgment of such diverse influences as Marx, Foucault, psychoanalysis, feminism, structuralism and deconstruction—often accomplished by cramming as many of these functions as possible into the appointment of one bright new member of faculty— this would imply an equalizing of discourses and their proponents. In the process the sincere personal pluralist who sees all points of view at once should remain a stalwart minority, steering the middle path and speaking for the generic humanist subject 'Man' who, hitherto, has usually succeeded in remaining white, male and middle-class. The longer the delay, the more a liberal education's doctrine of balance comes to resemble the one-handed juggling of the capitalist press and the mass-media. Meanwhile there are already signs that the humanist critic's anxieties in the face of the awful problem of life are being compounded by a meta-paranoia of theoretical reaction, running from the fear of 'foreign muck' expressed at Cambridge in 1980 to the gentler ironies directed more recently at the "*messieurs et mesdames* of New Accents".[9]

A picture emerges in Britain of a minor Reformation in English Studies, complete with a Church which shows signs of reneging on its central doctrines at the moment they are tested, well-meaning revisionists prepared to address the issues in the interest of unity, and a variety of more radical positions which have accomplished in relation to each other a more genuine pluralism and tolerance in the common cause of confronting the saints and holy images of literature and the practices of reading that keep them in place. If the main line of demarcation is an acknowledged theory of the sign, the subject and ideology, there is no reason why this should not be crossed in an attempt to test the doctrine of pluralism. Basic versions of materialism and vulgar feminism, for example, may need to be accommodated, with a Christopher Cauldwell possibly preparing the ground for a Macherey, and Marilyn French acting as a stepping-stone to Cixous and Kristeva. This would mean not only an end to the hounding of Marxist and feminist literature teachers in schools but positive discrimination in their favour to break the monopoly of vulgar liberal-humanism. Ideological determination does not suddenly begin at the level of higher education and published criticism, and the sky falling on Chicken Licken is as amenable to a rudimentary deconstruction as it is to an indoctrination in empiricism and idealism. Theory is what is happening from the outset, and those who feel that children are innately better equipped to absorb the 'unmediated' essences and phenomena of the self-naturalizing sign than the principles of system and structure should be seated in front of a computer next to the ten year olds who, in a decade, will be adding another twist to the spiral of liberal anxiety.

The variety of interpretations of Shakespeare proves not so much the inexhaustibility of the text as the productive, rather than merely parasitic, operations of all forms of critical discourse. The Prado Museum's *Guide* to its collections, having given a date for *Las Meninas* and identified its 'characters', praises Velazquez's mastery of perspective and colour before inviting the spectator to be "transported back" by his realism "into the Alcázar of Madrid to contemplate this intimate scene of court life at the time of Philip IV" (Prado, 1976, no. 16). This representation of the painting, with its unproblematic 'author', subjects and 'representation', is as different from Foucault's as Pierre Menard's *Don Quixote*, in Borges's story,[10] is from that of Cervantes or, indeed, Foucault's version of the same text. A revaluation of the subservient role of criticism, while banishing 'literature' or 'art' in an idealist sense, does not simply reverse the position of dominant and supplement, parasite and host, but holds both in the common category of discourse. The problem of distinguishing a 'literary' from a 'critical' language in the work of such modern writers as Borges, Barthes, Lacan, Derrida, A. E. Sims and Edward

Harrison only intensifies the dilemmas implicit in deciding, for example, what may or may not be called seventeenth-century English literature. This already fraught relationship is further complicated in the work of Shakespeare and other dramatic texts re-presented as literature by the level of dramatic production, in which the text may, traditionally, either become more fully and ideally itself or be subjected to less responsible forms of interpretation than those circumscribed by 'objective' and purely 'professional' standards of scholarship. The implication here for 'pluralism' and 'balance' in education is that the study of literature, however varied the critical 'approaches', is already a loaded activity unless made answerable to a larger discipline of semiotics or cultural studies which can theorize, among other things, the production of the literature-criticism pairing within a broader historical ensemble of discourses.

The Barbadian writer George Lamming describes Ariel as "a lackey", the "archetypal spy" and "the embodiment—when and if made flesh—of the perfect and unspeakable secret police". He also lists some of the early methods of persuading slaves to work, which stand between a modern reader and the "sadism" of Prospero when confronted with the threat of Caliban's revolt:

> In some cases, they were roasted, others were buried alive up to the neck, their heads smeared with sugar that the flies might devour them; they were fastened to nests of wasps, made to eat their excrement, drink their urine, and lick the saliva of other slaves. A great pastime too, was to fill them up with gunpowder and strike a match somewhere near the hole of the arse.
> (Lamming, 1960, pp. 98–9)

These comments appear in a critical essay, but one which has less in common with a detached humanist criticism than with other Caribbean and Latin American reworkings of *The Tempest*—in fiction, poetry, revolutionary pamphlets and in political theory—that seize a fable of colonial oppressor and slave and dialectically point its historical trajectory rather than bestowing on it hermeneutic rites appropriate to a sacred text.[11] This mode of *overtly* ideological criticism, which spans interpretation and 'fictioning', displaces the formalistic distinction between the inexhaustible 'literary' text and the parasitic commentary that text keeps in perpetual motion. From the vantage point of this ideological criticism the political dimensions of an essentialist 'literature' and the subjects it reaffirms are more clearly visible: "In France one says, 'He talks like a book'. In Martinique, 'He talks like a white man'" (Fanon, 1970, p. 16). Kermode's 'neutral' or 'white' *Tempest*, in contrast, while supplying invaluable information on sixteenth-century and early seventeenth-century discourses on exploration and colonization, deletes the part necessarily played in any reproduction of the play (critical, theatrical or fictional) by the subsequent history of these discourses. Kermode's presentation shares its ideological 'innocence' with other views of Shakespeare's skills and essential purpose which display more openly the relations of power that sustain a magisterial disinterestedness. In 1777, for example, Maurice Morgann praised Shakespeare for recognizing that in the portrayal of character "climate and complexion demand their influence", and that Othello's " '*Be thus when thou art dead, and I will kill thee, and love thee after*' is a sentiment characteristic of, and fit only to be uttered by a Moor" (Vickers, 1974–81, VI, p. 168), an insight into race only slightly modified in Laurence Olivier's interpretation of the same role for the 1964 National Theatre production: "It is the only play in the whole of Shakespeare in which a man kills a woman, and if Shakespeare has an idea he goes all out for it. He knows very well that for a black man to kill a white woman is a very big thrill indeed" (*cit.* Elsom and Tomalin, 1978, p. 161).[12]

In a traditional demarcation of disciplines this broad configuration of discourses, part of the material history that determines contemporary readings of *The Tempest* and *Othello*, would be dispersed in several directions—to Politics, French or Caribbean Literature, Theatre History, the History of Criticism. A conventional English course would have no place for most of them. Students might be encouraged to see the film of Olivier's *Othello*, which 'brings the words on the page to life', but not to spend a great deal of time on the production's specific racial or sexual presuppositions. Since the ultimate requirement will be essays on such topics as 'Art and Nature', 'motiveless malignity', tragic form, or experimentation in the late plays—all designed to limit discussion 'in the interest of the student' to *purely* literary or dramatic issues—Kermode's *Tempest* and other readings that share its discursive closures are much more likely to be recommended than Fanon, Césaire, Lamming or anyone else who offers temptations to 'wander off' into sociology, politics or 'subjective judgments'. In a broader discipline of semiotics or cultural studies—encompassing theories of the subject, the sign and ideology—the unity of an authorial intention hunted by Morgann, Olivier, Kermode and most modern Shakespeare criticism would, if recoverable at all, be subject to the discourses and social contradictions that constitute the text without ever being fully recognized or resolved in it.[13] Here the diversity of commentaries, theatrical productions and 'literary' reworkings become part of the subsequent history of these discourses, now encompassing the text itself and its modes of institutional reproduction. Brecht's revisions of Shakespeare, for example, or Césaire's *Une Tempête* amount to a criticism which denies the text its monumental, inviolable status and discovers its most important 'meanings' in the historical process in which that very status is eventually produced. Conversely, Kermode's type of criticism is a *mise en scène*, with its discursive emphases and exclusions, and a performance in the bourgeois theatre which aims to remain faithful to the canonized text is always already a 'literary' rewriting of Shakespeare.

A semiotics of discourse which goes beyond the immobilizing dogma of 'literature' and its critical 'approaches' also escapes the limiting vertical imperative of traditional English Studies, which directs criticism back to an original 'presence' in the literary work, produces its periods, authors and influences, and determines linear, empiricist histories of genre, criticism, the theatre, and so on. Olivier's *Othello*, for example, may be less significant in relation to Shakespeare's intentions or the history of the play in production than to a number of discourses that are 'extraneous' as far as the pedagogical presuppositions of English Literature are concerned but which nevertheless determine the meaning of such an authoritative reproduction of a canonical text in the 1960s. Olivier's comment on the "big thrill" experienced by black men who kill white women works in the same ideological context as the speeches of Martin Luther King, Eldridge Cleaver's *Soul on Ice*, and the production in the language of British politicians and the mass-media of the 'immigrant problem' as a racialist simplification of a number of strains and contradictions in the mixed economy. A truly 'liberal' education would be less concerned with the relation of Olivier's interpretation to other stabs at the inexhaustible essence of the play than to BBC television's "Black and White Minstrel Show", the emphasis on racial and national stereotypes in broadcast comedy, later legislation for civil rights and racial equality in the United States and the United Kingdom, and the role in bringing this about of both violent and non-violent protest. In relation to this analysis of Shakespeare the readings of Fanon, Lamming and Césaire become as important as that of Kermode, and the text is no longer simply its universal self, an island surrounded by strategic silences, but the history of its material production which, in this case, would include the fact that Olivier's National Theatre *Othello* was financed in part by black tax-payers statistically very unlikely to be there to ask for a refund or to experience the 'big thrill' of massacring the white audience.

The gains in redefining 'English', expanding the narrow focus on 'literature' into a broader concern with language, discourse and culture, must be balanced against the losses. Students would probably not read as many of the 'great works' so the consumption of the body of Arnoldian 'culture' leading to a personal cultivation and refinement would be scaled down. But the ability to be critical, perhaps more fully and flexibly so, would be fostered in other ways. If a study of literature, seen as something like "language charged with meaning to the utmost possible degree" (Pound) ever enabled pupils and students to master the discursive practices of vernacular English at large, it is doubtful if this remains true, particularly in the case of the mass media. The experience of having read *Romeo and Juliet* and analysed its characters and themes does less to 'humanize' sixteen-year-old school-leavers and equip them against the slick textuality of television commercials or the hidden persuasions of news and current affairs programming than a direct analysis of the codes of such discourses, which will continue to affect their lives daily. Earlier in the system the sky that terrorizes Chicken Licken might more profitably fall on Benny Hill. The transfer of resources and the retraining that such a shift in priorities would involve does not, of course, rule out the survival of literary production as an object of study, or of conventional English Literature in a more marginal and optional position comparable to that occupied by Cultural or Communication Studies in Britain at present. English Literature's central role is, however, no longer defensible in terms of the stated principles that have traditionally sustained it, and without some version of the Arnold/Newbolt theory of literary 'culture' as essentially a 'humanizing' force and a means of 'grace' the study of literature alone moves some way in the direction of an antiquarian specialism. At the beginning of 1984, when an American president whose sensibilities seemed to have been nurtured by Walt Disney, *Star Wars* and his own Hollywood westerns defended intellectual and artistic freedom against a former head of the KGB who was also a connoisseur of Beckett, the old theology of 'culture'—already haunted by the now familiar figure of the commandant who unwinds with Goethe and Beethoven after a day at the gas-ovens—seemed to be on its last legs. But its ideology was marked from the outset by the historical contradictions it claimed to resolve. The Victorian 'apostle of culture' had a professional role to fulfil among Welsh school-children, and Sir Henry Newbolt was also a poet, whose inexhaustible creations include "A Ballad of John Nicholson", on the 1857 Indian Mutiny, in which the "proud and sly" rebel leader, Mehtab Singh, finally surrenders recognizing that "when the strong command, obedience is best".[14] At stake is a critical awareness which may politely decline the Newbolt tradition's invitation to "play up, and play the game", and begin to re-examine the rules.

Mock Tudor

In his presidential address to the English Association in 1928 Newbolt, lamenting "our nine days' civil war" during the General Strike two years earlier, appealed for a sense of national unity in which everyone could forget that classes existed.[15] Here, re-emerging in a more openly political form, is the blend of nationalist idealism and pragmatic mystification characteristic of the Newbolt Committee's critical and educational theory. A voluntary freeze on class-consciousness could only be a dream of arresting history and indefinitely confirming the existing hegemonic order. The proposal that Newbolt English and its legacy should now, voluntarily and in the declared spirit of liberal pluralism and balance, give way to a broader and more genuinely critical discipline may itself be utopian. If so, it is still a means of confronting the dominant discourse on the ground of its own idealism, forcing it to disclose its contradictions, and developing the critical awareness of those who have nothing to gain from its spiritual riches or mystical unities—text, nation, culture, Man. This implies a continuous process of what Barthes called "semioclasm", directed against the self-naturalizing procedures of this discourse and coupled with a production of different texts and different criticisms. It also involves a revaluation of the historical 'backgrounds' produced in traditional criticism and the need, in Foucault's terms, to "fiction" a different history, which starts from an acknowledged "political reality" rather than a theology of disinterested idealism (Foucault, 1979, pp. 74–5). [16]

This need is particularly acute in relation to Shakespeare, whose work, in the critical tradition of Eliot, Leavis and Tillyard, emerges from and reflects the unity of "a lost Elizabethan Utopia", [17] an organic community of undissociated sensibilities experiencing together thoughts as immediate as the smell of a rose and an unbroken harmony of moral, religious and political perceptions. In this context the 'groundlings', who have also done service in the denigration of popular taste, become part of an idealized order in which the little world of the theatre stands in for a society which distils the virtues of national and cultural unity. [18] For anyone brought up on this view of history, in many ways an extension of Tudor propaganda, the conflicts of opinion on exploration and colonization, for example, or the emergence of active feminist protest in London from the 1580s on, come as something of a surprise, as does Marx's account of the suffering of large numbers of English men and women who were the victims of capitalism's period of "primitive accumulation". [19] The myth of a unified culture, an Eden before the division and Fall of the seventeenth century, has to be severely qualified by a history of rebellions against the crown, uneasy compromise in religion, the persecution of a mass driven from their land by enclosure and engrossment, and inflation, which became particularly acute in the years when Shakespeare was establishing himself in the theatre. During the sixteenth century as a whole, when increasing numbers of people were made dependent on wages, the real purchasing power of those wages fell by two-thirds. While earnings for artisans and agricultural labourers were at roughly the same level in 1610 as they had been in 1565, prices rose by fifty percent during the same period. This process was to continue into the seventeenth century, and for a labourer born in 1580 real earnings would never be more than half those of his great-grandfather.[20]

To conjure up an 'organic unity' from these crises in the course of a major transition from one social and economic order to another is as considerable a feat of the historical imagination as the construction of a Shakespearean text which, while producing an inexhaustible plurality of meanings for all people at all times, remains a paradigm of moral and aesthetic unity which captures both the essence of its particular cultural moment and the most abiding concerns of humanity. An initial breach in this extraordinary fiction may be brought about by readings that take up committed positions contrary to that of the idealized universal reader of humanism. These compel the text to signify not 'in its own terms' but in the context of a discourse—feminist, Marxist or anti-colonialist, for example—which recognizes that any production of the text is *for* a particular interpretation of history, which is not simply a disinterested chronicle but a selective production of the past for the present with a stake in *making* history or, in the case of the discourse under attack, prolonging the existing set of historical relations by transforming history into 'nature'.

These are the readings that the mainstream of criticism would regard as 'dogmatic', regretting their 'inflexibility' but patronizing any useful empirical insights they might happen to deliver in unguarded moments of intuition. On the edge of the dominant discourse, they are always faced with the temptation of lapsing back into confirming its aesthetics and only *revising* its view of the text and history by adding additional data. So Shakespeare might be seen as an author who marshals his characters and themes to make essentially "feminist" points, for example, or to reaffirm a repressive "gender principle".[21] A reading of *The Tempest* antagonistic to the values of Prospero might still discover Shakespeare's genius in his acute *anticipation* of "the psychology of colonization".[22] In departing from the limited pluralism of more familiar interpretations held in the dogma of no dogma, such readings may indirectly accentuate historical contradictions by giving priority to subject-positions invisible or supplementary in conventional histories, but at the cost of reproducing an authoritative source for the original text in the mind of the one who expresses his coherent vision. Unity, be it textual or cultural, is the fetish of humanist criticism and aesthetics.[23] And a materialism for which contradiction in the social formation and the subject takes priority as the dynamic of historical change must produce a text in which the fictional unity that cuts it free from history and gives it the status of a cultural commodity is also torn apart. The object of a theory which goes beyond an idealist distinction between literature and criticism and concerns itself with literary production is, as Macherey maintains, a determinate insufficiency and disorder, the "incompleteness which actually shapes the work" and bursts through its very "letter", which is "fissured, unmade even in its making" (Macherey, 1978, pp. 79, 155).

Graffiti

Foucault's recognition of a need to "fiction" a different history, "starting from a political reality", is extended by Catherine Belsey to the study and teaching of literature: "the literary institution has 'fictioned' a criticism which protests its own truth; we must instead 'fiction' a literature which renders up our true history in the interests of a politics of change" (Belsey, 1983, p. 26). Because they appear on every course, Shakespeare's plays are as good a place to start as any. Tolstoy regarded their survival and continuing reputation as one in a long series of "epidemic suggestions", comparable to the Crusades, the quest for the Philosopher's Stone, and the mania in Holland for tulip growing.[24] This explanation, however comforting, is clearly not good enough, but neither, at the other end of the scale, is the idealist belief in an objective test of time as proof of an immortal and universal value or significance.

Terry Eagleton argues that a future society may find nothing of interest in these plays and that such a society, in which "Shakespeare would be no more valuable than much present-day graffiti", might conceivably arise "from a general human enrichment" (Eagleton, 1983, pp. 11–12). If Shakespeare's expensive life-support systems in English education and subsidized 'culture' were turned off now and the resources transferred elsewhere, to the National Health Service for example, this society might well emerge sooner than expected, and it has always been here, at least in part, for most British men and women. In this case the Longinian test of time cannot itself be tested as long as Shakespeare's work remains an ideological stick for some and a carrot for those who come to fully appreciate it only as part of a much wider acculturation and privilege. The work's longevity cannot be entirely divorced from an inverted form of censorship which ensures an institutional boosting of the volume on certain texts and discourses. As far as Shakespeare is concerned it is rare for a moratorium on this boosting to be allowed. It was attempted in China during the Cultural Revolution and the experiment failed not because of a clamouring of starved sensibilities for nourishment but through a turning of political sights back to the West and the sunset of cultural imperialism. Shakespeare, in the form of an English production of *Measure for Measure*, returned to Beijing along with the Coca-Cola advertisements. But since they are inescapably *there*, Shakespeare's plays can be produced as texts for feminism, Marxism and other theories of discourse and ideology: as sites for a study of historical discontinuities in such areas as language, the subject, sovereignty, gender and race,[25] and as works that submit the material history of their reproduction for analysis rather than selective assimilation to the contraband courses concealed in the baggage of traditional English Literature—on history, moral philosophy, 'human nature' and elocution. Since all 'approaches' to literature are sustained by a theory, 'dogma' will no longer be useful as a term of abuse, except perhaps for a discourse which denies its status as such and attempts to silence those that do not.

This can only be a first step. The fact that a text has "no

single or uniquely privileged meaning" and that a critical reading *makes* it signify in relation to a particular set of priorities[26] does not imply that the canon and the 'great traditions' already produced within one critical ideology will be necessarily respected and left intact in others. There are clearly 'literatures' for feminism and Marxism, as well as writing from colonized and post-colonial cultures, that remain insufficiently represented on most existing courses. And for a discipline in which the relationship of literature to criticism is itself part of a larger theory of discourse, the Elizabethan rhetorics might be a better place than Shakespeare at which to begin a historical study. To "fiction" a new literature, then, implies more than refurbishing the old. In the topography of academic English, Shakespeare's plays, emanating from a unified Elizabethan culture, are the peaks every student must scale successfully on the road to refined sensibilities and an enhanced critical awareness. The process of shaping this journey and its setting must now be made an object of inquiry alongside a projection of other ways of landscaping discourse. In this inquiry the concept of an absolute aesthetic value is itself subject to the question "Valuable for whom, and for what?" Literature has always done more than to sit there being complex, harmonious and sublime. The propagation and funding of literary studies in education have been justified in terms of value *for* a particular construction of personal refinement and its relation to the life of the culture, literature's function being to humanize and make critical. But in a context of increasing theoretical and political conflict, such terms are rendered problematic, and with them the normative operations of how 'we feel' about a particular aesthetic effect or how 'one responds' to a text. "We", writes Michel Pêcheux, is now only a 'shifter' whose function is to support "the universal orator's unlimited persuasive power over himself as universal audience" (1982, p. 46). What 'we' prefer and value cannot ultimately be disentangled from either a conservatism of political renunciation or an activism in confronting a 'literature' which has become "a crucial mechanism by which the language and ideology of an imperialist class establishes its hegemony" (Eagleton, 1976, p. 55).[27] In this our response to 'we' is no longer one, and we respond to 'one' severally.

"If in time, as in place", wrote Thomas Hobbes, "there were

degrees of high and low, I verily believe that the highest of time would be that which passed between the years 1640 and 1660".[28] We can all agree that this high ground in English history is the best point at which to begin fictioning a new literature, drawn out of the silences around the hegemonic unities of the old. In the early sixteenth century Thomas Müntzer proclaimed that "authority should be vested in the Common people", declared princes worthy only of contempt and championed the peasants of the Harz and Thuringia in violent struggle against enclosures and evictions, sanctioning the Elect to kill those who stood in the way of freedom and equality.[29] As far as it could, the Elizabethan compromise squeezed out Anabaptism and the social implications of other radical religious ideologies while the monarchy consolidated its power and bureaucracy. By 1649, however, a revolution had been successfully begun in England and the reigning monarch despatched. In the process, those who benefited very little from the Elizabethan 'unity' idealized by Tillyard, Leavis and Eliot gained a voice and an increasing involvement in political activity. 'Masterless men' fought in the New Model Army and, along with artisans, farm labourers, small merchants and the poor of the larger towns and cities, made up the bulk of several large and over a hundred smaller radical sects devoted to different conceptions of a more just and egalitarian future. Arguments have been put forward for some improvement in the position of women in the sixteenth century, mainly through the influence of humanism and Protestantism,[30] although the presence of Elizabeth on the throne seems to have accomplished little for women in general.[31] But during the seventeenth century, and particularly in the religious movements of the 1640s, the opportunities available to women for participation and leadership increased dramatically. While only men could play an active part in the Catholic Church and the Church of England, in the sectarian congregations of the Civil War period women could debate, vote, prophesy and preach, enjoying the equal share in Church government denied to them during the reign of Elizabeth, when separatist groups with similar aspirations were compelled either to meet in secret or to emigrate to Holland or America.[32]

This unique period in English history produced a literature

which has no place in the official canon. It is much too extensive to consider here in any detail, but a number of general considerations arising from it have a bearing on the place of Shakespeare's text in the theorizing of a new 'literature' within the broader discipline that will come to occupy the place of academic English. If a feminist reading that remains at the level of plot, theme and what Shakespeare 'thinks' or 'reflects' is limited in comparison to one that can account for the text's particular production and problematization of gender, this more sophisticated reading must, in turn, open onto a historical analysis of discourse—an analysis in which Rosalind's "If I were a woman", for example, or the. polymorphous "nothing" between Ophelia's legs, can be seen to produce their contradictions with a different historical and institutional force from that of the language of women who, in the 1640s and 1650s, gained access to the means of literary production in their own capacity rather than that of 'representations' or surrogate men. In the prophecies of Eleanor Davies, Mary Cary and Anna Trapuel, for instance, the symbolic order which affirms an ideological division of gender as already accomplished outside language in 'nature' is disturbed, just as it is in Shakespeare's text, but in a discourse which involves women in an ecstatic 'fictioning' of political futures rather than an involuted and ideologically self-mutilating play of boys being girls being boys. [33]

The problematization of the subject generally is marked by a comparable discursive difference between, on the one hand, a displacement of historical contradictions onto the doubleness of language and dramatic action and, on the other, their insertion into forms of social action no longer held in an unrelenting supplementarity in the semiotic asylum of the theatre. By 1653 the morbid perception of Tourneur's Vindice, that "Surely we're all mad people, and they/Whom we think are, are not" (*The Revenger's Tragedy*, III. v. 79–80), had been translated into a cause for celebration—"If madness be in the heart of every man, *Eccles*, 9:3 then this is the island of Great Bedlam . . . come, let's all be mad together", [34] while the divided and broken 'characters' of Shakespeare's text had been overtaken by revolutionary subjects-in-process like Giles Calvert, whose "I" seeks both extinction and plenitude:

I, either am or would be nothing, and see the Lord all, in all, in me. I am, or would be nothing. But by the grace of God I am what I am in I am, that I am. So I am in the Spirit—The Kings and the Queenes and the Princely Progenies, and the Presbyters, the Pastors, Teachers, and the Independents, and the Anabaptists, and the Seekers, and the Family of Loves, and all in the Spirit; in a word God, Christ, the Saints.[35]

This subject, with its repetitions, tautologies and defamiliarized syntax, is at once an apotheosis and a scattering of individualism. It appears time and again in the late 1640s, particularly in the work of the Ranters whose leader, Abiezer Coppe, writes from a womb of "still Eternity" as one without mother, father, wife or name, proclaiming against distinctions of 'mine' and 'his' in a voice that has become all voices, human and divine.[36]

The crisis of the subject is also that of the naturalized sign, and the language of the antinomian millenium is an inversion of orthodox discourses. Coppe prophesies the overturning of a world already turned upside-down, in which the timidly and formalistically righteous "call Good Evill, and Evill Good; Light Darknesse, and Darknesse Light; Truth Blasphemy, and Blasphemy Truth", while Lawrence Clarkson proclaims that "Light and Darkness are both alike" to the enlightened, and that "Devil is God, Hell is Heaven, Sin Holiness, Damnation Salvation".[37] The links here with an earlier tradition of festive inversion and indulgence are much stronger than those in Elizabethan and Jacobean drama. Contemporaries describe the Ranters in terms of their revelry and familiarity—the customary term of address for all was "fellow creature"—their whistling, singing, dancing and enjoyment of sexual intercourse "which is not done in corners".[38] Coppe was an actor in a society in which drama was no longer cordoned off in the theatre. In *A Fiery Flying Roll* he describes his activities in London in 1649, charging the coaches of the wealthy and confronting "so many hundreds of men and women of the greater rank" in the streets, "with my hand stretched out, my hat cock't up, staring on them as if I would look through them, and day and night with a huge loud voice proclaiming the day of the Lord" (Coppe, 1649, II, p. 9). When finally arrested and investigated by a Parliamentary Committee, Coppe responded

by feigning madness, as a number of his revolutionary pre-
decessors had done in similar circumstances, throwing pears,
apples and nutshells around the room.[39] The only missing component in this theatricality is the clear institutional distinction
between stage and audience, fiction and reality, that would
render it innocuous, and the Ranter carnival differed from the
medieval popular feast primarily in that it envisaged no end.

In the literature of this period, during which censorship of
the press briefly lapsed,[40] social criticism and denunciation are
unequivocal. Gerrard Winstanley transforms a Jacobean 'handy
dandy' into the "plain truth" that "theeves and murderers,
upheld by preaching witches and deceivers, rule the Nations:
and for the present, the Laws and Government of the world, are
laws of darknesse, and the divell's Kingdome" (Winstanley,
1941, p. 316). The power of Abiezer Coppe's rhetoric makes
the language of the mad Lear sound like an exercise in under-
statement:

> I say (once more) deliver, deliver, deliver, my money which
> thou hast . . . to poor creeples, lazars, yea to rogues, thieves,
> whores, and cut-purses, who are the flesh of thy flesh, and every
> whit as good as thy self . . .
> The plague of God is in your purses, barns, houses, horses,
> murrain will take your hogs, (O ye fat swine of the earth) who
> shall shortly go to the knife, and be hung up i'th roof,
> except—blasting, mill-dew, locusts, caterpillars, yea fire your
> houses and goods, take your corn and fruit, the moth your gar-
> ments, and the rot your sheep, did you not see my hand, this
> last year, stretched out?
> You did not see.
> My hand is stretched out still.
> Your gold and silver, though you can't see it, is cankered, the
> rust of them is witness against you . . .
> The rust of your silver, I say, shall eat your flesh as it were
> fire . . .
> . . . give, give, give, give up, give up your houses, horses,
> goods, gold, lands, give up, account nothing your own, have
> ALL THINGS common.
>
> (Coppe, 1649, II, pp. 2–3)

English utopias of the seventeenth century are less dependent
on overtly imaginary elements than their more 'literary' pre-

decessors, and tend towards programmes that seek their vali-
dation in practice.[41] By any standard of absolute aesthetic
value, the utopian and millenarian writing of the 1640s
produced no single 'great work' and, as a whole, it may have no
major contribution to make to what one account of the genre
calls "a history of thought that frankly favours the high and
middle culture" (Manuel and Manuel, 1979, p. 332). Coppe,
for example, shows little concern for 'universal significance',
balance or complexity, and when God speaks in him His
preoccupations are often parochial, transient and not in the best
of taste.[42] If this type of work does not qualify for attention
under a traditional definition of literature, it has nevertheless an
important bearing on the institutional criteria that determine
what literature is, particularly as so many of the discourses that
cross the Shakespearean text are reproduced here, only a few
decades later, at a time when the historical contradictions
cosmetically sealed in the Elizabethan compromise, and displaced to the level of signs in the theatre, affirm their presence
in a crisis in which discourse shows more pressing concerns than
supplementarity, self-scrutiny and play.

In the case of the Ranters some of these continuities are
striking, particularly so in a "fair is foul" unseating of ethical
absolutes, the words of fools who restore 'truth' by doubly
corrupting an already corrupt language, the shaking of the
"single state" of man, and the festive tradition's combination of
inversion and social criticism. Yeats's view that our argument
with others produces only rhetoric while true poetry comes
from our argument with ourselves may be axiomatic in the
construction of a 'literature' in which complexity and the free
flow of the imagination can only be inhibited by unyielding
political conviction. But through the texts of the 1640s it is
possible to turn this formulation upside-down and discover
again in Shakespeare a rhetoric which is, in Foucault's terms,
"*only* literature", a language turned in on itself, capable of
producing its imaginary transcendences, distances and redou-
blings only within an ideology which masters it and always
draws it back into the finite historical processes of hegemony
and class struggle.

Coppe's partial recantation, written from Newgate Prison, is
an awakening from "such dainties, that the tongues of men &

angels cannot express", from "Unfathomable, unspeakable
mysteries and glories" of which the dreamer can say "I was
(really, in very deed) besides myself' and "I have been
conversant with BEASTS" (Coppe, 1651, preface)[43] Coppe was
born in Warwick, within spitting distance of Stratford-upon-
Avon, only three years after Shakespeare's death, and although
such pastimes would obviously have been low on his list of
priorities, there is no evidence to suggest that he was unaware
of the plays. For anyone so minded there might be a note or
query here in relation to the recantation, on a recurrence of
Bottom's dream in a backwater of English literature. But this,
and related works by Coppe and his contemporaries, suggest
other ways of fictioning a national literature, in which periods
of intense contradiction might take priority over those of
relative unity, and a play like *A Midsummer Night's Dream* could
itself be seen as one of the backwaters of a tradition which values
texts that point a continuing historical struggle for equality and
democracy. In *The Making of the English Working Class*, E. P.
Thompson notes that the plebeian theatre of the early nineteenth century had little "artistic merit" but that Shakespeare
was a positive influence on the "sensibility" of Radical and
Chartist journalists, who "were wont to cap their arguments
with Shakespearian quotations" (Thompson, 1968, p. 809).
Shakespeare's text, as is clear from this example, can be
appropriated to the needs of any political cause, but the cultural
presuppositions called into play when they are cited may, in
many cases, be counter-productive. A future in which a
developed "critical awareness" can be achieved without the help
of Shakespeare is no more intimidating than a present in which
English graduates need know nothing of Winstanley and
Coppe.[44]

In an investigation of the concealed political agenda of New
Criticism, Terence Hawkes touches on the criteria that determine which texts make up English Literature's informal history
of the best writing the language and culture has produced.
Ideological presuppositions and "the nature of man's moral,
psychological and social being" are, as Hawkes argues, evident
in the assumptions of New Criticism about such matters as
" 'taste' and 'sensitivity' " and in "its habit of speaking as if they
were objective and unchanging human qualities, unaffected by

historical and economic pressures". New Criticism's use of complexity, ambiguity and balance as aesthetic norms sustains, against single-mindedness, commitment and forceful direct action, "the characteristic bourgeois concern for a 'fixed' and established, unchanging reality", and does so by admiring a sophistication, poise and wit that represent the values of "a decaying aristocracy, characteristically revered by a sycophantic middle-class" (Hawkes, 1977, p. 155).

Exiled from this hegemony of taste, the texts that emerged from what Christopher Hill calls a "revolt within the revo-lution" also mark an ideological interregnum preceding the political alliance of the merchant classes and aristocracy which put an end to the programmes of Levellers, Diggers and Ranters. This alliance also brought the restoration of the House of Lords and, in 1660, inaugurated the constitutional monar-chy which now, on the level of British 'mass culture', is a resource as inexhaustible as 'literature' for the production of conservative ideologies re-presented as being 'above politics'. To fiction a different literature involves more than producing an inverted image of the old. The last thing we need is a "tasteless muddlehead" like Carlyle[45] to consolidate an imperial per-sonality cult of Abiezer Coppe, a Matthew Arnold to discover in Winstanley "the best that is known and thought in the world", or even an official blessing on *écriture* which will permit Ranter 'textuality' to be incorporated into the canon.[46] A contemporary critical awareness calls, rather, for a theory of discourse which can function without heroes, sacred texts and great periods, and which refuses to hold its silence on the institutional rhetorics that continually divert attention from more 'transient' concerns that can *only* be dealt with politically, and which threaten increasingly that there will be no posterity for *King Lear* and *A Midsummer Night's Dream* to prove their immortality to.

Any attack on the level of theory is clearly confronted by more than just New Criticism or the liberal-humanist 'plura-lism' of English Literature as a whole, and Winstanley's jeers at the "Parrat-like speaking, from the Universities, and Colledges for Scholars",[47] institutions excluded from his own ideal commonwealth, are a useful reminder of limitations, par-ticularly those of a branch of the academy that developed delusions of grandeur under the influence of F. R. Leavis and his disciples. Althusser too, while praising those who struggle inside the educational apparatus against the dominant ideology, expresses pessimism about what they can achieve and sees their devotion as a positive boost for the view which "makes the School today as 'natural', indispensable-useful and even beneficial for our contemporaries as the Church was 'natural', indispensable and generous for our ancestors a few centuries ago" (Althusser, 1971, p. 157).

The bleak determinism of this moment is relieved in part by the analogy Althusser uses. Religious ideologies were in time turned against the Catholic Church and the feudal order it represented, serving a positively *enabling* function in the mobilization not only of bourgeois revolution but also of early experiments in communism and other forms of radical egalitarianism. And for Hobbes, if not for Winstanley, the universities constituted "the core of the rebellion", breeding grounds for religious and political subversion—"to this nation as the wooden horse was to the Trojans" (Hobbes, 1969, pp. 58, 95). It may be naively utopian to think that a liberal education can be held to its democratic promises and turned against the forces that deploy the rhetoric of individualism and the Free World to produce subjects who are powerless in the face of the arms trade, the multinationals, mass-media propaganda and the global morality play staged against the background of nuclear terror. But Althusser's theorizing of the "relative autonomy" of ideology, coupled with other aspects of recent critical practice, allows some leeway for an occupation of institutional platforms and for some preliminary adjustments to the course of an unwieldy ensemble of discourses named 'English' which has traditionally proclaimed the virtue of flexibility. Whatever the frustrations of this struggle it brings at least the pleasures of an interregnum. And the alternative, which does not bear much looking into, is to go on fiddling with form, intention and eternity while Nero's bunker is furnished with copies of the *Complete Shakespeare*, evidence for someone of some kind of civilization.

Notes

1. *See* Holloway, 1961, pp. 1–15.
2. My italics.
3. Extending from the mid seventeenth century to the end of the eighteenth, a period when "unknown to themselves, the naturalists, economists and grammarians employed the same rules to define objects proper to their own study, to form their concepts, to build their theories" (Foucault, 1970, p. xi). This *"positive unconscious* of knowledge" during the Classical Age is also the object of Foucault's history of madness.
4. *See* Eagleton, 1983, pp. 27–8.
5. This heroism has been revamped and bolstered up against post-structuralism by A. D. Nuttall: "If we fully admit the mimetic dimension, literary criticism becomes harder. We are transformed from cartographers to explorers, exposed to dangers, difficulties and even actual pains unknown to the formalist" (1983, p. 190).
6. *See* Hawkes, 1983.
7. *See* Eagleton, 1981, pp. 145–6.
8. This was the underlying motif in the press coverage of the 1980–81 Cambridge 'structuralist' controversy.
9. See *The Sunday Times*, 25 January 1981, p. 13, and Bernard Bergonzi, "Reinstating Reference", *Times Literary Supplement*, 26 October 1983, p. 1178.
11. *See*: Lamming, 1971; Césaire, 1969; Fernández-Retamar, 1974; Fanon, 1970, pp. 75–6, 112–27; Sanchez, 1976; Monegal, 1977 and Griffiths, 1983.
12. Cf. the questionable liberalism of the introduction to the Arden *Othello*, reprinted in 1984—in particular the comments on negro features (Ridley, 1958, p. li).
13. *See* Eagleton, 1976, pp. 58–60, 62–3.
14. *Cit.* Howarth, 1973, p. 10.
15. Howarth, p. 12.
16. *Cit.* Belsey, 1983, p. 26. Catherine Belsey explains that Foucault "invents the verb 'to fiction' in order to undermine his own use of the word 'truth'".
17. Belsey, 1983, p. 17.
18. *See* Eagleton, 1983, p. 28.
19. Marx, *Capital*, I, Ch. 24.
20. Oulthwaite, 1969, p. 11; Shanker, 1975, p. 116; Hill, 1980, pp. 11, 18.
21. *See* Dusinberre, 1975, pp. 5–6, 136, 225, and French, 1981, respectively.
22. *See* Mannoni, 1956.

23. Raymond Powell, who is representative in this case, defines 'complexity' as a "mutually sustaining balance of conflicting qualities" and "the expression of a coherent intention", positive qualities absent or destroyed in "contradiction" (Powell, 1980, pp. 7–8).

24. *See* Orwell, 1962, p. 104.

25. This, slightly extended, is Catherine Belsey's list of "specific descontinuities" to be analysed (Belsey, 1983, p. 26).

26. *See* Bennett, 1979, pp. 135–7, 141.

27. *See also* Eagleton's essay "Marxism and Aesthetic Value" (1976, pp. 162–87).

28. Hobbes, 1969, p. 1.

29. *See* Manuel and Manuel, 1979, pp. 187–95.

30. Dusinberre.

31. Cf. Jardine, 1983, pp. 169–79.

32. Thomas, 1965, pp. 320–4, 330. *See also* Thompson, 1974, pp. 90–3 and Arblaster, 1981, p. 229.

33. *See* Berg and Berry, 1981, pp. 37–54, particularly their comments on Kristeva's "semiotic" and Luce Irigaray's "language of the feminine" in relation to female prophecy in the seventeenth century (pp. 39–41, 44f.). *See also* Mack, 1982.

34. W. Erbury, *The Mad Man's Plea. Cit.* Hill, 1972, p. 223.

35. G. Calvert, *Some Sweet Sips, of some Spirituall Wine*, 1649. *Cit.* Manuel and Manuel, 1979, p. 357.

36. Coppe, 1649, I, Preface; II, p. 15. Cf. "How long shall I heare the sighs and groanes, and see the teares of poore widowes; and heare curses in every corner; and all sorts of people crying out oppression, oppression, tyranny.—O my back, my shoulders. O Tythes, Excize, Taxes, Pollings, &c. O Lord! O Lord God, Almighty! . . . Mine eares are filled brim full with confused noise, cries and outcries; O the innumerable complaints and groanes that pierce my heart (thorow and thorow) O astonishing complaints" (I, p. 10).

37. Coppe, 1649, I, p. 8; Clarkson, *A Single Eye, cit.* Morton, 1970, p. 77.

38. *See* Morton, 1970, pp. 91, 96–7.

39. Morton, 1970, pp. 103–4; Manuel and Manuel, 1979, p. 357.

40. Manuel and Manuel, p. 333.

41. *Ibid.*, pp. 2–3.

42. At one point Coppe warns of the coming of the Archangel Michael, on a day when "purses shall be cut, guts let out, men stabb'd to the heart, women's bellies rip't up, specially gammer Demases, who have forsaken us, and imbraced this wicked world, and married *Alexander* the coppersmith; who hath done me much evill. The Lord reward him" (Coppe, 1649, II, p. 3).

43. Coppe recanted only under duress, still protesting the virtues of a

primitive Christian communism, "that Apostolical, Saint-like Community spoken of in the Scriptures". He continued to affirm, "I am for dealing bread to the hungry, for cloathing the naked, for the *breaking of every yoke*, for the *letting of the oppressed* go free" (Coppe, 165 1a, p. 5).

44. But *see also* Douglas Reid's comments on the popularity of Shakespeare with working-class audiences in Victorian Birmingham (1980, pp. 65, 69, 83–5).

45. One of Nietzsche's many apt and economical descriptions of Carlyle (1973, p. 164).

46. The crisis of subjects and signs in the Ranter text is compounded by its strands of biblical citation, in which scriptural fragments have a very ambiguous authority. The 'letter' and outward righteousness constituted, for Coppe, a "holy Scripturean whore", and his followers regarded the Bible as a collection of fables, valuable only as a supplement to the inner voice. In the delirium which is the mark of much Ranter writing, revolution is displaced onto language. The movement, according to A. L. Morton, came into its full prominence at a time when the radical sects were in retreat "and the turning point of the Revolution had already passed" (1970, p. 85). Unlike the Diggers and Levellers, who took direct political action, the Ranters relied on the imminent and miraculous arrival of the divine Leveller who would complete the work of overturning initiated with the death of Charles I. Insofar as it is marked by *political* pessimism and renunciation, the Ranter text may have a special affinity with post-1968 French deconstruction and its current chic in the United States (cf. Eagleton, 1983, pp. 141–3).

47. *Cit.* Manuel and Manuel, p. 354.

Bibliography

Abbott, E. A. 1870. *A Shakespearian Grammar*, London: MacMillan

Abrams, M. H. 1977. 'Behaviourism and Deconstruction', *Critical Inquiry*, 4, pp. 181–93

—— 1979. 'How to Do Things with Texts', *Partisan Review*, 46, pp. 566–88

Addenbrooke, D. 1974. *The Royal Shakespeare Company: The Peter Hall Years*, London: William Kimber

Adorno, T. W. & Horkheimer, M. 1979. *Dialectic of Enlightenment*, tr. J. Cumming, London: NLB

Albright, E. M. 1927. *Dramatic Publication in England 1580–1640*, New York: D. C. Heath

Althusser, L. 1971. *Lenin and Philosophy*, tr. B. Brewster, London NLB

Anderson, P. 1968. 'Components of the National Culture', *New Left Review*, 50, pp. 214–84

—— 1978. *Passages from Antiquity to Feudalism*, London: Verso

Arblaster, A. 1981. 'Revolution, the Levellers and C. B. Macpherson', in Barker *et al.* (eds.), 1981, pp. 220–37

Aristotle, 1926. *The Nichomachean Ethics*, tr. H. Rackham, London: Heinemann, *Loeb Classical Library*

Arnold, M. 1942. *Poetical Works*, ed. C. B. Tinker and H. F. Lowry, London: Oxford Univ. Press

—— 1962. *The Complete Prose Works*, vol. III, ed. R. H. Super, Ann Arbor: Univ. of Michigan Press

Artaud, A. 1958. *The Theater and Its Double*, tr. M. C. Richards, New York: Grove

Arthos, J. (ed.) 1965. *Love's Labor's Lost*, New York: NEL, *Signet Classic Shakespeare*

Asimov, I. 1960. 'An Immortal Bard', *Earth is Room Enough*, London: Panther

Bainton, R. H. 1951. *Here I Stand: A Life of Martin Luther*, London: Hodder & Stoughton

—— 1963. 'The Bible in the Reformation', S. L. Greenslade (ed.), *The West from the Reformation to the Present Day*, *Cambridge History of the Bible*, vol. III, pp. 1–37

Bakhtin, M. 1968. *Rabelais and his World*, tr. H. Iswolsky, Cambridge, Mass.: MIT Press

Baldwin, C. S. 1939. *Renaissance Literary Theory and Practice*, Gloucester, Mass.: Peter Smith

Balibar, R. 1974. *Les Français fictifs: le rapport des styles littéraires au français national*, Paris: Librairie Hachette

Barber, C. L. 1959. *Shakespeare's Festive Comedy: a study of dramatic form and its relation to social custom*, Princeton, N.J.: Princeton Univ. Press

Barker, F. et al. (eds.) 1981. *1642: Literature and Power in the Seventeenth Century*, Colchester: University of Essex

Barry, P. 1981. 'Is There Life after Structuralism?', *Critical Quarterly*, 23, pp. 72–77

Barthes, R. 1973. *Mythologies*, tr. A. Lavers, London: Paladin
—— 1974. *S/Z*, tr. R. Miller, New York: Hill & Wang
—— 1976. *The Pleasure of the Text*, tr. R. Miller, London: Cape

Belsey, C. 1980. *Critical Practice*, London, Methuen, (*New Accents*)
—— 1981. 'Tragedy, Justice and the Subject', Barker *et al.* (eds.), 1981, pp. 166–86
—— 1983. 'Literature, History, Politics', *Literature and History*, 9, pp. 17–27

Benjamin, E. B. 1958. 'Fame, Poetry and the Order of History in the Literature of the English Renaissance', *Studies in the Renaissance*, 6, pp. 64–84

Bennett, T. 1979. *Formalism and Marxism*, London: Methuen, *New Accents*

Bentley, G. E. 1964. *Shakespeare and his Theatre*, Lincoln: Univ. of Nebraska Press

Berg, C. and Berry, P. 1981. 'Spiritual Whoredom: An Essay on Female Prophets in the Seventeenth Century', Barker *et al.* (eds.), 1981, pp. 37–54

Berggren, P. 1980. 'The Woman's Part: Female Sexuality as Power in Shakespeare's Plays', in Lenz, Greene and Neely (eds.), 1980, pp. 17–34

Bethell, S. L. 1944. *Shakespeare and the Popular Dramatic Tradition*, Westminster: P. S. King & Staples
—— 1947. *The Winter's Tale: A Study*, London: Staples

Biggins, D. 1975. 'Sexuality, Witchcraft and Violence in *Macbeth*', *Shakespeare Studies*, 8, pp. 255–77

Borges, J. L. 1970. *Labyrinths: Selected Stories and other writings*, ed.

D. A. Yates and J. E. Irby, Harmondsworth: Penguin

Boss, J. E. 1972. 'The Golden Age, Cockaigne and Utopia in *The Faerie Queene* and *The Tempest*', *Georgia Review*, 26, pp. 145–55

Booth, S. 1969. 'On the Value of *Hamlet*', N. Rabkin (ed.), *Reinterpretations of Elizabethan Drama: Selected Papers from the English Institute*, New York: Columbia Univ. Press, pp. 137–76

—— (ed.) 1977. *Shakespeare's Sonnets*, New Haven: Yale Univ. Press

Bradbrook, M. C. 1964. 'St. George for Spelling Reform!', *Shakespeare Quarterly*, 15, pp. 129–41

Bradley, A. C. 1904. *Shakespearean Tragedy: Lectures on Hamlet, Othello, King Lear, Macbeth*, London: MacMillan

Brecht, B. 1964. *Brecht on Theatre: The Development of an Aesthetic*, tr. J. Willett, London: Methuen

Breuer, H. 1976. 'Disintegration of Time in Macbeth's Soliloquoy "Tomorrow and Tomorrow, and Tomorrow"', *Modern Language Review*, 71, pp. 256–71

Bridges, R. S. 1927–35. *Collected Essays, Papers etc.*, 10 vols., London: Oxford Univ. Press

Briggs, K. M. 1972. *Pale Hecate's Team*, London: Routledge & Kegan Paul

Brook, G. L. 1976. *The Language of Shakespeare*, London: André Deutsch

Brooks, H. F. (ed.) 1979. *A Midsummer Night's Dream*, London: Methuen, *Arden Shakespeare*

Brown, A. 1964. 'The Printing of Books', *Shakespeare Survey*, 17, pp. 205–13

Brown, J. R. (ed.) 1982. *Focus on Macbeth*, London: Routledge & Kegan Paul

Bullough, G. 1973. *Narrative and Dramatic Sources of Shakespeare*: Vol. VIII, *Major Tragedies*, London: Routledge & Kegan Paul

Calderwood, J. L. 1971. *Shakespearean Metadrama*, Minneapolis: Univ. of Minnesota Press

—— 1983. *To Be or Not to Be: Negation and Metadrama in Hamlet*, New York: Columbia Univ. Press

Carlisle, C. J. 1967. 'Hamlet's "Cruelty" in the Nunnery Scene: the actors' Views', *Shakespeare Quarterly*, 18, pp. 129–40

Carlyle, T. 1841. *On Heroes, Hero-Worship and the Heroic in History*, London: James Frazer

Caspari, F. 1968. *Humanism and the Social Order in Tudor England*, New York: Teacher's College Press, *Classics in Education*, 34

Castelvetro, L. 1570. *Poetica d'Aristotele*, Vienna: G. Stainhofer

Castiglione, B. 1900. *The Book of the Courtier, tr. Sir T. Hoby (1561)*, London: David Nutt

Caxton, W. 1928. *The Prologues and Epilogues*, ed. W. J. B. Crotch, *Early English Texts Society*, 176, London, 1928

Césaire, A. 1969. *Une Tempête*, Paris: Editions du Seuil

Chambers, E. K. 1930. *William Shakespeare: A Study of Facts and Problems*, 2 vols., Oxford: Clarendon Press

Charlton, K. 1965. *Education in Renaissance England*, London: Routledge & Kegan Paul

Charney, M. & Charney, H. 1977. 'The Language of Madwomen in Shakespeare and his Fellow Dramatists', *Signs: Journal of Women in Culture and Society*, 3, pp. 451–460

Chemnitz, M. 1582. *A Discoverie and Batterie of the Great Fort of Unwritten Traditions*, London: T. Purfoot & W. Pounsonbie

Cicero, 1913. *De Officiis*, tr. W. Miller, London: Heinemann, *Loeb Classical Library*

Cinthio, G. 1968. *Giraldi Cinthio on Romances*, ed. H. L. Snugges, Lexington: Univ. of Kentucky Press

Cipolla, C. M. 1969. *Literacy and Development in the West*, Harmondsworth: Pelican

Cixous, H. 1974. 'The Character of Character', *New Literary History*, 5, pp. 383–402

―――― 1981. 'The Laugh of the Medusa', E. Marks and I. Courtivron (eds.), *New French Feminisms: An anthology*, Brighton: Harvester

Clarke, M. V. Cowden 1850–52. *The Girlhood of Shakespeare's Heroines*, 3 vols., London: Simpkin, Marshall & Co.

Cohen, B. 1954. 'Note on Letter and Spirit in the New Testament', *Harvard Theological Review*, 47, pp. 197–203

Cohn, N. 1970. *The Pursuit of the Millenium: Revolutionary Millenarians and Mystical Anarchists of the Middle Ages*, revised ed., London: Temple Smith

Colie, R. L. 1966. *Paradoxica Epidemica: The Renaissance Tradition of Paradox*, Princeton, N.J.: Princeton Univ. Press

Collier, J. 1698. *A Short View of the Immorality and Profaneness of the English Stage*, London: S. Keble

Cook, J. 1980. *Women in Shakespeare*, London: Harrap

Coppe, A. 1649. *A Fiery Flying Roll*, 2 pts., London

—— 1651a. *A Remonstrance of the sincere and zealous Protestation of Abiezer Coppe*, London: James Cottrel

—— 1651b. *Copp's Return to the wayes of Truth*, London: T. Newcomb

Coward, R. and Ellis, J. 1977. *Language and Materialism: Developments in Semiology and the Theory of the Subject*, London: Routledge & Kegan Paul

Cox, C. B. and Dyson, A. E. 1965. *The Practical Criticism of Poetry: A textbook*, Oxford: Blackwell

Cressy, D. 1980. *Literacy and the Social Order: Reading and writing in Tudor and Stuart England*, Cambridge: Cambridge Univ. Press

Crewe, J. V. 1982. *Unredeemed Rhetoric: Thomas Nashe and the scandal of authorship*, Baltimore: Johns Hopkins Univ. Press

Culler, J. 1975. *Structuralist Poetics: Structuralism, Linguistics and the Study of Literature*, London: Routledge & Kegan Paul

Curtius, E. R. 1953. *European Literature in the Latin Middle Ages*, tr. W. R. Trask, London: Routledge & Kegan Paul

Danson, L. 1974. *Tragic Alphabet: Shakespeare's drama of language*, New Haven: Yale Univ. Press

David, R. 1978. *Shakespeare in the Theatre*, Cambridge: Cambridge Univ. Press

—— (ed.) 1951. *Love's Labour's Lost*, London: Methuen, *Arden Shakespeare*

Davis, D. R. 1982. 'Hurt Minds', J. R. Brown (ed.), 1982, pp. 210–27

Davis, J. C. 1981. *Utopia and the Ideal Society: A Study of English Utopian Writing 1516–1700*, London: Cambridge Univ. Press

Dawson, A. B. 1982. 'Much Ado About Signifying', *Studies in English Literature*, 22, pp. 211–21

Deanesly, M. 1920. *The Lollard Bible and other Medieval Biblical Versions*, Cambridge: Cambridge Univ. Press

Della Casa, G. 1892. *Galateo, tr. R. Peterson (1576)*, ed. H. J. Reid, London

Derrida, J. 1972. *La Dissémination*, Paris: Éditions du Seuil

—— 1976. *Of Grammatology*, tr. G. C. Spivak, Baltimore: Johns Hopkins Univ. Press

—— 1977. 'Limited Inc. abc', *Glyph*, 2, pp. 162–254.

—— 1978. *Writing and Difference*, tr. A. Bass, London: Routledge & Kegan Paul

—— 1979a. 'Living on: Border Lines', tr. J. Hulbert, G. Hartman (ed.), *Deconstruction and Criticism*, London: Routledge & Kegan Paul

—— 1979b. *Spurs: Nietzsche's Styles*, tr. B. Harlow, Chicago: Chicago Univ. Press

—— 1981. *Positions*, tr. A. Bass, London: Athlone Press

Dickens, A. G. 1964. *The English Reformation*, London: B. T. Batsford

Dollimore, J. 1984. *Radical Tragedy: Religion, Ideology and Power in the Drama of Shakespeare and his Contemporaries*, Brighton: Harvester

Dollimore, J. and Sinfield, A. 1985. *Political Shakespeare*, Manchester: Manchester Univ. Press

Donne, J. 1952. *Essays in Divinity*, ed. E. M. Simpson, Oxford: Clarendon Press

Dowden, E. 1885. 'Shakespeare's Portraiture of Women', *The Contemporary Review*, 47, pp. 517–35

Doyle, B. 1982. 'The Hidden History of English Studies', P. Widdowson (ed.), *Re-Reading English*, London: Methuen (New Accents)

Drakakis, J. (ed.) 1985. *Alternative Shakespeares*, London: Methuen (New Accents)

Dryden, J. 1668. *Of Dramatick Poesie, an Essay*, London: H. Herringman

Dunn, E. C. 1968. *Shakespeare in America*, New York: B. Blom. First published 1939

Dusinberre, J. 1975. *Shakespeare and the Nature of Women*, London: MacMillan

Eagleton, T. 1976. *Criticism and Ideology: a study in Marxist Literary Theory*, London: NLB

—— 1981. *Walter Benjamin: Or Towards a Revolutionary Criticism*, London, NLB, 1981

—— 1983. *Literary Theory: An Introduction*, Oxford: Blackwell

Ebeling, G. 1970. *Martin Luther: An Introduction to His Thought*. London: Collins

Eckener, H. 1958. *My Zeppelins*, tr. D. Robinson, London: Putnam

Egan, R. 1975. *Drama Within Drama: Shakespeare's Sense of His Art in King Lear, The Winter's Tale and The Tempest*, New York: Columbia Univ. Press

Elam, K. 1984. *Shakespeare's Universe of Discourse: Language-Games in the Comedies*, London: Cambridge Univ. Press

Eliot, T. S. 1965. *To Criticize the Critic and Other Writings*, London: Faber

Elliott Leigh-Noel, M. L. 1885. *Shakespeare's Garden of Girls*, London: Remington

Ellis, H. A. 1973. *Shakespeare's Lusty Punning in Love's Labour's Lost*, The Hague: Mouton

Elsom, J. & Tomalin, N. 1978. *The History of the National Theatre*, London: Cape

Empson, W. 1953. *Seven Types of Ambiguity,* 3rd ed., revised, London: Chatto & Windus

Engels, F. 1947. *Anti-Dühring*, Moscow: Progress Publishers

—— 1968. *Socialism: Utopian and Scientific*, in Marx and Engels: *Selected Works*, London: Lawrence & Wishart

Erickson, P. B. 1982. 'Review of Marilyn French, *Shakespeare's Division of Experience'*, *Women's Studies*, 9, 189–202

Evans, M. 1985. 'Deconstructing Shakespeare's Comedies', J. Drakakis (ed.), *Alternative Shakespeares*, London: Methuen, New Accents

Evans, M. & Vaughan-Lee, L. 1980. 'The Vernacular Labyrinth', *Shakespeare Jahrbuch* (West), pp. 167–73

Fanon, F. 1970. *Black Skin White Masks*, tr. C. L. Markmann, London: Paladin

Farnham, W. 1950. *Shakespeare's Tragic Frontier: The World of His Final Tragedies*, Berkeley, Univ. of California Press

Faucit, H. (Lady Martin), 1891. *On Some of Shakespeare's Female Characters*, 4th ed., revised, Edinburgh: Blackwood

Fekete, J. 1977. *The Critical Twilight: Explorations in the Ideology of Anglo-American Literary Theory from Eliot to McLuhan*, London: Routledge & Kegan Paul

Fernández-Retamar, R. 1974. 'Caliban', tr. R. Gorafola, D. A. McMurray and R. Marquez, *Massachussetts Review*, pp. 7–72

Felperin, H. 1977. *Shakespearean Representation: Mimesis and Modernity in Elizabethan Tragedy*, Princeton, N.J.: Princeton Univ. Press

Ficino, M. 1944. *Commentary on Plato's Symposium*, tr. S. R. Jayne, Columbia: Univ. of Missouri Press, *Univ. of Missouri Studies*, 9

Fish, S. 1972. *Self-Consuming Artifacts: The Experience of Seventeenth-Century Literature*, Berkeley: Univ. of California Press

Fitz, L. T. 1977. 'Egyptian Queens and Male Reviewers: Sexist attitudes in *Antony and Cleopatra* Criticism', *Shakespeare Quarterly*, 28, pp. 297–316

Flaubert, G. 1954. *Dictionary of Accepted Ideas*, tr. J. Barzun, London: Max Reinhardt

Forker, C. R. 1963. 'Shakespeare's Theatrical Symbolism and its Function in *Hamlet*', *Shakespeare Quarterly*, 14, pp. 215–30

Foucault, M. 1967. *Madness and Civilization*, London: Tavistock

—— 1970. *The Order of Things: An Archaeology of the Human Sciences*, London: Tavistock

—— 1972. *The Archaeology of Knowledge*, tr. A. M. Sheridan Smith, London: Tavistock

—— 1977. *Language, Counter-Memory, Practice*, tr. D. F. Bouchard & S. Simon, New York: Cornell Univ. Press

—— 1979. *Power, Truth, Strategy*, ed. M. Morris and P. Patton, Sydney: Feral Publications

Foxe, J. & Haddon, W. 1581. *Against Jerome Osorius*, London: J. Daye

Franck, H. A. 1920. *Roaming Through the West Indies*, New York: D. Appleton-Century Co.

French, M. 1981. *Shakespeare's Division of Experience*, New York: Summit Books

Freud, S. 1960. *Complete Psychological Works*, Vol. 8: *Jokes and Their Relation to the Unconsicous*, ed. J. Strachey & A. Freud, London: Hogarth

Frye, N. 1962. 'Recognition in *The Winter's Tale*', *Essays on Shakespeare and Elizabethan Drama in Honor of Hardin Craig*, ed. R. Hosley, Columbia: Univ. of Missouri Press

Fulke, W. 1579. *D. Heskins, D. Sanders and M. Rastel . . . overthrowne*, London: G. Bishop

Furness, H. H. (ed.) 1896. *As You Like It*, Philadelphia: J. B. Lippincott (New Variorum Shakespeare)

—— 1963. *Hamlet*, reprint of 10th ed., New York: Dover (New Variorum Shakespeare)

Gann, T. 1927. *Maya Cities: A Record of Exploration and Adventure in Middle America*, London: Duckworth

Gerschenkron, E. & Gerschenkron, A. 1966. 'The Illogical Hamlet: A note on Translatability', *Texas Studies in Literature and Language*, 8, pp. 301–6

Girard, R. 1980. 'Myth and Ritual in Shakespeare: *A Midsummer*

Night's Dream', J. V. Harari (ed.), *Textual Strategies*, London: Methuen

Gosson, G. 1869. *The School of Abuse (1579)*, ed. E. Arber, London: *English Reprints*

Grant, R. M. 1963. *A Short History of the Interpretation of the Bible*, London: A. & C. Black

Granville-Barker, H. 1927–48. *Prefaces to Shakespeare*, 5 vols., London: Sidgwick & Jackson

Greenfield, T. N. 1968. '*A Midsummer Night's Dream* and *The Praise of Folie*', *Comparative Literature*, 20, pp. 236–44

Griffiths, T. R. 1983. '"This island's mine": Caliban and Colonialism', *Yearbook of English Studies*, 13, pp. 159–80

Grivelet, M. 1963. 'Shakespeare as "Corrupter of Words"', *Shakespeare Survey*, 16, pp. 70–6

Gollancz, I. 1916. *Shakespeare Day 1916*, London: Geo. W. Jones

Guazzo, S. 1925. *The Civile Conversation*, tr. G. Pettie and B. Young, 2 vols., London: Constable, *Tudor Translations*, 2nd series, vols. 7–8

Guevara, A. de 1574. *The Familiar Epistles*, tr. E. Hellowes, London: H. Middleton & R. Newbery

Haley, D. 1978. 'Gothic Armaments and King Hamlet's Poleaxe', *Shakespeare Quarterly*, 29, pp. 407–13

Halliday, F. E. 1957. *The Cult of Shakespeare*, London: Duckworth

Harbage, A. 1941. *Shakespeare's Audience*, New York: Columbia Univ. Press

Hart, H. C. (ed.) 1906. *Love's Labour's Lost*, London: Methuen, *Arden Shakespeare*

Hattaway, M. 1982. *Elizabethan Popular Theatre: Plays in Performance*, London: Routledge & Kegan Paul

Hawkes, T. 1971. 'Shakespeare's Talking Animals', *Shakespeare Survey*, 24, pp. 47–54

—— 1973. *Shakespeare's Talking Animals: Language and Drama in Society*, London: Arnold

—— 1977. *Structuralism and Semiotics*, London: Methuen (*New Accents*)

—— 1983. 'Telmah: to the Sunderland Station', *Encounter* (April), pp. 50–60

Haywood, C. 1966. 'Negro Minstrelsy and Shakespearean Burlesque', B. Jackson (ed.), *Folklore and Society: Essays in Honor of Benjamin A. Botkin*, Hatboro, Penn.: Folklore Associates

Hegel, G. W. F. 1977. *Phenomenology of Spirit*, tr. A. V. Miller, Oxford: Clarendon Press

Heilbrun, C. 1957. 'The Character of Hamlet's Mother', *Shakespeare Quarterly*, 8, pp. 201–6

Hibbard, G. R. 1969. 'The Year's Contribution to Shakespearian Study: 1. Critical Studies', *Shakespeare Survey*, 22, pp. 145–66

Hill, C. 1972. *The World Turned Upside Down: Radical Ideas During the English Revolution*, London: Temple Smith

—— 1980. *The Century of Revolution 1602–1714*, reprint of 1961 ed., Wokingham: Van Nostrand Reinhold

Hinman, C. (ed.) 1968. *The Norton Facsimile: The First Folio of Shakespeare*, New York: Norton

Hobbes, T. 1969. *Behemoth or the Long Parliament*, ed. F. Tönnies, 2nd ed., London: Cass & Co.

Holloway, J. 1961. *The Story of the Night: Studies in Shakespeare's Major Tragedies*, London: Routledge & Kegan Paul

Honigman, E. A. J. 1965. *The Stability of Shakespeare's Text*, London: Arnold

Horwich, R. 1978. 'Integrity in *Macbeth*: The search for the Single State of Man', *Shakespeare Quarterly*, 29, pp. 365–73

Howarth, P. 1973. *Play Up and Play the Game: The Heroes of Popular Fiction*, London: Eyre Methuen

Huarte Navarro, J. de. D. 1594. *Examen de Ingenios*, tr. R. Carew, London: R. Watkins

Hulme, H. M. 1962. *Explorations in Shakespeare's Language: Some Problems of Word Meaning in the Dramatic Text*, London: Longmans

Hulme, P. 1981. 'Hurricanes in the Caribbees: The Constitution of the Discourse of English Colonialism', Barker *et al.* (eds.), 1981. pp. 55–83

Hunter, G. K. 1978. *Dramatic Identities and Cultural Tradition: Studies in Shakespeare*, Liverpool: Liverpool Univ. Press

Hunter, J. A. 1926. *The South American Handbook*, London: South American Publications

Hyppolite, J. 1974. *Genesis and Structure of Hegel's Phenomenology of Spirit*, tr. S. Cherniaky and J. Heckman, Evanston: Northwestern Univ. Press, *Northwestern University Studies in Phenomenology and Existential Philosophy*

Jackson, R. 1979. '"Perfect Types of Womanhood": Rosalind, Beatrice and Viola in Victorian Criticism and Performance', *Shakespeare Survey*, 32, pp. 15–26

James, D. G. 1951. *The Dream of Learning: An Essay on The Advancement of Learning, Hamlet and King Lear*, Oxford: Clarendon Press

Jameson, A. B. 1904. *Shakespeare's Heroines*, 9th ed., London: Ernest Nister

Jameson, F. 1981. *The Political Unconscious: Narrative as a Socially Symbolic Act*, London: Methuen

Jardine, L. 1983. *Still Harping on Daughters: Women and Drama in the Age of Shakespeare*, Brighton: Harvester

Jedin, H. 1961. *A History of the Council of Trent*, tr. Dom. E. Graf, 2 vols., London: Nelson

Jenkins, H. 1955. 'As You Like It', *Shakespeare Survey*, 8, pp. 40–51
—— (ed.) 1982. *Hamlet*, London: Methuen, *Arden Shakespeare*

Johnson, S. 1969. *Dr Johnson on Shakespeare*, ed. W. K. Winsatt, Harmondsworth: Penguin

Jones, A. R. 1981. 'Writing the Body: Toward an Understanding of *l'Écriture feminine*', *Feminist Studies*, 7, pp. 247–63

Jonson, B. 1925–52. *Works*, ed. C. H. Herford, P. and E. Simpson, 11 vols., Oxford: Clarendon Press

Joseph, B. L. 1971. *Shakespeare's Eden: The Commonwealth of England 1558–1629*, London: Blandford Press

Kamen, H. 1976. *The Iron Century: Social Change in Europe 1550–1660*, 2nd ed., revised, London: Cardinal

Kaiser, W. 1963. *Praisers of Folly*, Cambridge, Mass.: Harvard Univ. Press

Kantak, V. Y. 1963. 'An Approach to Shakespearian Tragedy: The Actor Image in *Macbeth*', *Shakespeare Survey*, 16, pp. 42–56

Kermode, F. (ed.) 1954. *The Tempest*, London: Methuen, *Arden Shakespeare*

Kettle, A. 1964a. 'From *Hamlet* to *Lear*', Kettle (ed.), 1964, pp. 146–71
—— (ed.) 1964. *Shakespeare in a Changing World*, London: Lawrence & Wishart

Klein, J. L. 1980. 'Lady Macbeth: "Infirm or Purpose"', Lenz, Greene & Neely (eds.), 1980, pp. 240–55

Knight, G. W. 1949. *The Wheel of Fire: Interpretations of Shakespearian Tragedy*, 4th ed., London: Methuen
—— 1951. *The Imperial Theme: Further interpretations of Shakespeare's Tragedies*, 3rd ed., Methuen, 1951.

Knights, L. C. 1931–32. 'Education and Drama in the Age of Shakespeare', *Criterion*, 11, pp. 599–625

—— 1946. *Explorations: Essays in Criticism, Mainly on the Literature of the Seventeenth Century*, London: Chatto & Windus

Kojève, A. 1980. *Introduction to the Reading of Hegel: Lectures on the Phenomenology of Spirit*, tr. J. H. Nichols, Jr, Ithaca: Cornell Univ. Press

Kökeritz, H. 1953. *Shakespeare's Pronunciation*, New Haven: Yale Univ. Press

Kott, J. 1964. *Shakespeare Our Contemporary*, tr. B. Taborski, London: Methuen

Kristeva, J. 1980. *Desire in Language: A Semiotic Approach to Literature and Art*, tr. L. S. Roudiez, T. Gora, & A. Jardine, New York: Columbia Univ. Press

Kuhn, M. S. 1977. 'Much Virtue in If', *Shakespeare Quarterly*, 28, pp. 40–50

Lacan, J. 1977a. *Écrits*, tr. A. Sheridan, London: Tavistock

—— 1977b. 'Desire and the Interpretation of Desire in *Hamlet*', *Yale French Studies*, 55–6, pp. 11–52

Ladurie, E. Le Roy 1980. *Carnival In Romans: A People's Uprising at Romans 1579–1580*, tr. M. Feeney, London: Scholar Press

Lamming, G. 1960. *The Pleasures of Exile*, London: Michael Joseph

—— 1971. *Water with Berries*, London: Longman Caribbean

Latham, A. (ed.) 1979. *As You Like It*, London: Methuen, *Arden Shakespeare*

Lawrence, W. W. 1960. *Shakespeare's Problem Comedies*, New York: Frederick Ungar (first publ. 1931)

Leavis, F. R. 1963. '*Scrutiny*: A Retrospect', *Scrutiny*, 20, 1963, pp. 1–26.

—— 1982. *The Critic as Anti-Philosopher: Essays and Papers*, ed. G. Singh, London: Chatto & Windus

Lentricchia, F. 1980. *After the New Criticism*, London: Athlone Press

Lenz, C. R. S., Greene, G. and Neely, C. T. 1980a. 'Introduction', Lenz, Greene and Neely (eds.), 1980, pp. 3–16

—— 1980b. 'Women and Men in Shakespeare: A Selective Bibliography', Lenz, Greene and Neely (eds.), 1980, pp. 314–35

—— (eds.) 1980. *The Woman's Part: Feminist Criticism of Shakespeare*, Urbana: Univ. of Illinois Press

Lever, K. 1938. 'Proverbs and *Sententiae* in the Plays of Shakespeare', *Shakespeare Association Bulletin*, 12, pp. 173–83, 224–39

Leverenz, D. 1978. 'The Woman in Hamlet: An Interpersonal View', *Signs: Journal of Women in Culture and Society*, 4, pp. 291–308

Levin, R. 1979. *New Readings vs. Old Plays: Recent Trends in the Reinterpretation of English Renaissance Drama*, Chicago: Univ. of Chicago Press

Lévi-Strauss, C. 1961. *A World on the Wane*, tr. J. Russell, London: Hutchinson

—— 1966. *The Savage Mind*, London: Weidenfeld & Nicholson

Lodge, D. 1981. *Working with Structuralism: Essays and Reviews on Nineteenth and Twentieth-Century Literature*, London: Routledge & Kegan Paul

Lyman, S. M. & Scott, M. B. 1975. *The Drama of Social Reality*, London: Oxford University Press, 1975

Macherey, P. 1977. 'An Interview with Pierre Macherey', ed. C. Mercer & J. Radford, *Red Letters*, 55, pp. 3–9

—— 1978. *A Theory of Literary Production*, tr. G. Wall, London: Routledge & Kegan Paul

Macherey, P. and Balibar, E. 1978. 'Literature as an Ideological Form: Some Marxist Propositions', *Oxford Literary Review*, 3, pp. 4–12

Mack, P. 1982. 'Women as Prophets during the English Civil War', *Feminist Studies*, vol. 8, no. 1, pp. 19–46

Macpherson, C. B. 1962. *The Political Theory of Possessive Individualism: Hobbes to Locke*, Oxford: Clarendon Press

Madariaga, S. de 1948. *On Hamlet*, London: Hollis & Carter

Mahood, M. M. 1957. *Shakespeare's Wordplay*, London: Methuen

Mannoni, O. 1956. *Prospero and Caliban: The Psychology of Colonization*, tr. P. Powesland, London: Methuen

Manuel, F. E. & Manuel, F. P. 1979. *Utopian Thought in the Western World*, Oxford: Blackwell

Marder, L. 1964. *His Exits and Entrances: The Story of Shakespeare's Reputation*, London: J. Murray

Marotti, A. F. 1982. '"Love is not Love": Elizabethan Sonnet Sequences and the Social Order', *English Literary History*, 49, pp. 396–428

Marston, J. 1934–39. *Plays*, ed. H. H. Wood, 3 vols., Edinburgh: Oliver & Boyd

Marx, K. 1976–81. *Capital*, 3 vols., Harmondsworth: Penguin
—— 1973 *Grundrisse*, tr. M. Nicolaus, Harmondsworth: Penguin
McDonald, D. J. 1978. '*Hamlet* and the Mimesis of Absence: A Post-structuralist Analysis', *Educational Theatre Journal*, 30, pp. 36–53
Mehl, D. 1975. 'King Lear and the Poor Naked Wretches', *Shakespeare Jahrbuch* (West), pp. 154–62
Monegal, E. R. 1977. 'The Metamorphoses of Caliban', *Diacritics*, 7, pp. 78–83
Montaigne, M. E. de 1892. *Essays*, tr. J. Florio, 3 vols., London: Constable, The Tudor Translations, vol. I
Montrose, L. A. 1981. ' "The Place of Brother" in *As You Like It*: Social Process and Comic Form', *Shakespeare Quarterly*, 32, pp. 28–54
More, Sir T. 1557. *The English Works*, ed. W. Rastell, London: J. Cawood, J. Waly & R. Tottell
Morton, A. L. 1970. *The World of the Ranters: Religious Radicalism in the English Revolution*, London: Lawrence & Wishart
Muir, K. 1963. *Shakespeare: Hamlet*, London: Arnold
—— 1964. 'Shakespeare and Politics', Kettle (ed.), 1964, pp. 65–83
—— (ed.) 1953. *Macbeth*, London: Methuen, *Arden Shakespeare*
Mulhern, F. 1979. *The Moment of Scrutiny*, London: NLB
Naipaul, V. S. 1976. *The Overcrowded Barracoon*, Harmondsworth: Penguin
Nashe, T. 1904–10. *Works*, ed. R. B. McKerrow, 5 vols., London: A. H. Bullen
Newbolt, Sir H. 1921. Board of Education, *The Teaching of English in England*, London: HMSO
Nietzsche, F. 1910. *Human All-Too-Human*, tr. H. Zimmern, London: T. N. Foulis
—— 1911. *Twilight of the Idols*, tr. O. Levy, London: T. N. Foulis
—— 1956. *The Birth of Tragedy and the Genealogy of Morals*, tr. F. Golffing, New York: Doubleday
—— 1960. *Joyful Wisdom*, tr. T. Common, New York: Frederick Ungar
—— 1973. *Beyond Good and Evil*, tr. R. J. Hollingdale, Harmondsworth: Penguin
Norman, R. 1976. *Hegel's Phenomenologic: A Philosophical Introduction*, Brighton: Sussex University Press

Northbrooke, J. 1843. *Treatise Against Dicing, Dancing, Plays and Interludes, with Other Idle Pastimes . . . 1577*, ed. J. P. Collier, London: *Shakespeare Society Reprint*

Nuttall, A. D. 1983. *A New Mimesis: Shakespeare and the Representation of Reality*, London: Methuen

Olson, P. A. 1957. '*A Midsummer Night's Dream* and the Meaning of Court Marriage', *Journal of English Literary History*, 24, pp. 95–119

Orgel, S. 1975. *The Illusion of Power: Political Theater in the English Renaissance*, Berkeley: Univ. of California Press

Orwell, G. 1962. 'Lear, Tolstoy and the Fool', *Inside the Whale and Other Essays*, Harmondsworth: Penguin, pp. 101–19

Oulthwaite, R. B. 1969. *Inflation in Tudor and Early Stuart England: Studies in Economic History*, London: MacMillan

Palmer, D. J. 1970. 'Art and Nature in *As You Like It*', *Philological Quarterly*, 49, pp. 30–40

—— (ed.) 1968. *Shakespeare, The Tempest: A Casebook*, London: MacMillan

Pêcheux, M. 1982. *Language, Semantics and Ideology: Stating the Obvious*, tr. H. Nagpal, London: MacMillan

Peele, G. 1970. *The Life and Works of George Peele*, vol. III, ed. R. M. Benbar, E. Blistein & F. S. Hook, New Haven, Yale Univ. Press

Pierce, R. B. 'The Moral Languages of *Rosalynde* and *As You Like It*', *Studies in Philology*, 68, pp. 167–76

Pitt, A. 1981. *Shakespeare's Women*, London: Chatto & Windus

Plato, 1952. *Phaedrus*, tr. R. Hackforth, Cambridge: Cambridge Univ. Press

Poulantzas, N. 1975. *Political Power and Social Classes*, tr. T. O'Hagan, London: NLB

Powell, R. 1980. *Shakespeare and the Critics' Debate: A Guide for Students*, London: MacMillan

Prado, 1976. *The Prado Museum Guide to its Collections*, 5th ed., Madrid: Patronato Nacional de Museos

Prosser, E. 1971. *Hamlet and Revenge*, 2nd ed., revised, Stanford: Stanford Univ. Press

Puttenham, G. 1589. *The Arte of English Poesie*, London: Richard Field

Quiller-Couch, Sir A. & Wilson, J. D. (eds.) 1923. *Love's Labour's Lost*, Cambridge: Cambridge Univ. Press (*New Cambridge Shakespeare*)

—— 1926. *As You Like It*, Cambridge: Cambridge Univ. Press (*New Cambridge Shakespeare*)

Quinn, D. B. & Quinn, A. M. (eds.) 1973. *Virginia Voyages from Hakluyt*, Oxford: Oxford Univ. Press

Rabkin, N. 1981. *Shakespeare and the Problem of Meaning*, Chicago: Univ. of Chicago Press

Raggio, O. 1958. 'The Myth of Prometheus', *Journal of the Warburg and Courtauld Institutes*, 21, pp. 44–62

Reid, D. A. 1980. 'Popular Theatre in Victorian Birmingham', D. Bradby, L. James and B. Sharratt (eds.), *Performance and Politics in Popular Drama*, London: Cambridge Univ. Press

Rice, E. F. 1958. *The Renaissance Idea of Wisdom*, Cambridge, Mass.: Harvard Univ. Press

Richards, I. A. 1929. *Practical Criticism: A Study of Literary Judgment*, London: Routledge & Kegan Paul

Ridley, M. R. (ed.) 1958. *Othello*, London: Methuen, *Arden Shakespeare*

Righter, A. 1962. *Shakespeare and the Idea of the Play*, London: Chatto & Windus

Rosenberg, M. 1978. *The Masks of Macbeth*, Berkeley: Univ. of California Press

Rossiter, A. P. 1961. *Angel with Horns and other Shakespeare Lectures*, ed. G. Storey, London: Longmans

Rowse, A. L. 1976. *Matthew Arnold: Poet and Prophet*, London: Thames & Hudson

Ryan, M. 1982. *Marxism and Deconstruction: A Critical Articulation*, Baltimore: Johns Hopkins Univ. Press

Sadoleto, J. 1916. *Sadoleto on Education*, ed. E. T. Campagnac & K. Forbes, London: Milford

Salgado, G. 1977. *The Elizabethan Underworld*, London: Dent

Sanchez, M. E. 1976. 'Caliban: The New Latin-American Protagonist of *The Tempest*'', *Diacritics*, 6, pp. 54–61

Schanzer, E. 1963. *The Problem Plays of Shakespeare*, London: Routledge & Kegan Paul

Schoenbaum, S. 1975. *William Shakespeare: A documentary life*, Oxford: Clarendon Press

Schofield, R. 1968. 'The Measurement of Literacy in Pre-Industrial England', Literacy in Traditional Societies, ed. J. R. Goody, Cambridge: Cambridge Univ. Press

Seabrook, W. B. 1929. *The Magic Island*, London: Harrap

Searle, C. 1973. *The Forsaken Lover: White Words and Black People*, Harmondsworth: Penguin

Shakespeare, W. 1598. *Love's Labour's Lost*, London, Cuthbert Burby

Shanker, S. 1975. *Shakespeare and the Uses of Ideology*, The Hague: Mouton

Shattuck, C. H. 1976. *Shakespeare on the American Stage: From the Hallams to Edwin Booth*, Folger Shakespeare Library

Sibony, D. 1977. '*Hamlet*: A Writing-Effect', *Yale French Studies*, 55–6, pp. 53–93

Sidney, Sir P. 1966. *A Defence of Poetry*, ed. J. A. Van Dorsten, London: Oxford Univ. Press

Simon, J. 1966, *Education and Society in Tudor England*, Cambridge: Cambridge Univ. Press

Sims, A. E. n.d. *A Shakespeare Birthday Book*, London: Harrap

Sinfield, A. 1983. *Literature in Protestant England 1560–1660*, London: Croom Helm

Skipp, V. H. T. 1970. 'Economic and Social Change in the Forest of Arden 1530–1649', *Agricultural History Review*, 18, supp., pp. 84–111

Slater, P. 1977. *Origin and Significance of the Frankfurt School: A Marxist Perspective*, London: Routledge & Kegan Paul

Smith, R. 1980. 'A Heart Cleft in Twain: the Dilemma of Shakespeare's Gertrude', Lenz, Greene and Neely (eds.), 1980, pp. 194–210

Somerset, J. A. B. 1975. '"Fair is foul and foul is fair": Vice-Comedy's Development and Theatrical Effects', *The Elizabethan Theatre*, vol. V, ed. G. R. Hibbard, London: MacMillan

Spivack, B. 1958. *Shakespeare and the Allegory of Evil: The History of a Metaphor in Relation to His Villains*, New York: Columbia Univ. Press

Spufford, M. 1981. *Small Books and Pleasant Histories: Popular Fiction and Its Readership in Seventeenth-century England*, London: Methuen.

Spurgeon, C. F. E. 1933. 'Shakespeare's Iterative Imagery', *Aspects of Shakespeare: British Academy Lectures*, Oxford: Clarendon Press
—— 1935. *Shakespeare's Imagery and What It Tells Us*, Cambridge: Cambridge Univ. Press, 1935

Stallybrass, P. 1982. '*Macbeth* and Witchcraft', J. R. Brown (ed.), 1982, pp. 189–209

—— 1983. 'Rethinking Text and History', *LTP: Journal of Literature Teaching Politics*, 2, pp. 96–107

Starnes, D. T. & Talbert, E. W. 1955. *Classical Myth and Legend in Renaissance Dictionaries*, Chapel Hill: Univ. of N. Carolina Press

Stone, L. 1964. 'The Educational Revolution in England 1560–1640', *Past and Present*, 28, pp. 41–80

—— 1965. *The Crisis of the Aristocracy 1558–1641*, Oxford: Clarendon Press

—— 1977. *The Family, Sex and Marriage in England 1500–1800*, London: Weidenfeld & Nicolson

Stubbes, P. 1585. *The Anatomie of Abuses*, London: R. Jones

Sweet Silvery Sayings 1887. *The Sweet Silvery Sayings of Shakespeare on the Softer Sex*, compiled by an Old Soldier, London: Trubner & Co.

Talbert. E. W. 1963. *Elizabethan Drama and Shakespeare's Early Plays*, Chapel Hill: Univ. of N. Carolina Press

Thomas, K. 1971. *Religion and the Decline of Magic: Studies in Popular Beliefs in Sixteenth and Seventeenth-Century England*, London: Weidenfeld & Nicolson

Thompson, E. P. 1968. *The Making of the English Working Class*, revised ed., Harmondsworth: Pelican

Thompson, R. 1974. *Women in Stuart England and America: A Comparative Study*, London: Routledge & Kegan Paul

Tinkler, F. C. 1937. 'The Winter's Tale', *Scrutiny*, 5, pp. 344–64

Van Laan, T. F. 1978. *Role-Playing in Shakespeare*, Toronto: Univ. of Toronto Press

Veszy-Wagner, L. 1968. '*Macbeth*: "Fair is Foul and Foul is Fair"', *American Imago*, 25, pp. 242–57

Vickers, B. 1974–81. *Shakespeare: The Critical Heritage*, 6 vols., London: Routledge & Kegan Paul

Vološinov, V. N. 1973. *Marxism and the Philosophy of Language*, tr. L. Matejka & I. R. Titunik, London: Seminar Press

Vonnegut, K., Jr. 1974. *Breakfast of Champions*, London: Panther

Weimann, R. 1978. *Shakespeare and the Popular Tradition in the Theater: Studies in the Social Dimension of Dramatic Form and Function*, ed. R. Schwartz, Baltimore, Johns Hopkins Univ. Press

Weitz, M. 1972. *Hamlet and the Philosophy of Literary Criticism*, London: Faber

Wells, S. 1970. *Literature and Drama*, London: Routledge & Kegan Paul

—— (ed.) 1973. *Shakespeare: Select Bibliographical Guides*, London: Oxford Univ. Press

Welsford, E. 1927. *The Court Masque*, Cambridge: Cambridge Univ. Press

Westfall, A. V. R. 1939. *American Shakespeare Criticism 1607–1865*, New York: H. W. Wilson

White, H. 1973. *Metahistory: The Historical Imagination in Nineteenth-Century Europe*, Baltimore: Johns Hopkins Univ. Press

Wilbern, D. 1980. 'Shakespeare's Nothing', M. M. Schwartz and C. Kahn (eds.), *Representing Shakespeare: New Psychoanalytic Essays*, Baltimore, Johns Hopkins Univ. Press

Wilkins, J. 1641. *Mercury or the Secret and Swift Messenger*, London

Williams, R. 1974. *Television: Technology and Cultural Form*, London: Fontana

Wilson, F. P. 1945. 'Shakespeare and the "New Bibliography" ', *The Bibliographical Society 1892–1922: Studies in Retrospect*, ed. F. C. Francis

Wilson, J. D. 1951. *What Happens in Hamlet*, 3rd ed. revised, London: Cambridge Univ. Press

—— 1962. *Shakespeare's Happy Comedies*, London: Faber

Wilson, R. F., Jr 1978. 'Macbeth the Player King: The Banquet Scene as Frustrated Play within the Play', *Shakespeare Jahrbuch (Weimar)*, 114, pp. 107–14

Wilson, T. 1909. *Arte of Rhetorique, 1560*, ed. G. H. Mair, Oxford: Clarendon Press

Winstanley, G. 1941. *Works*, ed. G. H. Sabine, Ithaca: Cornell Univ. Press

Yates, F. A. 1947. *The French Academies of the Sixteenth Century*, London: Warburg Institute, *Studies of the Warburg Institute*, vol. 15

—— 1964. *Giordano Bruno and the Hermetic Tradition*, London: Routledge & Kegan Paul

Ziegler, G. 1982. 'A Supplement to the Lenz-Greene-Neely Bibliography on "Women and Men in Shakespeare" ', *Women's Studies*, 9, pp. 203–14

Index

287